Deepak Bajaj is a bestselling author, motivational speaker, breakthrough trainer and high-performance coach. Deepak was a regional manager with an MNC when he started in network marketing in 2007. He resigned from his job to build his business, and in a really short period attained great success and earned a luxurious lifestyle.

Deepak devotes most of his time to his ever-growing business empire. He has already trained more than 7 lakh people in the last 16 years and his videos on social media get over 3 million views every month, globally. Today, after many flourishing years in the business, Deepak Bajaj has become a brand unto himself, and has garnered an iconic stature in the network marketing industry. He has made it his life's mission to impart the techniques for success that he has developed over the years in the direct selling business to people, helping them on their path to success.

Be a Network Marketing Millionaire

Proven step-by-step formulas to achieve your dream life faster

DEEPAK BAJAJ

NEW EDITION

Manjul Publishing House

First published in India by

Manjul Publishing House
• 7/32, Ansari Road, Daryaganj, New Delhi 110 002 – India
Website: www.manjulindia.com

Registered Office:
• 10, Nishat Colony, Bhopal 462 003 – India

Copyright © by Deepak Bajaj, 2018
All rights reserved.

This edition first published in 2019

ISBN 978-93-88241-65-6

Cover design by Bhavi Mehta

This publication is designed to provide competent and reliable information regarding the subject matter covered. However, it is sold with the understanding that the author and publisher are not engaged in rendering legal, financial, or other professional advice. If legal or other expert assistance is required, the services of a professional should be sought. The author and publisher specifically disclaim any liability that is incurred from the use or application of the contents of this book.

All rights reserved. No part of this publication may be reproduced, stored in or introduced into a retrieval system, or transmitted, in any form, or by any means (electronic, mechanical, photocopying, recording or otherwise) without the prior written permission of the publisher. Any person who does any unauthorized act in relation to this publication may be liable to criminal prosecution and civil claims for damages.

*This book is dedicated to
every human being who has dreams and
who is committed to do everything it takes
to make those dreams a reality.*

Introduction to this new revised edition

What you hold in your hands is the improved and updated version of the number one bestselling book in network marketing/direct selling industry. People working in all different companies with different products and income plans have multiplied their incomes and have grown their business many times with this book. All successful teams are using this book as an essential guidebook and building large business empires using the principles and tools given in this book.

New chapters and new tools have been added in this book because I want to see my readers at the top, living their dreams and becoming top achievers of their company in record time.

I believe time is the most important resource in a person's life and this book is my attempt to save at least 6-8 precious years of your life. I have worked in network marketing with my heart and soul for more than 12 years. I have created new records of income and achievement and created thousands of achievers using the same principles, tools and techniques that are there in this book in your hands now.

Now is your time.
This is your moment.
Follow the success system given in this book.
Give this book to all your teammates.
And don't stop till your reach the top.
I am with you.

Your success partner,
Deepak Bajaj

WHAT READERS ARE SAYING ABOUT THIS BOOK

Every direct seller and those who target to become a millionaire should read this book.

–Kailash Bhattad, CEO,
Mi Lifestyle Marketing Global Private Limited

One of the best books on how to achieve big in network marketing. It's a perfect gift for the teammates to make them serious in business.

–Mubeen Muhammad

Excellent book. Highly recommended. I have read so many books but never come across such appropriate and structured content that is there in every page of this book.

–Gaurav Mehra

Leverage your human networking skills to beat artificial intelligence. Everyday reference book to meet goals and life skills.

–Payal Kothari

A masterpiece on network marketing. This is not just a book but a mentor with a capability to take its reader to the top. One stop solution on network marketing. Strongly recommended for those who want to avoid mistakes and achieve success faster in Network Marketing.

–Vijay Tetarwal

It's ultimate. Deepak Sir you have done exceptionally great for network marketing industry with this book.

–Dr Shiv Gautam

After reading this book I am feeling more confident, proud of my business and action oriented towards my goals. You can build a strong network and achieve your goals by help of this book and with experience of Mr Deepak Bajaj.
—Ravi Nandan Sharma

Ordinary to extraordinary. Awesome book on how a common and ordinary human can become extraordinary.
—Nishant Choudhary

It is as sacred as Gita. It's a guide for those seeking success and striving hard.
—Himangi

It is not just a book but a self-awakening tool. It's a guide of ingredients required to become millionaire.
—Varun Dua

This book will help all those people who really want to do something in life.
—Mahender Singh Rawat

Speechless. Fantastic book. This book really gives you a way of approaching problems and keeps you on the edge of your seat.
—Sanjay Suryan

Awesome book. Must read for everyone who is taking network marketing as a career.
—Samkit Jain

A new person can achieve his goals with easy learning from this book.
—Neha Rana

King of network marketing. Mind-blowing book by a mind-blowing leader.
—Zishan

Life changing book. This book is not only about network marketing but also about how a person can change himself, his living status and develop his personality.
—Rekha Sharma

Beyond description. Marvelous book covering every single point about network marketing. It seems like experience of many decades not just one.
—Dr Neelam

WHAT PEOPLE ARE SAYING ABOUT DEEPAK BAJAJ

Deepak Bajaj is an excellent leader and doing wonders in network marketing. He is my role model and he has played a vital role in my overall success and development. He is bound to change the world with his wisdom and hard work.

–Gaurav Mehra,
TVS Motor Company, Noida

I started network marketing casually but attended one program by Deepak Bajaj and it showed me my purpose. Today I am a successful network marketer and have accomplished all my childhood dreams. Credit for all my success goes to Mr Deepak Bajaj. Anyone can change his/her life by listening to his words. He is doing a great work of changing this world. I am sure millions of people will be benefitted with this book and will get a new direction in life. Love you, Deepak Sir. Thank you for giving me a new life.

–Chintan Arora,
Real Estate and Insurance, Gaziabad

Deepak Bajaj is my life coach and mentor. His quotes 'Fill up your calendar' and 'No rest till we become the best' have become the essence of my life. He has a big vision not only for himself but also for people around him and for our country. Anyone will be super charged in his presence. He taught me that real enjoyment lies in giving and empowering others.

–Divya Saberwal,
Bharti Walmart, Gurgaon

Deepak Bajaj's leadership is a great inspiration in my life. He is a hero of network marketing. My life has totally changed after attending his training program. I have resigned my government job of 20 years and taken path to entrepreneurship under his guidance. Today Deepak Bajaj is the most important person in my life and I am happy that I have been blessed with a great leader like him.

–Pratap Singh Arya, Lecturer,
Haryana Government

I had one life before 15th July, 2017 and one after that. That was the day when I attended Deepak Bajaj's training program. Me and my mom got a new life that day. He is an intuitive, persuasive and passionate leader who is doing extra ordinary things with ordinary people. Impact of his training programs is magical that can only be experienced by being there. Everyone who attends his programs comes out transformed as a different person. Thanks is small word to express my gratitude. Deepak Bajaj is God and mentor to me and many more people.

–Nitu Jindal, Senior Lecturer,
Sirsa (Haryana)

I was mesmerized when I heard him in an event for the first time. He is a passionate man with dreams. He is warm, upcoming and is willing to solve others' problems. Blessed are those who are mentored by him. I pray to almighty to give him all the happiness and reward for the endeavors he is making towards empowering individuals, creating entrepreneurs and making India a better place to live.

–Gaurav Vatsaya, Managing Partner,
Hutsmith Gourmet LLP, Delhi

Everyone who attends your sessions falls in love with you, I am not exception. When I went for your first training program, that very day I resigned my job and took the path of entrepreneurship. Thousands of people have already taken to entrepreneurship by listening to you. What is different about you from all other speakers is that you inspire everyone from deep within to take action. I feel blessed to know Deepak Bajaj.

–Ashish Chadha, IT Professional,
Amritsar

I was well settled in Australia but was looking for a better career opportunity in Delhi. Doubtfully started network marketing but Deepak Sir's training and 24 x 7 unconditional support made me a successful network marketer. He transformed me from a pessimist to optimist. His trainings are like a *breath of fresh air with new content that is relevant to real life. True to his name Deepak, the light, he is showing right path to people.*

—Saurabh Mehra, Hotelier & Sales Professional,
Australia

I was amazed when I listened to Deepak Bajaj's training first time in 2014 and since that day I have been following him. I was on a bike when I met him 4 years back and today I drive a top model Verna. Not only my income and lifestyle but also my whole personality has changed under his influence. His trainings have got unbelievable impact on me and thousands of my teammates. Blessed to have a mentor like him. Love you, Sir.

—Nishant Chaudhry,
Telecom Sales, Karnal

I was brought up with typical values of scoring good and getting a job. When I first met Deepak Bajaj I saw a true Indian with a mission of creating successful people with high moral values. I admire his commitment for his people and his convictions to make them succeed. He is the man of magical words and his trainings have given stability and sustainability to my team. My team and I blindly follow every word of his like verses of Bhagwad Gita.

—Abhishek Mishra, Engineer & MBA,
Gwalior

Deepak Bajaj is a man of vision and is the mentor for next generation. He has influenced thousands of Indians through his speeches and mentorship. He has changed my life and I am able to transform my team under his guidance. He is taking Indians to next level. His training can change lives drastically for both men and women.

—Debashish Khuntia, Mechanical Engineer,
Orissa

Deepak Bajaj is a powerhouse of energy for me and my team. He reminds me of the leader in Guru movie. His trainings have changed my whole thinking process. I built my network marketing team with his knowledge and wonderful trainings. I salute him for his valuable contribution for the society and for changing lives of thousands of people. He is a great dreamer who can make all dreams possible.

—Harkesh Aroa,
Tata Communications, Delhi

I started network marketing business as an obligation. I never thought I can uplift people and grow this big until I met Deepak Bajaj. You are a man with wise and clear vision and under your guidance we will reach the sky. Thank you, Deepak Sir, for you contribution in my life.

–Chanchal Vats,
ICICI Bank, Delhi

Mr Deepak Bajaj is one of the few precious pearls our country has. He is the best leader I have seen in my life who is growing himself and helping others to grow. Your one session can totally change the mindset of any person. You can make people laugh and cry in the same program, inspiring them to be a different person altogether. I wish him best of luck for his next mega project.

–Rahul Chanda,
Pharmaceuticals Sales & Marketing, Faridabad

Deepak Bajaj's training programs have greatly impacted my life. He is visionary, dreamer, honest and always ready to help his people. I have attended many of his trainings and it has totally changed my life. I have a special place in my heart for Deepak.

–Inderjit kataria, Teacher,
Delhi Government

Deepak Bajaj is a source of great positive energy to me. I started believing on my dreams after attending his trainings. His impactful training have changed the attitude of my entire team and they have started taking right actions. He has changed lives of millions of people and still he is a simple, down to earth and friendly person. I am lucky to have him in my life.

–Amit Arsh, Educator and Vastu Consultant,
Bokaro (Jharkhand)

WHAT THIS BOOK CAN DO FOR YOU?

Your life doesn't get better by chance; it gets better by change.
—Jim Rohn

Dear Reader,

Congratulations on selecting this book for changing your life and business. This shows you have dreams and you are serious about them. This book is full of powerful and time-tested knowledge that has already changed lives of thousands of people for so many years. The wisdom, tools, techniques and principles contained in this book have already created thousands of millionaires and now it's your turn. Whether you are a professional, student, employee, business owner, retired person or anyone, this book is a practical and step-by-step guide to your dreams.

Use this book like a dictionary or encyclopedia of network marketing. Read it fully once and come back to it every time you need a solution for anything. The principles and techniques given here will work with every product, every company and every income plan everywhere in the world. So whichever company you are working with, whatever is your product or service, which ever is your team, just use these principles and be a top performer there.

Actually there is no secret to success but there is a system to success. Doing anything will not give you results in spite of years of hard work, motivation and commitment. But only doing right things in the right way will give you massive success. This book will teach you the proven system for massive success in your business in a record time.

I know for a fact that there are millions of people with dreams, who are looking for a right opportunity, the right training and the right guidance to achieve their dreams. I was also one of them: an ordinary boy froma middle class family staying in a small town who wanted to make it big in life. I got these 3 things—right opportunity, right training and right coaching and it changed my life forever. I consider it to be a God's gift in my life.

Now, it's time to give it back and I want to return the favor by helping as many people as I can to fulfill their dreams. I sincerely believe I owe it to the world to share with them everything that has brought me financial abundance and happiness. This book is my way of thanking the universe. I have only one intention in writing this book —to impact millions of lives around the world and to empower people in fulfilling their dreams. I have genuinely poured in this book everything I learnt in my life.

The purpose of this book is not to impress you with my achievements but to impress upon your heart that we can achieve anything and everything in life if we make a decision to do so. Whatever you are doing, whichever company you are working with, whatever is your profession, I want you to shine there and be a source of inspiration for your family, your neighborhood, your country and for the world.

Each one of us has got dreams, talent and capability to achieve whatever we want. But we have imprisoned ourselves and have compromised with our situation. Through this book I invite you to begin the journey to your dream life. Take a step forward. I am with you. Open up, learn new skills, try new things, meet new people, travel to new places, attend new events, and find new ways of doing things. Who knows when you will find the turning point in your life?

Even if you are not into network marketing, the concepts in this book will propel you and empower you to fulfill your dreams. If you are already doing Network Marketing with any company anywhere in the world, there is no point in doing this wonderful business if you cannot become a millionaire in 3 – 5 years. This book will give you everything you need to be a millionaire.

Why wait for a lifetime to get something that can be earned now.

–Deepak Bajaj

My question to the world is, why wait? You've only got one life. If something has already fulfilled the dreams of millions of people for more than 70 years, across 100+ countries, why don't you use it to fulfill your dreams as well? Why wait for 20-30 years to get something that can be earned right now in just 3-5 years. Things are changing faster than our wildest imaginations. Old concepts about jobs and businesses are changing. If you don't take a step now, it may be too late. Give it a shot. Why not you? Why not now?

Read this book as a guide and act on it. All knowledge is useless if it is not acted upon. The right training in our business is like oxygen for a human being. Statistics show that most of the people leave this business because of a lack of training. Now with this book, you have world's best training available for you and your team right in your hands.

This book is your friend and partner and will help you fulfill your dreams.

I wish you super success. Be a multi-millionaire and create millionaires in your team.

Your success partner,
Deepak Bajaj

THE NETWORK MARKETING JOURNEY OF DEEPAK BAJAJ

From being brought up in a small village with a population of some 1000 odd people to becoming one of the top performers of network marketing industry and being considered as #1 authority in this industry, Deepak has travelled a long journey and is a living proof of what can be achieved with vision, faith, determination and unconditional hard work.

Deepak was born in a family of government employees and was brought up in a small village, Jatusana in Haryana, India. His family moved to different towns because of parents' job. Deepak studied in government schools and completed his B.Com from Government National College, Sirsa. He wanted to do MBA from a leading institution, which meant clearing the CAT exam. It was tough for someone who had only studied in Hindi medium. But with sheer determination, Deepak secured the admission to T.A. Pai Management Institute, Manipal—ranked among the top 20 management institutes in India. With an education loan to fund his fees, blessings and support from his mother and a bicycle to commute, Deepak completed his MBA in 2003.

He got a campus placement in TVS Motors and worked at different positions in Bihar, Jharkhand, UP and Delhi NCR. Due to his extraordinary performance, he got promoted to regional manager at the age of 25 for Chandigarh, Punjab, HP and J&K. He was one of the youngest people to hold this position and established new benchmarks of performance.

In 2006, he was approached for network marketing business, but he was not convinced. After 13 months, he started this business after attending a network-marketing event. He was desperate to be successful, but his job did not allow him any time. He counselled with his upline and made a massive 90-days action plan. At the end of the 90 days, he was a record-breaking leader of his company and resigned from his job.

Deepak was a top performer, but he didn't know how to build this business in the right way. He was an achiever, but he didn't have the training and support system to create more achievers in his team. Hence, the business crashed and his family went through their worst financial crisis for the next 9 months. But he persisted and rebuilt the business with the right foundation. He created programs and systems that were never heard of in the industry and created record after record in the business. To make success easier and faster for everyone, he created India's finest school of network marketing, Multipliers, that has been creating big number of achievers day after day for more than 11 years now.

Today, after many glorious years in the business, Deepak Bajaj has become a brand and is considered as a living legend of the network marketing industry. With his proven principles and techniques, thousands of people are fulfilling their dreams, and his business empire is growing everyday even without his active involvement.

He has earned millions from this business and maintains a luxurious lifestyle. He lives in a joint family of 10, with his wife, Dr Tanima and three kids Saksham, Nirbhay and Prashansa. He loves travelling, adventure sports, marathons and reading. Deepak has already visited 28 countries with his family.

Today Deepak Bajaj is India's #1 authority on network marketing and direct selling. He is a motivational speaker, breakthrough trainer and high performance coach. He is famous for his unique, life changing live training events that are always jam-packed. He is a leading social media influencer. His videos get more than 3 million views every month.

His passion and life mission is to inspire and empower people to fulfill their dreams through his books, videos, speeches and training events by teaching the same techniques and principles that got him this legendary success. Deepak says that his biggest income is not what is lying in his bank accounts, but the love and blessings of people. He always says, 'The real joy comes from seeing people fulfill their dreams with your inspiration, coaching and training.' Deepak has dedicated his life in developing tools and techniques to make success easier and faster for people.

Find more about Deepak and his work at www.deepakbajaj.biz.

TABLE OF CONTENTS

Dedication		v
Introduction to this new revised edition		vii
What Readers are Saying About this Book		viii
What People are Saying About Deepak Bajaj		x
What this Book Can Do for You?		xiv
The Network Marketing Journey of Deepak Bajaj		xvii
I.	The World of Network Marketing	1
II.	Principles to Give Foundation to Your Business	13
	1. Unshakable Faith	17
	2. 100% Submission to the System	20
	3. It's a Business, it Will Take Time	24
	4. Programs are Lifeline	26
	5. Pulse of the Business: Numbers and ratios	31
	6. Upline is Your Best Friend	36
	7. Power of Mentorship	38
	8. Ownership and Mastery	41
	9. Time Management – Your Winning Edge	45
	10. Daily Choices: the Unseen Side of Success	49
	11. Use the Power of SURGE	53
	12. Communication and Relationships	65
	13. Personal Sponsoring is a Game Changer	68
	14. Depth-building	72

	15.	Duplication – The Backbone of the Business	77
	16.	Edification – The Glue that Keeps the Team Together	81
	17.	No Accounts Policy	84
	18.	Sponsor Many Choose Few	86
	19.	Positive and Empowering Self-image	89
	20.	Growing Customer Base	92
III.	**The Success Process**	**95**
	1.	Let's Solve the Puzzle Called Selling	99
	2.	List Building and Selection	103
	3.	Approaching your List and Securing Appointments	112
	4.	Sharing the Opportunity	125
	5.	Follow Through and Sales Closing	134
	6.	Right Takeoff for New Associates	142
	7.	The Triangle of Massive Success	146
IV.	**Success Accelerators**	**149**
	1.	Work with Big Dreams	153
	2.	Get MAD (Massive Action Daily)	155
	3.	Convert Individuals to Teams Faster	158
	4.	Power Shots	160
	5.	Make your Team a Leaders' Creation Factory	162
	6.	Creating and Sustaining Speed in your Entire Team	167
	7.	Developing Business in Multiple Locations	171
	8.	Reinvestment	173
	9.	Build Your Brand: Your Most Valuable Asset	175
	10.	Contests: Be a Winner, Create Winners	179
	11.	Social Media – Turbo Charger for Your Business	181
	12.	Clarity and Focus	187
V.	**Qualities of a Successful Network Marketer**	**189**
	1.	Burning Desire	193

	2.	Integrity and Reputation	195
	3.	Attitude of Service and Gratitude	199
	4.	Leadership	203
	5.	Enthusiasm	206
	6.	Always Ready to Learn and Change	208
	7.	Drive for Action	210
	8.	Discipline and Consistency	213
	9.	Perseverance	215
	10.	Committed for Continuous Personal Growth	218
	11.	Pleasing Personality and Dress Up for Success	220
	12.	Punctual and Prepared	223
	13.	Ability to Lead a Balanced Life	225
	14.	Financial Discipline	228
	15.	Building and Nurturing Relationships	232
	16.	Emotional Resilience	235
VI.	**9 Core Actions**		**239**
VII.	**Business Code of Conduct**		**245**
VIII.	**Tools for Excellence**		**251**
	1.	596 System for Massive Success	253
	2.	Universal Framework for Choosing the Best Network Marketing Company	255
	3.	Write Tour Million Dollar Story	258
	4.	Top Success Drivers (TSD) Chart	260
	5.	5 Lists for Success	264
	6.	Power Connectors	266
	7.	Programs Progress Monitor (PPM)	270
	8.	Active Distributor Scorecard (ADS)	272
	9.	Getting the Best Results from Programs	274
	10.	Recommended Books	277
	11.	Things to Do Immediately After Starting the Business	278

12.	Action Plan for the First 90 Days in the Business?	280
	Social Media Planning Guide for Big Success in Network Marketing	283
IX.	**Frequently Asked Questions (FAQs) Answered**	**285**

The Next Steps	294
Deepak Bajaj's Network Marketing Millionaires Academy	297
Deepak Bajaj's High Performance Coaching	299
Acknowledgement	300
About Deepak Bajaj	302

SECTION-I
THE WORLD OF NETWORK MARKETING

THE WORLD OF NETWORK MARKETING

I can do things you cannot, you can do things I cannot; together we can do great things.

–Mother Teresa

Having lived in this world of network marketing for 11 years, I have literally breathed this business every single day. I am yet to come across a more pious, more democratic and more economically and socially sustainable way to be a millionaire. Incidentally, the people outside the industry have a variety of opinions about it, but those who are in the industry are madly, truly and deeply in love with this business. I believe this industry is full of happy, optimistic, growth oriented, positive and hard working people who love helping others. The most incredible virtue of this business is its foundational principle that you cannot grow big without helping your fellow associates. Your only job here in this business is to help people fulfill their dreams.

Life's most persistent and urgent question is, 'what are you doing for others?'

–Martin Luther King Jr

What I have observed is that doing this business is easy, but making a decision to do this business and committing yourself to your dreams is tough. In this section, let's look at the network marketing industry, the scope, the future projections, the benefits it offers and many other things around this business. Let's explore what makes people flock to this business and what makes people succeed or fail in this business. Before we go to the science of building this business, let's set the right foundation for doing this business and develop the right mindset required for success in this business.

Network marketing industry is also called direct selling, personal franchising or consumer distribution system by different agencies and people. Essentially, it means a distribution of products or services through a network of consumers. Here, the consumer uses the products and once convinced, recommends the products to others. Some take it up as a serious business and start working as distributors, while some stay as consumers.

Network Marketing/Direct Selling – History and Global Scenario: Network marketing/direct selling business started somewhere in the 1930s in USA and gradually spread across the globe because of its values and benefits. As per the FICCI Report 'Ease of Doing Business in India' submitted on Dec 05, 2017, 'The global Direct Selling industry generated a retail sales of US $18,356 crore in 2016 and provided part-time employment to 10.7 crore direct sellers worldwide.' The top 10 direct selling markets are USA, China, Japan, Korea, Brazil, Germany, Mexico, France, Malaysia, and UK. Together, these markets accounted for 78% of the global direct selling volume, and the largest 23 markets accounted for 93% of the global market share.

Network Marketing/Direct Selling Indian Scenario: Direct Selling has been practiced in India for hundreds of years and continues to be practiced today. The modern format of direct selling/network marketing, as we know it today, started in India around the mid-1980s. Some major international players entered the Indian market in 1990s. The industry kept growing at a steady pace, but several illegal pyramid schemes also mushroomed to get the benefit of a growing industry, which brought a bad name to the industry.

In the last few years, several industry bodies and government agencies have worked to create a positive environment and a robust regulatory framework for a massive growth of the industry in India. FICCI has been playing a key role in the same and various reports on the industry can be found on the FICCI website. Government has already issued the guidelines for direct selling in India in 2016 and since then, the industry has taken a big boost. A recent report by FICCI-KPMG projected that the retail sales in Direct Selling could reach Rs 64,500 crore by 2025 and provide self-employment opportunities to 1.8 crore Indians, 60% of which are women.

A golden period for the network marketing industry in India is starting now and the industry is ready with huge opportunities for everyone.

What all a network marketing business can give you? People flock to network marketing business for a variety of reasons. Whatever may be your key reason, once you build this business successfully with the right foundation and system, you can get all of these benefits together.

1. Extra income/second income source
2. Financial freedom/being rich and wealthy
3. Security for the family for generations to come
4. Being your own boss (low risk and low cost entrepreneurship opportunity)
5. Own dream house or mansion
6. Luxury international holidays
7. Opportunity for public speaking and stage presence
8. Collection of luxury cars
9. Fame and recognition/being a celebrity
10. Lifestyle of your choice
11. Your own personal growth and personality development
12. Contributing for a better country and society
13. Early retirement
14. Quality time with family
15. Freedom and flexibility to pursue your hobbies
16. Meeting new people and developing a social circle
17. Helping others

Unique Features of Network Marketing Industry: There are a few distinct features of this industry that make it easier and lucrative for people to start their network marketing business:

1. Low entry cost – This business can be started by shopping for a few products or services that we generally buy from somewhere else any way. You can start this business simply by being a customer.
2. Zero exit cost – You can close this business simply by deciding to discontinue it. Since you never had a set up for this business and you have already used the products or services, there is practically zero exit cost.

3. Zero set up cost – You don't need an office/staff/working capital/stock or any other fixed costs for doing this business.
4. No hassles of a traditional business – Credits, payment defaults, accounting, bank limits, rental of the premises, staff costs, manpower issues, working capital, etc.
5. Working hours as per your convenience.
6. System support – Get excellent support from a training and development system which has already produced thousands of achievers.
7. Low investment – You just need to do some shopping to start this business.
8. Get partners who will support you fully for your success.
9. The whole family can do it together.
10. No need to leave your current profession or job for it.
11. Possibility of creating passive income – From the best of my knowledge, network marketing business is one of the best and easiest ways for a common person to create passive income.
12. Mentorship and training from people who are already successful.
13. Life changing education that can make you a totally different person.
14. Equal opportunity for everyone – Anyone can be successful here, irrespective of age, education, gender, location, financial background or religion.
15. Tax advantages, just like in any other business.

Why do people fail?

When this business is so good and there is so much support available, why do people fail in this business? Before I answer this question, let's discuss something fundamental – 'What do you mean by failure in a business?' Although everyone has got their own parameters for defining success and failure, broadly a failure is someone who has given his or her best in the business for a few years and in spite of doing everything that the person could have done, the person is not able to make that business profitable.

Generally, every business takes a few years to be profitable and even in the same industry, every business owner takes a different amount of time before he or she starts making profit. While people are fine with waiting for a few years to make profit in any other business, when it comes to network marketing, suddenly they start expecting profit within a few days or some even within a few hours of starting.

You will come across many people who will say things like – 'I also tried this business; but it didn't work for me. Such businesses don't work. Oh, I know this. My cousin tried this, but he lost everything, etc.' For most of these people, such statements simply mean any of these:

1. Someone gifted them some products;
2. They just purchased the products;
3. They attended one or two meetings;
4. They arranged 2-3 meetings with their Upline half-heartedly; or
5. They tested this business with some people over the phone.

Most of these people quit at this stage, making a wrong opinion that this business doesn't work.

In my experience, the majority of people who say that they tried but failed have not even put in 6-10 hours in the business before making this judgment. Most of them have not even attended 2-3 programs. You need to work on something to make it work. Purchasing of products is not doing the business, or testing the business by talking to a few people is not called building the business. I can assure you, if anyone is ready to follow the principles and the working system of network marketing business for a few months to a few years, this business will offer the highest success ratio.

Typically, people call themselves or the business a failure because of a few simple reasons:

1. Unrealistic expectations:

People start this business with unrealistic expectations and when those expectations are not fulfilled, they quit and start blaming the business. Some people think it's a lottery. Like in a lottery, you just buy the ticket and wait to hit the luck, these people buy some products and wait to get rich. Some other people introduce 2-3 people and stop working with an expectation that now their work is over and now these teammates will do all the work. It doesn't work like this. A few others expect their uypline and the system to do everything for them, because they feel they have already done a big favor by purchasing a few products.

Some people want the world to come knocking at their door, even when they haven't told anyone about it. While people consider it normal in a traditional business to get success after 3-5 years, those same people expect massive success here within a few days or weeks and that too while working part time. Sometimes, even the sponsor sets the wrong expectations by over committing a few things that he or she is not able to deliver later. Some people start the business thinking that it will not involve too much work, but after a few meetings, they realize that they'll have to work hard and feel that they are not ready for the same.

The irony is, many people quit even before realizing that it is such a life transforming business. Wrong expectations are a major cause of disappointment and quitting.

2. Low entry cost allowing non-serious people to start:

This business starts with a negligibly low amount of money, which also gets recovered immediately in the form of products or services. Due to this low entry cost, anybody and everybody can start this business. Most of these people don't even know what it takes to be successful at business. They have no clue of what kind of hard work and commitment is required in this business every day or every week.

Actually, they never started the business; they just did some shopping. They bought a lottery ticket with the products as consolation. Neither did they attend any training, nor did they organize any proper meetings. Most of these people quit within a few days or weeks, and become a part of that crowd that says this business doesn't work.

3. Zero exit cost making it easier to quit:

Ups and downs are part of a business. Every business passes through a good and a bad phase, but business people don't quit because they have a huge investment, manpower, working capital, receivables from the market, stock, a well-done premises and other infrastructure. All of these will become zero when the owner quits. This huge exit cost keeps people in the business in spite of losses or challenges. Since network marketing is a business with zero set up costs, there is no financial loss in closing this business. This zero exit cost makes it easier for people to quit at the very first challenge they come across.

4. Lack of dreams:

Most people don't really have big dreams. They may not be happy with their current lifestyle, but they are not willing to work to change their situation. Most of them wish to get rich, but are not committed to get rich, and commitment comes from dreams and a clarity of purpose.

5. Lack of focus:

Most people start this business part time along with their other job or profession. People give time to this business only if they have any time left after their work, family, recreation, etc. There is already immense pressure in the jobs/professions and family life has also come under pressure, so this business gets neglected and doesn't get any time. If we don't water a plant, howsoever good it may be, it is bound to perish.

6. Lack of willingness to learn the system and work as per the system:

Everyone has got their own ideas and opinions about doing this business and they feel they know how to do it. People are not willing to invest the time in learning the principles and the right working system for this business. Doing this business in the wrong way brings zero results and disappointment, and they quit.

Generally, the people who quit are the ones who have not attended the programs or understood the business properly.

7. Working with the wrong beliefs:

A wide majority of people start this business with some wrong beliefs about themselves and about this business. Some of the wrong beliefs that people have are: *I can't do sales, this business is very difficult, I can't talk to people, I don't think anyone will agree for this business, my friends and relatives may not like me doing this business, I am not competent enough to build a business, this business doesn't suit me, etc.*

If you are willing to look at all these beliefs with an open mind and have the courage to test them, you will easily figure out the truth. When you talk to people in the business, read books, research the business and attend a few events, you will come to know the real truth about this business. This will remove your wrong beliefs and develop the right and empowering beliefs about yourself and about this business.

Most of the people are not willing to work on their beliefs and hence they quit, further strengthening their already wrong beliefs.

Being in this business for 11 years now, I can say with utmost faith and conviction that network marketing is definitely a better way to fulfill your dreams. You compare it with any other business on any parameter like the initial investment, the return on investment, profitability, gestation period, generation to generation transferability, zero risk, fixed costs, ease of setting up, time freedom, money freedom, tension free operations etc., you will find network marketing better than any other practically available business opportunity.

The features of this industry, its foundational principles, working philosophy and the benefits this industry can give in a short span of time are simply incredible and too good to be true. Just start it with the faith that you are doing the right business at the right time with the right company and the best team. Follow the system 100% and do your share of work with utmost honesty. Have patience, success may take some time, but the best part is you will get help throughout this journey and will make awesome friends on the way.

This business has only three basic requirements from you:

1. You have dreams. You have a reason why you want to do this business.
2. You are willing to learn and willing to change as per the requirements of this business.
3. You are ready to work hard for the next few months to a few years as per the new system.

If you have all the above, no one can stop you from fulfilling all your dreams with network marketing. You are in the right business at the right time in the best market of the world. The world needs this business today more than ever before and millions of people are looking for the right person to start this business with.

I urge you to be that right person and become a source of prosperity for millions of people through this business. This book will give you the complete knowledge, skill and the right mindset to be a successful network marketer. Just follow the principles given in this book, keep coming back to this book whenever and wherever you are stuck, and all your dreams will soon turn into reality.

> *I wish you will be the next network-marketing millionaire and create many more millionaires in your team.*

SECTION-II
PRINCIPLES TO GIVE FOUNDATION TO YOUR BUSINESS

PRINCIPLES TO GIVE FOUNDATION TO YOUR BUSINESS

An army of principles can penetrate where an army of soldiers cannot.

–Thomas Paine

What is a principle?

As per Cambridge dictionary, 'A principle is a rule that controls how something happens or works. Principles simply work on cause and effect model and if followed correctly, produce the same result every time for every person at every place. If anyone works on the cause, the desired result is guaranteed.' For example, as per the principle of gravity, if anything is dropped, it will fall downwards; be it a piece of jewellery or a stone, be it in London, Delhi or Sydney and irrespective of whoever is dropping it.

As there are principles for Physics and Mathematics, there are certain principles for success in network marketing business also. These guiding principles have been used by every successful network marketer for decades, and will give you the same success if you apply these principles in your business. With principles you will reach your goals faster and with surety. Observing countless number of people succeed and struggle in this business, I realized that there is one key factor in all big achievers' success—following the principles 100%.

The 20 principles presented in this book have been time-tested and are doable by everyone. They have already made me earn millions of rupees in a record time and empowered me to create hundreds of millionaires in my team. They have the power to put your business on fast track and will take you to your dream income faster.

You can come into this business by chance, but you cannot be successful by chance.

–Deepak Bajaj

I have repeatedly seen that these universal principles will give desired results to each and every person, working in any company, anywhere in the world. Whatever the product line, income plan or other policies may be, following these principles will definitely give you success in record time.

1
Unshakable Faith

> *Whatever the mind of man can conceive and believe, it can achieve.*
>
> –Napoleon Hill

Faith is complete trust and confidence in someone or something. Faith is believing in something much before it has actually even happened. Having faith is the starting point of every achievement. Things will happen only when you believe in them. Why would you even try to do something if you have a feeling that it will not work out? Faith will get you started and will also determine how far you go.

> *It's the repetition of affirmations that leads to belief and once that belief becomes a deep conviction, things begin to happen.*
>
> –Muhammad Ali

To be successful in this business, you need to have faith in two forces: Outside forces and Inside forces.

You need to have complete and absolute faith in these five forces that are outside of you: your upline, your training and development system, your own team, your company and the network marketing industry. I understand building faith is a process and takes time. You may not have total faith when you start off, but the fact that you have started this business with someone and with some company indicates that you have some degree of faith, else you would not have started. Now, begin honestly with whatever faith you have, and books, videos, tools, programs and regular association with uplines will strengthen your faith over time.

Many people leave this business before they even explore the basics of it completely. Give yourself at least a year and if you are ready to be a student of the business, you will thank God for bringing the world's most beautiful business into your life.

> *What lies behind us and what lies ahead of us are tiny matters compared to what lives within us.*
> –Henry David Thoreau

Have faith in yourself. It is your fuel to action and at the same time, it's your pillar of strength when you face rejection, ridicule, and disappointment. Your faith will wake you up every morning to start your day with hope that you will get a champion performer in your team today. When you face challenges, failures or setbacks, your faith will again come to your rescue and will give you the hope to start afresh the next day. There will be times when doubts creep in and your faith starts shaking, it's normal and happens to everyone. It has sometimes happened to me as well, particularly in the initial days of my business, but my close association with my upline, books and programs kept me going. **I call these three as vaccines for your business: Recommended books, programs, and association with active uplines.** As long as you are connected to these three, you will never have any problem in maintaining and multiplying your faith. It's always a fight between your faith and fear. Your faith tells you that you can do it and fear will keep shouting that you cannot do it and what if you fail. **Let your faith be bigger than your fears.**

Your faith can move mountains and your doubts can create them.

–Unknown

Generally, every team in a network marketing company has a pre-developed training and development system. Your job is to plug into that system and start working as per that system. If this training and development system has successfully worked for so many people for so many years, it will work for you too. Your team's success system is the most critical aspect of this business. Just surrender to that system 100%. If your team is yet to develop such a system, you can follow the success system given in this book and achieve your dreams. The system given in this book has already fulfilled dreams of countless number of people for so many years. Work with the faith that success may be delayed, but success will not be denied.

You cannot believe in God until you believe in yourself.

–Swami Vivekananda

Nothing is permanent, not even problems.
Four months into the business, I was growing fast but made a few mistakes and my income crashed to zero. I had an option to go back to my job or to accept my mistakes and grow through them to achieve what I had come for. Me, my wife and brother all had resigned jobs. Our credit cards were full and we had exhausted every resource but we worked everyday with faith that today we will get the right person. We spoke to our upline daily, read books, showed more plans and managed to attend every event even though there was no one to go with us for many events. But whatever I am today is because I didn't quit in those tough 9 months.

2
100% Submission to the System

> *There is no secret to success; there is always a system to success.*
>
> –Deepak Bajaj

As per businessdictionary.com, 'A system is a set of detailed methods, procedures and routines created to carry out a specific activity.' In our business, a system is a set of programs, activities and tools designed to guide you on what to do and how to do, so that you get quick and remarkable results for your time and effort invested in the business. A good system is developed by the serious efforts of thousands of people over a period of many years and once established, paves a proven and time tested way for fellow distributors/associates to be successful in the business.

The chances of success in network marketing business are higher than in any other business because here there is a full training and development system to support a new comer, which is not the case anywhere else. By following the system, new associates can fulfill their dreams in a much lesser time and with least amount of pain and suffering. The best thing about a system is that it works equally well for each and every person. Your education, schooling, financial background, gender, location, work experience etc. do not matter in this business, what really matters is how fast you can adapt to its system and start functioning according to that system.

Once there was a famous music teacher who was known not only for his musical genius but also for his wisdom. One day, a 40-year-old man came to see him and expressed his desire to learn music from him. The teacher asked what this man knew about music. He replied that he had learnt music for 5-6 years and used to perform for one group, but he stopped practicing a few years back. The teacher told him that it would take him 3 years and Rs 80,000 to be a master of music. The man found it very expensive and sat there to think about it. Just then, a 12-year-old child came to visit the teacher and expressed his desire to learn music. The teacher asked this young boy what he knew about music. The child replied he knew nothing about it. The teacher said it would take the child 1 year and Rs 20,000 to be a master of music. Now, this man who had been sitting there hearing all of this, became really furious and asked, 'I know quite a lot about music and I already have good experience, then why would this child with no experience take 2 years and Rs 60,000 less to be a master?' The teacher replied, 'To be a master, it only requires one year and Rs 20,000, but to unlearn what you have already learnt, it will take 2 years and Rs 60,000.'

> *New learning is easier and faster when we are ready to unlearn some of what we have already learnt.*
>
> –Deepak Bajaj

As a matter of fact, there is a unique system for success in every profession or business. A doctor, a lawyer, an accountant, a shopkeeper, a police officer—all have different ways and principles of working. If you are successful in any profession, it is because you followed the system of that particular profession and not of any other profession. You cannot be successful as a police officer by following systems required for a nurse or an architect. Likewise, if you want to be successful in network marketing, you need to keep aside your current system and like a beginner, learn the best system for network marketing. The faster you adapt to this new system of working, the quicker you will be able to make it big in the business.

Actually this is one of the major causes of failure for a majority of people in this business. People come from different backgrounds in this business and they carry with them their experiences, systems, thinking and unique ways of working. They start operating this business with that old thinking and approach and then suffer setbacks and disappointments. Since entry and exit costs are negligible in this business, those initial setbacks make a majority of the people quit the business. If people can just give themselves some time to learn and practice the principles of this business, they will realize that network marketing is the easiest and the most rewarding business in the world.

A tree is hidden inside a seed, but it comes out only with a system.

A beautiful statue is hidden in a stone, but it comes out with a system. There is a system even to give birth to a child in 9 months.

I always insist whenever you choose a team or a company to work with, make sure they have an established training and development system. After working with thousands of people, I have developed a system that has given me legendary success in this business and also great success to thousands of other people who followed it. This system has worked equally well for every network marketing company with any product line or income plan.

This book will tell you everything about this success system. I strongly believe that if you can understand and implement everything that has been given in this book, you will definitely fulfill all your dreams and be amongst the top performers of your company. You can apply this same system as it is or consult your upline and modify it as per your specific requirements. The adjacent diagram explains this complete system.

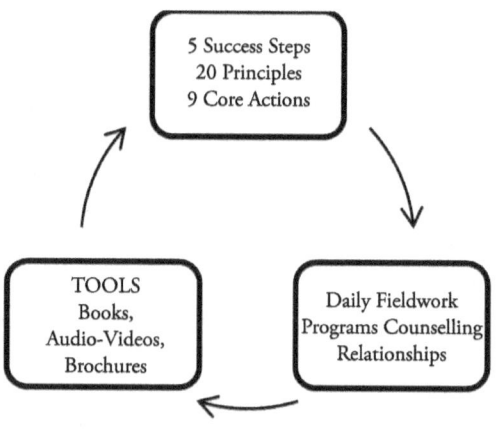

The Network Marketing Success System

First you work for the system and then the system will work for you.

A good system supports you in many ways:

✓ When you start the business, you can recruit people but you cannot train them. The programs and the tools provided by the

system will train and develop your team members and help in establishing your team.
- ✓ System will help you in developing teams at different locations.
- ✓ People come to network marketing for passive income. Most of the companies offer nomination facility also which means your hard work will benefit your children and their children also. This ongoing passive income is possible only if you work with a powerful system.
- ✓ Whatever you cannot teach to your team, some trainer in some program or in some video will be able to teach it better.

So, 100% submission to the system is the smartest thing to do. Be a student of the business and build a stable and growing business empire.

System is your insurance against ignorance.

–Deepak Bajaj

How life taught me the power of a system.
I started my business with massive activity and within 14 weeks I touched a particular income level that a good leader takes 2-5 years to achieve. But after 4 months my business started slowing down. My list was over, no one was visible in my team, my income crashed to zero and I had no clue what was going on. I approached my upline and he asked how many training centers I had? I was shocked because I thought our job was only to sell and add people. Actually I was so busy collecting new sales that I never cared for training, counseling and building relationships. Losing a big team was like a catastrophe. I was exhausted physically, emotionally and financially but I started again. It took me 9 months but this time I had wonderful relationships and training centers full of awesome people.

3
It's a Business, it Will Take Time

Anything long lasting or worthwhile takes time and complete surrender.

–Ryan Hidinger

Network marketing is like any other business and it needs to be nurtured daily, like any other business. Every business needs a huge initial investment, working capital, vision, passion, commitment, hard work, willingness to follow the basic rules of the industry, reinvestment, determination to not quit in the face of adversities, constant learning, patience, etc. You don't need a huge initial investment and working capital in network marketing business, but all other things listed above are essential for success here too.

Success in any endeavor doesn't happen by accident. Rather it's the result of deliberate decisions, conscious effort and immense persistence…all directed at specific goals.

–Gary Ryan

Network marketing business is built by becoming a leader and by developing leaders in your team. Developing a leader is like growing a tree; it needs regular care and patience. It's a process of constantly growing yourself and building a large team, one person at a time. Like it takes 5-10 years of training and education to become a doctor, lawyer, engineer or chartered accountant, it will take a few years for one to become a successful network-marketing businessman. Since you have started this business, commit yourself not to quit before at least one year, and in this one year, be committed to attend every event and follow the success system 100%. Be a student of the business and master it.

The growth in your business will be directly proportional to your personal growth. Sometimes, a few people get quick initial success, but if they don't develop their character and capability simultaneously, their business will also come down. God will fulfill every dream of yours only if you prove that you deserve it, and you prove it by following the system daily for a few years.

So start your network marketing business with a vision and stay committed to not quitting until you make that vision a reality.

> *Champions don't become champions in the ring; they are merely recognized there.*
>
> –John C Maxwell

Growing a tree takes much longer than growing a plant.
In 2008, I started building business in a city in Haryana (India) that was 5 hours drive from my home. Our company didn't have a store there so I had to carry products in my car every week. I couldn't afford a driver and drove late nights managing with jugs of tea and repeatedly washing my face. For the first 13 months, the cost of travel and stay was more than the money I earned from that team. For 2 years, I travelled to that city for 105 weeks without a single break and that city became one of the biggest business centers for me.

4
Programs are Lifeline

> *Program numbers are like blood test reports. I need not ask you how your business is doing? You show me your program numbers for last 3 months and I will tell you current and future position of your business.*
>
> –Deepak Bajaj

Be it a political party or an NGO or any private corporation, for every organization to function and grow, the team needs to meet up regularly. For a job, people work 8-12 hours a day for 5-6 days every week in an office. Since we network marketers don't operate from an office, we need programs/events to get our people together under one roof regularly. It gives a common purpose or mission to the team and keeps everyone motivated. Programs are the lifeline of this business. Network marketing business runs only on programs. While there are different types of program, they all fall into two major categories:-

1. Big events with more than 500+ people organized in hotels, auditoriums or stadiums. It may include training, experience sharing, recognition, award ceremony, etc. or a combination of two or more things from this list. These are generally grand events with lot of excitement and energy.
2. Training programs or workshops: Small events specifically focused on skill building for distributors and include product training, selling skills, stage performance, etc.

When I use the word program here in this book, it represents the first set of events.

I have observed many a times that when we share our opportunity with someone in their office or home, everybody is willing to start with us, but they have a few concerns. Does this thing really work? Is it really a business? Are people actually making money and fulfilling their dreams? Is there only a particular category of people who are successful in it or is everyone successful? Can I also be successful in this business?

You can give best possible answers to these questions but still people will not believe you completely. Making them attend a program and seeing it for themselves is the best answer anyone can give to any of their questions. It's like if you want to show the power of water to someone, you need to take them to the seashore. Pointing to a glass of water in somebody's drawing room will never convey what all the water can do. You cannot really make someone visualize a tsunami holding a small glass of water. What a program can do in a few hours is not possible to convey during a one to one chat or in small group meet-ups. One answer that I give to all the questions thrown at me is – 'Why don't you attend this program and find it out for yourself?' The answer to this question tells me the authenticity of the questions and the interest level of the person asking the question. Every time people have agreed to come for the program, it has saved me months of hard work.

You ask any network marketing leader where did they make their decision to take up this business seriously, and invariably all of them will tell you about one program after which their life was entirely different.

–Deepak Bajaj

Since distributors have easy access to the top leadership in network marketing, sometimes they try to bypass the system by arranging a small meeting for their team with the top leader, thinking that it will substitute for the program. It's a wrong assumption. Nothing can substitute for a program. All leaders need the platform, energy, edification and setting of a program to deliver their full potential. What a leader can do from a program stage is infinitely larger than what the same leader can do at a home meeting or in a small meeting of 4-10 people.

It can best be explained by the theory of Thermometer vs. Thermostat. The leaders in this business are like thermometers and the programs work as thermostat. Like a thermometer can only tell you the temperature and cannot change it, a leader can at best tell you if right now the other person has got drive and commitment to build a big business. Howsoever impactful and powerful the leader is, he or she cannot change your people's fire and passion during one to one counseling. But a program works like a thermostat and it actually enhances the drive, vision and commitment of a person. All the great leaders I have in my team, I got them through some program.

> *One program will change you or your distributor forever; we don't know which one. So keep getting maximum associates to every program.*
>
> –Deepak Bajaj

Programs have the power to change beliefs:-

People perform according to their beliefs. Programs can magically thrash wrong beliefs and build new empowering beliefs. When you see 1000-2000 or sometimes even more people gathered under one roof, having purchased tickets for the event, all dressed up professionally with never before seen energy, excitement and positivity, many of your old assumptions are bound to be shattered and you come out with a new and empowering set of beliefs. Three main new beliefs that a program can establish for people are as below:-

1. When they see thousands of people queuing up for the event, they get to believe that it's not one or two people doing it, the whole city has converged to do this business. Suddenly, the company that was non-existing a few days back appears now to be the most famous company in town. One fact is clearly established in their mind that whether **they do it or not, this business is going to flourish and prosper in their city anyway**.

   When they listen to the real life experiences of many people being shared from the stage, they develop this faith that everyone has their share of struggles and disappointments. Everyone has a small beginning. Everyone has doubts, but all winners overcome their fears, struggles, rejections and disappointments to be on stage one day as achievers. They get hope that if they don't quit, one day they will also be an achiever. They see multiple demonstrations of the fact that winners are over-comers. Another big confidence booster is the fact that they have access to all these overcomers who are willing to help them too. All network marketing achievers share everything they have to help new people become successful.

2. When they see achievers on stage from different age groups, gender, financial background, location, educational qualification, professional degrees etc. they are made to believe that people from all these different categories are doing it equally well and everyone can be successful at it. They develop a belief that **if they all can do it, so can we**.

Once the program is over, don't analyze if the program was good or bad based on the feedback of people. People's feedback may be used to make the event better next time, but not to understand the impact or long term results of the program. To me, what a program does is build faith and develop empowering beliefs about self and the business. Program works at different levels with different people and we really don't know what will work with whom, but it leaves an impact for sure. Results may be visible in a few weeks or in a few months.

If your answer to this one question is YES, whichever corner of the world you are in and whatever may by your product line and compensation plan, you will be super successful in this business – ***Are you growing from program to program? Have you got more people in this program than the last program?'***

This is the yardstick. This is the litmus test. If there is one thing for which you should be concerned the most in this business, it is your program numbers.

Strike when the iron is hot: You should be working really hard when you know there is a program coming up in the next 4-6 weeks. That is like the peak season for network marketing. Go for maximum recruitments. Build a recruitment drive and make sure everyone is working on personal lists. Simultaneously, start doing small events to promote the program. Your whole group should be promoting the event. Carry all program promotion tools with you all the time: videos, brochures, etc. Talk about the program wherever you can. Start selling tickets as soon as you can. Talk only about the next program. You should promote only one event at a time.

Don't worry about special techniques for promoting an event. If you genuinely believe that this program can change your life and the lives of those who attend it, that excitement and conviction will radiate in your speech and body language. You cannot lie all the time. It will be visible to all. Just make sure you reach out to maximum people possible and invite maximum people personally. This is the time to reignite old distributors. Bring up all your lists and invite everyone you can. Programs by themselves are not big or small, special or regular; your promotion makes it big and special. How you visualize it and how you transfer that faith to the people to whom you are promoting this program is what makes it big or small. Approach every program as a life-changing event. Give it all you got and you will grow bigger, better and faster in this business.

Just remember when you invite someone to give you one hour; there will be 20 more people/things asking for the same one hour. Your invitation must be strong enough to win over these 20 invitations. Remember Invitation vs. Intimation: Most people think that they are inviting others, but what they are doing generally is an intimation. Forwarding messages on WhatsApp, social media, sms, etc. are all intimations. Invitation has to be personal and persuasive. You may have to visit repeatedly for inviting people for special events.

> *Number one skill required to reach the top rank of your company is your ability to get people to the programs.*
>
> –Deepak Bajaj

Visit www.deepakbajaj.biz to get tips on designing the best programs for your team and to find out programs that can help you grow faster.

A program can save you months of hard work.
I was told to start this business in May 2006 and I started it in June 2007. You can attribute this delay to my degrees, salary, status, ego or ignorance. Many good leaders approached me in this period, but I started the business only after attending a program in June 2007 in Mandi, HP, India. I had gone there casually just to have a look but I was surprised to see the achievements of people there. With the magic of that event, I signed up on the same day and took off to become the fastest man in my company in whole of North India. I still regret wasting those 13 months that could have been saved if I would have attended any program earlier. But I also got 4 good friends from that event - Jairo K James, Ashish Mathew, Dr AR Mohite and Dr Shiv Gautam.

5
Pulse of the Business: Numbers And Ratios

Whatever gets monitored gets improved.

Network marketing is simply a numbers game. What I love the most about this business is its predictability. By all means, this is the simplest business on earth because by taking care of few numbers, you can take care of your entire business. The rule here is very simple:

Know your numbers. Work as per your ratios. Improve your ratios.

What are the key numbers in our business?
- ✓ How many names are there in your prospect list?
- ✓ How many new names you are adding to your prospect list every week?
- ✓ How many new guests are attending your business presentations every week?
- ✓ How many Home Meetings are happening in your team every week?
- ✓ How many new rank/pin achievers have you planned for this month?
- ✓ How many product training workshops are happening in your team this month and how many people are attending it?
- ✓ How many people are getting regular weekly/monthly income in your team?
- ✓ How many people are full timers and how many more are planning to come full time this month?

✓ How many distributors in your team are showing plans every day?

If you know your numbers and if you are working to improve your numbers, you are definitely moving towards a stable and growing business.

I have seen people telling stories of how hard they have been working and what all sacrifices they are making, but when you ask them to put their numbers on paper, it's a different story. People will tell you they are working hard, but not getting results. You put their numbers on paper and you will realize the problem doesn't lie with results; the problem is inadequate working. What I have learnt from my long career in this business is that never review people in general terms, always talk in terms of numbers. Never ask how a business is going, just discuss what the numbers are. It has got two key benefits:-

1. The discussion stays focused on the development areas and not on people.
2. There are no blames and criticism, numbers serve as the mirror. Numbers show the true picture.

Not only are numbers good for reviewing our teams, but it is also the best way to review us and improve ourselves.

Ratios:

We are in a business of numbers, and a relationship between different numbers is called the ratio. A ratio defines a relationship between two different numbers in such a way that if you change one number in the ratio, the others will change automatically in the same proportion. Ratios set the roadmap for your success. We need to understand three aspects of ratios:-

Know your ratios, work as per your ratios and improve your ratios.

Know your Ratios:

If you keep track of your numbers and their ratios, you will realize that success or failure in this business is not dependent on anything else but numbers. In fact, your success lies to a great extent not on your selling skills, but on your time management skills to manage maximum number of presentations.

Success is a game—the more times you play, the more times you win. And the more times you win the more successfully you will play.

—Allan Pease

We have two basic jobs in network marketing business:-

1. People should start the business.
2. People should actively build the business.

Since you have decided to take up this business, you must understand the basic operational ratios in our business for these 2 processes.

For the first one, I have typically observed a **Recruitment Ratio of 10: 7: 2**.

For 10 calls you make for setting appointment, you can actually do a meeting with 7 people, out of which 2 people start the business/buy the products.

For the second process, **Activity Ratio of 10: 5: 2: 1**.

Out of 10 distributors who start with you, 5 will attend the training program, 2 will be product customers and 1 will be a serious business builder.

These ratios are average ratios calculated over a period of 11 years working with thousands of people, but they purely depend on the individual.

Work as per Ratios:

We are in numbers business and numbers don't lie.

—Deepak Bajaj

Now, since we recognize that the success in business depends purely on numbers, our key task is to do the numbers. This realization came to me when one of my associates asked me a question – 'I show an opportunity presentation to 10 people, but only 1 person starts my business. What to do?' I asked him what does he want. He said he wanted 10 people to start business with him. I said, 'Show the plan to 100 people and 10 will start your business.' Ratios are powerful and numbers don't lie.

Ratios gave me an understanding that every activity in the ratio is important and pays me.

If you get Rs. 1000 per sale and your ratio is 10:7:2, then your income will look like this:

Income earned on 2 sales = Rs. 2000

Income per sale = Rs. 1000

Income per meeting = Rs. 286 (2000/7)

Income per phone call = Rs. 200 (2000/10)

You can have your own numbers in this ratio but when you work on this format, you are certain that every phone call and every meeting gives you income irrespective of it getting converted to a sale or not. Just imagine working with this attitude and you will always have that smile on your face. Your income doesn't depend on sale, but on doing that meeting and making that phone call. Thus your only job will be to book the meetings.

> 'Make more calls and book more meetings. You can be the best presenter or speaker on earth but if you don't give enough presentations, you will be out of business.'
>
> –Deepak Bajaj

Improve your Ratios:

Once you have started working as per ratios, next intelligent move is to improve yourself and your numbers. Make yourself better, develop right skills so that when you make 10 calls, you can book all 10 meetings and not 7. Why not close 4 sales and not 2 from every 7 meetings? Find out ways to add more people to your list and to make more calls every single day.

Essentially what we face in this business is not a selling problem but a planning problem. Network marketing business will grow exponentially for decades to come and the person who will be at the top is the one who reaches out to maximum people faster.

The sole purpose of this book is to empower you and your team to improve your numbers and get you massive success in a short period of time. You can access a lot of tools available on my website www.deepakbajaj.biz and attend my live training event—network marketing Millionaires Academy to get more cutting edge tools and to prepare yourself for big success in this business.

In network marketing business, the person who wins is not essentially the smartest one but definitely the one who shows more number of presentations.

–Deepak Bajaj

> **Track your numbers.**
> *While finding principles for success in network marketing, I got to hear some pearls of wisdom from two great leaders from USA - Paul Miller & Angelo Nardone. They made me realize that the right numbers can give you total control and big growth in the business.*

6
Upline is your Best Friend

> *The biggest reward of this business is not the money you make, but the friends who always stand by you and who always lift you up however deep you may fall.*
>
> –Deepak Bajaj

If there is one person who always has your best interest in his/her mind, it is your upline. If there is one person who is available to help you unconditionally, it is your upline. If there is someone who can forgive you for all your mistakes and stand by your side as you move towards your dreams, he/she is your upline. Upline is your best friend, partner, well-wisher and coach in this business. Half of your battle is won once you have a good upline.

The first person that you meet in this business is your upline. In fact, he/she is the person you meet even before you start the business. He/she is the one who ignited your dreams and convinced you to get into this business. Many a times I feel I can never thank my upline enough for what he has done for me. I am always full of gratitude when I think of my upline.

Network marketing business has been designed in such a way that people helping people is the inherent philosophy of the business. This model makes team work a necessity and makes the upline and downline work closely with each other. But if this arrangement gets converted into a friendship, that is the best thing that can happen to you and it will give 10 times the speed to your business.

Submit totally to your active and growing upline. Always stay connected to your upline. Have regular conversations with your upline. Use your upline wherever required, but don't misuse him/her. Give him/her all the respect he/she deserves and edify your upline at every platform. More than anything else, it will set the right example for your own team. When your team sees you edifying your upline, they will also start edifying you. An upline can help you in more ways than you can imagine. How to use your upline is also an art; master it. **Your upline is your biggest resource.** Use it judiciously.

Ironically, some people, after they achieve a certain rank or income, stop edifying their upline and stop acknowledging the contribution their upline has given in taking them to this particular position. Some even become arrogant and start criticizing their upline. You can tear your upline down but when you need help, you can't get the same person to motivate your team whom you yourself tore down sometime back. With my decade long experience in this business, I have seen that often there will be situations where you will need your upline to set things right in your team. Ours is a very dynamic business and howsoever smart you may be, certain things can be managed easier and faster with the help of your upline.

Till the time you have faith in yourself, have faith in your upline's faith in you.

You plus your upline makes a winning team and together you can give the right direction to your team and build the right momentum.

Not only look for a good upline but you also be a good upline.

–Deepak Bajaj

An upline can help you stretch your goals.

One of my associates, Chintan Arora achieved his dream income of Rs 3.5 Lac in a week. Everyone including me congratulated him. It was indeed a great feat. This was equal to a whole year's income for Chintan when he started with us few years back. He has grown 50 times in a couple of years with us. Next week I asked Chintan, 'When are you going to cross Rs 4 Lac income per week.' He immediately said 'I love you, Deepak sir. We all are growing because you keep pushing us to stretch and to set higher goals.' Sometimes you need that extra push and a good upline can do that for you.

7
Power of Mentorship

Mentorship is the key to extraordinary success.
                                            —Mike Murdock

Be it a sports person, a businessman or a politician, every successful person in any field will always have a coach or a mentor. In fact, every successful person advises, 'Hire a coach.' It's because when you have a coach who is mentoring you and monitoring you, your chances of reaching your goal multiplies many times. As per Merriam-Webster dictionary, **'a mentor is a trusted counselor or guide'**. A mentor helps you in many ways including:-

- ✓ Clarifies questions and doubts.
- ✓ Empowers you to set goals.
- ✓ Provides guidance on how to work and how to handle difficult situations.
- ✓ Makes an action plan and monitors your progress.
- ✓ Gives you emotional support and counseling.
- ✓ Stands with you like a friend and well wisher.
- ✓ Inspires you to achieve more.

Typically hiring a coach means lacs of rupees in fees, but in network marketing business you need not pay lacs of rupees for a coach, you always have the best coach in the form of your upline who will be working with you shoulder to shoulder in your journey towards your dreams without charging a single rupee.

A mentor is someone who sees more talent and ability within you than you see in yourself, and helps bring it out of you.
                                                    –Bob Proctor

In network marketing, working with a mentor is absolutely necessary for two reasons:-

1. In network marketing there is no boss, no major set up or investment. You are your own boss and the responsibility for your success is entirely on you. Almost everyone starts this business as a part time business. Your family and current profession or job also keeps you busy. In this scenario, if you have a mentor who can guide you, support you and inspire you when you face rejections, disappointment or setback, you can be successful faster.

2. By its very nature, network marketing is not a subject like mathematics and physics where you can just remember things from some textbook; it is more like learning a sport or a music instrument where you need regular practice and someone to be with you during this practice. A mentor can play this role for you.

Remember mentoring is an overlooked area and since mentoring is available freely in network marketing, people don't value it. But you need a mentor all the time: when your business is going great, when your business is stuck, or when your business is going down.

So, find an active and growing upline whom you can access and make him/her your mentor. Submit totally to your mentor and work as per the plan you have made with him or her.

I also provide one on one coaching to high dreaming individuals who want to achieve big in lesser time. You can find more details about my High Performance Coaching on my website – www.deepakbajaj.biz.

Every great achiever is inspired by a great mentor.
                                                    –Lailah Gifty Akita

> ***Mentors can do wonders.***
> *I have learnt the power of mentorship from two great men from USA whom I really admire – Kanti Gala and Shivaram Kumar. They have always talked about the power of submission to the right mentors and to the right system.*

8
Ownership and Mastery

The ones that take ownership of their lives are likely to be more successful.

—Gbatiste

Ownership is the total and absolute responsibility for your business. You take ownership of the business when you stop blaming others for your success or failure and when you stop looking at others for running your business. That is the first day of your business. Majority of the people who fail to build a big business are the ones who want to build their business with an employee attitude, but if you seriously want to build a big business, you need to work with an owner's attitude and be in the driving seat of the business.

What are the signs of someone who has taken full ownership in network marketing?

- ✓ You show your own presentations.
- ✓ You can do follow up meetings yourself and can close the sale without anyone's help.
- ✓ Your calendar is full of appointments.
- ✓ You don't criticize and don't blame others for your success or failure.
- ✓ You do what is required and some more.
- ✓ You reach to the events before time along with your teammates and guests.
- ✓ You don't run away from problems, you grow through them.
- ✓ You don't quit on the first signs of setbacks or rejections.

- ✓ You regularly call your uplines and seek counseling and solutions.
- ✓ You take initiatives in the organizing of events and not stay a participant only.
- ✓ You have your own written goals and you are committed to do whatever it takes to achieve those goals.

Your business is yours and not that of your upline or downline. It's your dream and it starts working the day you take a decision to do whatever it takes to fulfill those dreams through this business.

> *It all begins with ownership. No ownership no business. Ownership is not given; it is taken.*
>
> –Deepak Bajaj

You need to take full responsibility of continuously improving yourself and to be the person you want to be. You need to invest in yourself by attending programs and by reading recommended books. Many people feel training programs and tools are expenses but the fact is that they are not expenses they are an investment. This investment in yourself will give you highest returns for decades to come. Empower your team also through books, tools and Empower your team through books, tools and training programs. Many a times the books or tools you lend will not come back; that's part of the business. You need to buy more tools than you personally need, you need to stock for your team also. If you get even one good new distributor every month through this, you will recover your money. So keep reinvesting in yourself and in your business regularly.

> *God will give you a big team only if you are ready for the same.*
>
> –Deepak Bajaj

There are three upline types we should never become:-

(a) a **Postman** who keeps sending messages on groups;

(b) a **cheerleader** – clapping in programs, motivational forwards on social media, clapping and encouraging people the most in WhatsApp chat, they never post their work and achievements; and

(c) **Relative upline** – they are like relatives who will be seen only in functions and programs, they will never work on ground with their teams. Take the ownership of becoming what you want your team to be. Your team will be your copy. So make yourself worth copying.

Whenever you are stuck and the business seems to be slow or not moving, dress up, show up and show the plan. Lead from the front with the power of basics.

–Deepak Bajaj

Ownership and mastery go hand in hand. To take absolute ownership you need to master the basics of the business. Business basics in network marketing are really simple, that's why anyone can build this business successfully. All it needs is your willingness to learn and practice the 'Core Activities'—sharing the business presentation, handling objections, follow through, registration, product details, usage of business tools, knowledge about business system and code of conduct, etc. Once you become an expert in all these activities, your business will take off in a big way and how do you become an expert—by doing these activities more often. Just keep repeating these things and in no time you will be a master.

Repetition is the mother of all skills.

Master the use of tools too. The best network marketers use tools instead of showing off their knowledge and skills. They prefer events/programs than their own presentations. They use other peoples' testimonies and presentations than their own. The masters don't present themselves as experts; they just invite people to learn more about their opportunity and products using third party tools. The best network marketers bring passion, faith and conviction. Their energy and commitment is contagious. So, make passion, faith and commitment your priority, invite with conviction and let the third party tools do the rest.

Everyone starts amateur; mastery comes with constant practice. Everything that you need to grow big in network marketing is a learnable skill. Just take ownership of your business and work towards mastery of business basics.

I fear not the man who has practiced 10,000 kicks once, but I fear the man who has practiced one kick 10,000 times.

–Bruce Lee

Choose the right role models and set higher benchmarks for yourself. Your Uplines or any other leader is at a particular rank or income level because of their personal goals and actions. If you see people above you or around you as slow performers, it's not a limitation of the industry; it is a limitation of those people. You need not follow them in this aspect. Spot the fastest earners in the company and work to better their achievements. Your business starts with you.

Stand up, be bold, be strong. Take the whole responsibility on your own shoulders and know that you are the creator of your own destiny.

–Swami Vivekananda

Practice and patience leads you to the top.
When I introduced Gaurav Bajaj into the business in 2007 he was a Software Consultant in a leading American company, Sapient Corporation. He was a typical introvert and only knew how to deal with computers. His entire body used to shiver and sweat at the time of presentations. He was 300 km away from me and used to record his presentations so that I can give him feedbacks later. He travelled 14 hours every weekend in public buses to learn how to succeed in this business. His constant and untiring practice made him one of the youngest top rank achievers in the company within 3 years. Gaurav Bajaj is one of the most respected network marketers in the country today.

9
Time Management – Your Winning Edge

Time is not the main thing. It is the only thing.
—Miles Davis

We all have the same 24 hours everyday; the success lies in how efficiently we use those 24 hours. In this age of technology, social media and thousands of other distractions, the ultimate key to success is time management. Success in our business goes not to the ones with the best selling skills, but to the one with the best time management skills. Time management is nothing but prioritizing our activities and ensuring that we finish the most important ones before anything else. One key quality I have seen in people who are successful in this business: they mind their own business.

Mind your Own Business:

The main thing is to keep the main thing the main thing.
—Stephan R Covey

Always remember why we started this business: to fulfill our dreams, to become rich, to get recognition and to leave a legacy. But for some people, ironically as the business progresses and they build a team, they start devoting their time to activities, which will not propel them towards fulfilment of these goals.

You know what will propel you towards success: prospecting more people, showing more plans, closing more sales, being counseled by uplines and counseling your teammates, inviting more people to your events and organizing relevant events for your team. Everything else is a distraction and most of the times, the distractions are easier, tempting and you have others to give you company on the way.

Don't get side tracked by people who are not on track.

Time Drainers:

- ✓ Staying too engaged on social media/WhatsAap. Social media can help you in building business also, but generally we start by doing one small thing on Facebook or Instagram and end you being there for an hour or so.
- ✓ Resolving futile conflicts among repeated complainers. They are generally the same people with the same conflicts.
- ✓ Doing things for people that they should do for themselves. Help them to stand on their feet and not to be handicapped.
- ✓ Repeated discussion about other companies. They are too many to last a lifetime.
- ✓ Event management without focusing on getting maximum people to events.
- ✓ Too much involvement with cross-lines.
- ✓ Showing plans for people for whom you have already showed 4-6 plans.

Getting unnecessarily involved into issues that are out of the scope of this business, and many more.

> *The toughest thing in this business is to stay focused on doing what you have come for.*
>
> –Deepak Bajaj

Focus is the key to success in this business. My mentor, Tony Robbins says, 'Where your focus goes, energy flows.' Wherever you focus your time and energy, you will start getting results there. If you focus on the business, you will get success in the business; if you focus somewhere else, you will get results in that area. You need full focus on business all the time but there are two typical situations where many distributors lose focus and damage their business:

1. **Initial stages of business when you are a part timer:-**
   You have just started this new business along with a job or profession that you have already been doing. Plus you have family commitments and a few other things that you are used to doing.

In the middle of this, now a new business has come into your life that is asking you to learn new things and to do new things. You don't like a few of those things and results are also small in the beginning. To focus on your new network marketing business in this situation and to nurture it with daily commitment is tough. Inability to give required focus on business in the initial days is the key reason for majority of people to quit this business. Building this business on weekends is also not a problem as long as you are fully devoted to this for weekends.

2. **When your business is growing big independently without you:-**

    There will be a stage when your business will be running in auto mode without your active involvement. If you are doing personal sponsoring and building new teams you will be busy but otherwise you are free. When you have established yourself as a leader and you have free time, you will interact with cross lines or people from other companies or other so called wise men and advisors who will keep suggesting you highly profitable instant money making ideas. All these three sets of people will slowly take your time away from the business and when you stop giving focus to the business, it will slowly go down.

    Always remember to stay fully focused on your business at each and every stage of business development. Your business is your most valuable asset. Protect it with undivided focus.

To get the most value out of your day, please keep the following in mind:

- ✓ Fix your time slots for social media and adhere to it.
- ✓ Keep your calendar full of appointments for sharing products or business presentations.
- ✓ Stay away from a few selected people who you know are time drainers.
- ✓ Have momentum in your business and create so much work that there are more than two people calling you at the same time for help or for attending their events. Then you choose the ones who deserve your time more. **Teach your teams to earn your time.**

✓ **Remember your top 2 tasks for the day – make more calls and show more presentations.**

Check out latest time management techniques at www.deepakbajaj.biz.

Productivity is never an accident. It is always the result of a commitment to excellence, intelligent planning, and focused effort.

–Paul J Meyer

Time Management is a learnable skill.
I have a dear friend and my business associate from Punjab, India —Vikas Garg. He was a very successful traditional businessman for two decades when he started network marketing with me in 2007. It took him almost three years to close all his old businesses and to take up network marketing full time with me. But after 2 years of that decision he was happily making 10 times more income from network marketing than what he was making from his factories. He is an active political worker, actively involved in several social service organizations, has a big extended family and has a very active social circle. His success in this business is a living proof that we can do everything we want by developing our time management skills.

10
Daily Choices: The Unseen Side of Success

Everything in your life is a reflection of choices you have made. If you want different results, make different choices.

We all are very good at making big decisions in life, but majority of us struggle to make the right decisions when it comes to those everyday, seemingly insignificant situations. But actually, these are the decisions that define our future. This chapter will empower you on making right daily choices that will make you a winner.

I have simplified success in life to a 3-step process:-

Quickly write down a few things that are close to your heart and that you want to achieve through this business in a few months to few years period. Make as big a list as you want and select the top 3 goals that you are absolutely serious about. Now list down daily actions that will enable you to achieve those goals and start doing these actions everyday.

Show me your daily schedule and I will tell your priorities and the size of your achievements.

–Deepak Bajaj

What differentiates an achiever from everyone else are the things they do every single day. Actually, why people fail is simply because they don't do those things that are necessary for success. Why the failures don't do these things is because they don't like doing those things. On the other hand, what makes winners successful is that they do the things that are necessary for success. The winners also don't like doing those things, but they do it anyway. Winners are committed to do everything it takes to win, every single day and that makes all the difference.

> *Two roads diverged into the woods and I took the one less travelled by and that has made all the difference.*
>
> –Robert Frost

You have to live your dream every single day through the right choices you make. For next 1-3 years, keep this business at the center of your life and modify your schedules to give more time for your dreams. I did exactly the same when I started in 2007. I was clear my network marketing business is my top most priority and I planned all other activities around it. A few examples of how I made my daily choices are:-

- ✓ Since most of my business was done on weekends, I never attended any social function on a weekend.
- ✓ I never celebrated any of my own family events on a weekend.
- ✓ If it was about choosing whether to go to a business seminar/meeting or to a birthday party/wedding reception, my choice was clearly to attend the business meeting every single time.
- ✓ Since I had realized that success in my business depends on how many new plans I share every day, I scheduled business presentations as first and foremost activity of my day.
- ✓ I understood having a pipeline of prospects is important and I need to add names to my list, hence I cultivated this new habit of talking to strangers and starting new relationships every day.
- ✓ I realized that the way I look is an integral part of my communication; I chose to wear formals and look sharp and bright every time I stepped out of my home.
- ✓ When I understood the importance of reading books and preparing my mind for success, I made it a part of my daily schedule to read for at least 15-30 min every day.

- ✓ I reached the programs on time and sat in the front row in every program. I always took some of my teammates for the programs.
- ✓ I had written goals for myself and I pasted them in my home where I could see them many times every day.

Your calendar shows your priorities.
–Deepak Bajaj

My calendar was filled with all the right activities every single day and that brought me all the success. It's time for you now to identify what I call your **Primary Daily Actions (PDAs)**. You know your goals from this business. Now decide what are the actions you must perform on a daily basis starting from today to achieve those goals. If you can determine that, you have won half the battle. From this list of daily actions identify top 3 actions that are most important in achieving your goals; these are your Primary Daily Actions (PDAs). Write down your three PDAs and get compulsive and obsessive about doing them every single day.

It all comes down to small and sometimes boring daily choices. The choices we make daily, consistently over a period of time, will determine the type of life and lifestyle we will live. The right choices consistently executed every day over time will activate the compound effect that will lead to unprecedented success in years to come. We overestimate what can be done in one year but grossly underestimate what can be achieved in one day.

Making those choices may be tough for first few days or weeks but if you do them consistently over a period of time, they become your habits and once you develop the right habits, you are already on your way to success.

People plan their years and months, but achievers plan their days also.
–Deepak Bajaj

Stay focused on your Daily Actions

The successful warrior is the average man with laser-like focus.
–Bruce Lee

Once your goals are defined and your daily actions are clear, it's time to work on these actions with a laser like focus. Remember, focus is not only about saying 'Yes' to your three PDAs, but also saying 'No' to all the other activities that will need your time and attention. You need to guard your time and focus every waking hour for your PDAs. Other activities are also important and need to be done, but those will be done only once your PDAs have been successfully implemented for the day.

Focus will give you productivity and highest returns on the amount of time invested. An average student spends only 20% of time on actually doing homework and the rest 80% of time is wasted in things like sharpening pencils, staring out of the window, antagonizing siblings, whining, researching stuff on the internet, asking on snacks, etc. Similarly, an average employee produces an effective working of only 2-3 hours out of 8 hours being in office every day. It is the case with most of the people in almost all fields. But if you want to be a network marketing millionaire, set your priorities right, determine your PDAs and stay focused on doing them. Success will be all yours.

A 1% improvement everyday will make you a completely different person in 3 months. It adds up to 100% improvement in three and a half months.

Big dreams demand sacrifice and daily actions.
I had seen the power of this business and I knew this business could fulfill all our dreams. But knowing will not make you rich, doing will. I told my wife to give me 24 months to build this business properly but after 24 months I will keep a globe in front of her on 1st of every month and wherever she will put her finger, I will take her there in 24 hours. We worked together and those 24 months made us financially free for life. Now I have already taken her and our kids to 25 countries for holidays.

11
Use the Power of SURGE

Living with network marketing for so many years, I have witnessed five powers crossing my path every single day. These five powers determine how far any person will go in this business. These are simple, doable, duplicable and powerful, yet most of the people miss one or more of them. I have brought them together for you in a unique concept called SURGE. Cambridge dictionary defines SURGE as 'a sudden, strong increase or burst' and I strongly believe as you start using the power of SURGE in your life, you will see your business skyrocketing in no time.

The power of **SURGE** comes from five powers working together:-

1. **S**poken Words
2. **U**nity
3. **R**ight Association
4. **G**oals: Written
5. **E**xpectations: Big

Let's explore the five driving powers of SURGE one by one:-

1. Power of Spoken Words

You can change your world by changing your words. Remember, death and life are in the power of the tongue.

–Joel Osteen

The most powerful tool available to mankind is their words. Big revolutions, freedom struggles and life changing decisions have taken place because of choice of certain words by certain people in

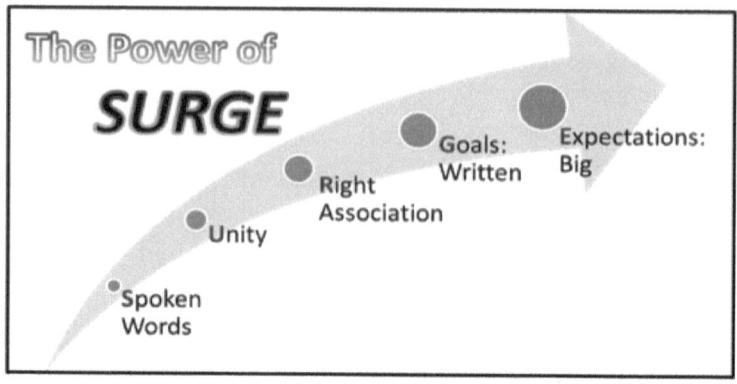

a particular situation. There are lives made out of speeches and there are speeches made out of lives. Words can touch someone without us touching that person or even without us being with that person. We read books written by authors whom we have never met and probably who may not even be alive, but their words make an impact on us. Words have the power to uplift or destroy someone.

> *Words are, of course, the most powerful drug used by mankind.*
> –Rudyard Kipling

When I talk about spoken words I talk about words said in two situations: Words that you speak to others and words that you speak to yourself. There has been countless books written on what to say and how to say when you talk to others and I have also covered that in this book in different chapters but people often tend to ignore the kind of words they use then they talk to themselves. Here, let's discuss both these situations separately.

Speaking to Others:

Ours is a people business and all the time we are talking to people. We communicate with people through various mediums: On stage, during counseling or one to one meetings, on messages, on phone calls and the often neglected communication areas: casual discussion with people while having meals or at airports or before or after programs or home meetings/visits and on countless other occasions every day. Follow these principles while communicating with people for a great impact:-

- ✓ Have one communication: the same communication on stage and off stage. Same communication with everyone. Same words during formal and informal meetings. Be particularly careful when you are not in a formal setting. People will observe you keenly even when you are not aware of the same. They want to see if you are real and genuine and the easiest way for them to do that is by matching what you say on stage and off stage.
- ✓ Don't complain, criticize or condemn anyone, particularly behind their back.
- ✓ Your non-verbals talk more than verbals. Your body language, your clothes, your hygiene and the way you conduct yourself talks more loudly than your words. Take care of it.
- ✓ Be polite, be respectful and be kind.
- ✓ Be sure to taste your words before you spit them out.
- ✓ Choose your words carefully. Have an uplifting vocabulary. Only those words are allowed to leave your mouth that will uplift another human being.
- ✓ Use THINK principle as given in adjoining table before you speak.

Before you speak THINK	
T	Is it True?
H	Is it Helpful?
I	Is it Inspiring?
N	Is it Necessary?
K	Is it Kind?

Be careful with your words. Once they are said, they can only be forgiven, not forgotten.

Speaking with Yourself:

Your words are your communication with the universe.

Your talking to yourself means your dominant thoughts that you choose to think over repeatedly. This is also called self-talk. These are also first reactions that come to you whenever you encounter any tough situation. This is what you are telling your subconscious repeatedly. This is what you expect from life and this is what life is going to give you. Your thoughts are the command you give to your mind. Have empowering and optimistic thoughts. Always use uplifting words when you think and talk to yourself.

2. Unity is Strength

We all have grown up with stories that taught us the moral value of Unity is strength. While this is a good moral to read and preach, very few people practice this principle in reality. But this one principle if followed in this business, can multiply your business growth. At the very core of network marketing business is the philosophy of people helping people. This business model itself makes it necessary for people to work closely with others in their team.

People may have their own reasons or nature for working individually but those who learn to work in cohesive teams with a spirit of unity have stable and growing team. Things become easier when we work together as a team. While people are generally together in initial stages of business, issues and disputes start when people move higher in ranks and achievements. But if you can hold your team together it is very good for everyone in the team. Even if you have always worked alone, let's change this habit now. If working together is fun and more profitable, why not change that old habit.

Legendary author Dr Stephan R Covey mentioned three levels of leadership in his book 'Seven Habits Of Highly Effective People: Dependence, Independence and Interdependence'. As per Dr Covey, when all independent leaders come together in a sprit of interdependence, they are able to create legendary success. Good relationships are important for maintaining unity. Read the chapter on relationships and communication in this book for proven tips on developing strong relations.

Also, network marketing business is highly profitable when there is momentum in the organization and momentum is possible only when all leaders jointly work together and give their best efforts. So when unity can give profits, stability and achievement, why not stay united. Build a culture of unity and cooperation in your team and grow bigger faster.

3. Impact of Association

Alien yourself with people that you can learn from, people who want more out of life, people who are stretching and searching and seeking some higher ground in life.

–Les Brown

Association is everything. Where will you be five years from now simply depends on people you meet, books you read, audios/videos you watch and programs you attend. It's simple: first you decide your associations and then your associations decide your future. So be very careful about whom you decide to spend your time with. Attitudes, beliefs, confidence, faith level, etc. everything gets transferred from one person to the other and this transfer happens when you are aware and also when you are not aware.

You may feel you are a highly positive, optimistic and determined individual and nothing can affect you. But no one is immune from the influence our associates and their interactions have on us. This impact may not be visible instantly but it will definitely show over a period of time.

One interesting thing about bad company or low dreamers is that they are all around in abundance and are easily accessible. So its very likely that if you don't make serious attempt to look for the best, you will end up being around people who will pull you down.

But if you want to move ahead faster than ever, look for association of high dreaming and growing people; people whom you adore, who are your role models, who know where they are going and are moving towards their goals. Look for people who are best in the industry and who have reached where you aim to reach. Sometimes right people will stretch you and their company will make you uncomfortable, but that's the sign of growth. That's the time to hold on and enjoy the growth that it brings along. Stick with them and never ever go back to old company. Buy them dinners, volunteer for some work where you get access to such people or grab every possible opportunity to spend time with them. Also I have personally observed that people, who are at the top of their industry love to mentor and guide people. They are generally open about sharing their success secrets and in fact love to see other people rising. But for them to mentor you they should also like you. So be genuine, work hard, be passionate and right people will also spot you. The better you become in life and in your chosen field, the greater are the odds of you reaching out to the best.

Also success in every field is based on the same fundamental principles. Legend in other fields can also teach you as much about being the best as the legends of your own field. Be open to learning from the best in other fields also. In network marketing business, right association automatically comes by attending all programs, reading right books, listening to right audio and video programs and staying in touch with your active line of sponsorship. So wherever you find the right people, just stick around them and make your way to the top. Remember your association determines your destiny.

> ***Wrong company is fatal.***
> *Without taking their names, I want to tell about a few promising associates in my team who grew really fast and earned big income in quite a short time, but they suddenly quit the business. Today, even after many years they are still struggling to survive. When I dig dipper into why these people quit at the peak of their careers, I found out in many cases that they started some new friendships with some wrong people 3-6 months before quitting. The influence of those people slowly poisoned their thought process and they made this mistake of quitting the business. One advice I repeatedly give in all my trainings is to choose your friends carefully. This includes your Facebook friends also.*

You are an average of five people you closely associate with.
–Jim Rohn

4. Power of Written Goals

People with clear, written goals, accomplish far more in a shorter period of time than people without them could ever imagine.
–Brian Tracy

Simply put, goals are dreams with deadlines. While dreams spring up from our vision and purpose in life, goals bring the necessary urgency towards fulfillment of those dreams. Goals are like milestones in our journey towards our dreams. You can use goals as your propelling system that will take you to where you want to be. Goals should be Short Term, Medium Term and Long Term.

Type of Goals as per the time frame for completion

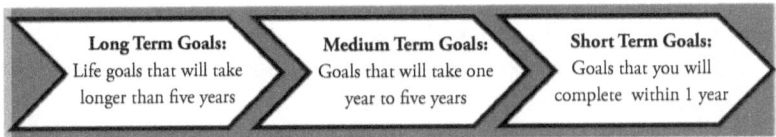

Long Term Goals: Life goals that will take longer than five years

Medium Term Goals: Goals that will take one year to five years

Short Term Goals: Goals that you will complete within 1 year

First you set your long-term goals. They are driven from your dreams, vision and purpose in life. Once you have set your long-term goals, you have the destination and direction. Now you need to set the milestones that you need to achieve year on year to accomplish your long-term goals. These are your medium term goals. The next step is to arrive at immediate goals that you want to fulfill within next twelve months. Write down your long term, medium term and short-term goals on a diary or laptop or your mobile right now and you are ready to take off.

Smart Goals

If your goals are SMART, you have far greater chances of achieving them. You can use the guidelines below to convert your goals into SMART goals. Many people are not able to accomplish their goals because they work on their goals at a surface level, but if you do everything I am recommending in this book, you will achieve your goals definitely and that too faster than ever before.

SPECIFIC	Define your goals as much as possible. Who, what, where, when, why, which, etc.
MEASURABLE	How will you know you have achieved? Can you track it? –Volume, money, time, etc.
ATTAINABLE	Challenging but not impossible. Time frame for achievement should be worth going for.
RELEVANT	Is the goal worthwhile and will help you achieve your long term goals and vision.
TIME BOUND	By when do you plan to achieve your desired results? – Exact date-month-year.

Whatever goals you have, convert them into SMART goals using the guideline above and create SMART goal statements for everything you want in life.

Written Goals

> *Write it down. Written goals have a way of transforming wishes into wants; cant's into cans; dreams into plans; and plans into reality. Don't just think it—ink it!*
>
> –Michael Korda

After defining your goals, now you must put your goals in writing. Write your goals on a notebook or a diary or loose sheets of paper or your laptop or iPad or smart phone or your favorite app, the bottom line is you should have written goals.

In a book named 'What They Don't Teach You At Harvard Business School' by Mark McCormack, it is mentioned that a study was conducted in 1979, wherein the passing students were asked, 'Have you set clear, written goals for your future and made plans to accomplish them?' Their response was:-

- ✓ 3% had written goals and plans;
- ✓ 13% had goals, but they were not in writing;
- ✓ 84% had no specific goals at all.

Ten years later, the 3% that had written goals and plans were earning, on average, ten times as much as the other 97 percent put together.

Simply writing your goals improves the chances of their accomplishment many times more. Write your goals regularly. Involve your family also in making your goals. Your spouse and your children are part of your home team and their support is very critical in achieving your goals. Involve them in goal setting. They will help you the maximum they can. When you are away from home working on family goals, they will understand that you are not working for yourself alone you are working for your family. That will help you maintain your life balance also.

Once you have written your goals, add some **SPARK** to them. This SPARK will definitely help you achieve your goals faster.

SPARK is simple:

1. **Speak your goals out.** Talk about them everywhere and also when you are alone.
2. Write your goals on 2x4 or 3x5 size **pocket cards** and carry them with you everywhere to look at them while you are travelling or working.
3. Every time you get a chance to speak to an audience, **announce your goals**. Whether it's a big program or a home meeting or even if you are doing a one to one meeting, always tell your goals. People love to be with someone who knows where he/she is going. When you tell your goals, it shows your conviction and faith in yourself and in your business.
4. **Read your goals daily.** Start and end your day by reading your goals. This ritual will help transfer your goals from your conscious to sub-conscious mind and your sub-conscious mind which is infinitely more powerful than your conscious mind will start working for fulfillment of your goals.
5. **Keep your goals around you.** See them often. Create posters and paste them in your home or in your study or your work desk. Keep them on your computer screen or mobile home picture or DP in your WhatsApp or Facebook profile or wherever possible. Seeing them repeatedly will strengthen your conviction on your goals and also help them to transfer to sub-conscious mind.

Breakthrough Goals:

Now I want to take you to the next level of goal setting, that is setting Breakthrough goals. When you are setting goals anyway, why not set breakthrough goals, the goals which will transform you and which will make you so incredibly better by the time you achieve them. Goals that will set you free forever, goals that are once achieved will altogether change the pedestal from which you look at the world, goals so big that after achieving them your life will never be the same again.

'A breakthrough goal is a goal that once achieved, changes everything in your life or your company's life'. It moves you from total anonymity to stardom, it opens doors that were closed earlier, it automatically puts you in the top 1% of achievers, and suddenly you become a person who is sought after. The best part that I personally admire about breakthrough goals is not what you get once you achieve that goal, but what you become in the process of achieving that goal. When you work towards achieving a breakthrough goal, you need to change yourself completely in all areas of your life. You need to go through a total transformation to achieve those goals, and that is awesome.

As you are in network marketing business, I can guarantee you, this is one business where you can achieve everything you set your eyes on. Network marketing industry has a track record of several decades of creating success stories and breakthrough successes. In network marketing, it does not matter who you are, what have you achieved till date, etc. What matters is do you have a dream and are you willing to work for that dream as per the system. Now is the time to take the leap. Now is the time to think big. Yes. Set some big, bold and life changing goals and start working towards them: Why not you, why not now. Once you achieve your goals, do write me a word. I would love to hear your story.

Breakthrough goals bring out your hidden powers.
I was offered this business in May 2006 but I started in June 2007. I always had this regret that I was 13 months late in the business. To cover it up, I set a crazy goal of achieving a particular level in 3 months. 99% people never reached that level and those who did took 3-5 years. To get there in 3 months, I did presentations for 16-18 hours a day. I was in my job and I had my first child who was barely a month old. But those 3 months, I don't know when I ate and what I ate. I slept in cars and on my office conference table. I was caught sleeping in my office meetings because of whole night working. Once I travelled 500 kilometers to give just one presentation. It was madness. I don't know how it happened and how I got the strength to do it but I achieved that level within 14 weeks and became the fastest person in North India. When I look back, I believe, it was power of that goal. Breakthrough goals bring out the best in us that never comes out otherwise.

During our live event—Network Marketing Millionaires Academy, we do a lot of exercises to define your goals and every participant goes back with a customized action plan.

> *The greatest danger for most of us lies not in setting our aim too high and falling short; but in settling our aim too low and achieving our mark.*
>
> —Michelangelo

5. Power of Big Expectations

> *Expect big from people and expect it genuinely. They will do everything in their power to live to your expectations.*
>
> —Deepak Bajaj

Expectation is where it all starts. You came to this business only because you expect big from life. You will continue doing this business while many others may quit because you expect this business can fulfill your big expectations and dreams. So expect big from yourself, expect big from life, expect big from God and expect big from Universe. The next step would be to expect big from your team. Expect big from every meeting. Expect big from every associate. Expect big from every program. When God has given you the power of choosing your expectations why not choose to expect big.

I have realized that the people do their best to live up to the expectations others have from them. When you repeatedly tell people what all they can do and achieve, slowly they start believing it and do their best to fulfill those expectations.

Let the big expectations radiate in your body, on your face, in your energy levels, in the words that you choose and in fact all around you. You should have an aura of big expectations all around you all day throughout the year. Everyone who comes across to you should not go without being affected by this aura of big expectations. Gradually you will find things around you changing and this one change in attitude can turnaround your life. Big expectations from life, business or people indicate your hope, optimism and positive thinking and these virtues will give you a big fan following and people will be glued to you.

What to do when some people don't perform as you expect them to perform. Please note that the performance and output of every person in your team is the combined effect of yours and their expectations and hard work. If any one of you is lacking anywhere, the results will never match the desired expectations. You can mentor people, you can offer the best possible support, you can even go out of the way but if the other people don't have dreams, commitment, hard work or expectations from themselves then your expectations alone will not work. Keep expecting good from everyone, but you focus your time and energy on people who expect big from them.

Few people may not be performing today as per your expectations but any moment they can get one right person and business will change forever. Success is one contact away in our business, so always expect good.

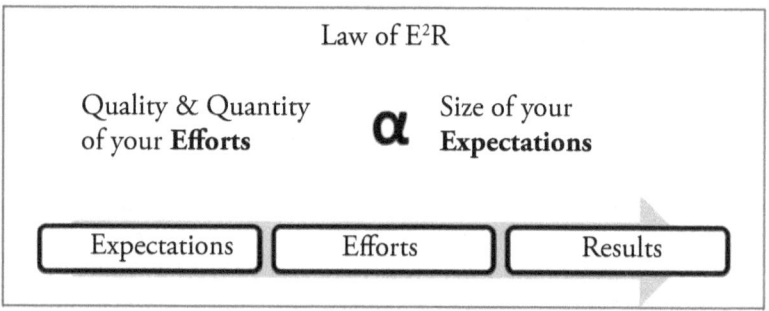

With my experience of working with thousands of people, I have developed a powerful key to excellent results that I call the law of E^2R. As per this law: *The quality and quantity of efforts undertaken by any person is directly proportional to the size of his/her expectations that in turn would determine the results produced.*

Typically the intensity of our commitment and efforts for any work depends on what kind of results we are expecting by putting those efforts. Zero expectation will bring zero effort to the work, mediocre expectations will generate mediocre efforts and big expectations will generate insurmountable efforts that in turn will lead to legendary success. The size of your expectations and your faith in your expectations actually determines the extent of efforts you will put towards your goals. Then the quality and quantity of your efforts will determine the size of your achievements. Start with big expectations and it will definitely change everything forever. Big expectations will propel great efforts and then great efforts will produce outstanding results.

Stay connected @ www.deepakbajaj.biz and my various social media channels for latest tools and research to improve your results.

12
Communication and Relationships

> *Communication to a relationship is like oxygen to life. Without it, it dies.*
> –Tony Gaskins

Regular communication between upline and downline is the primary element of our business. It's like oxygen. Ours is a dynamic business. Every individual is different; every meeting is different and things change really fast in our business. Upline and downline should be updated in real time on what is happening in the team and with the teammates. Teams that grow really big are the ones where upline and downline are almost in daily communication with each other particularly in the initial few months of the business. Communication is the foundation of relationships and it keeps the relationships and business alive. We can start and nurture relationships any time but they are particularly vital when things are not going well. I have observed that whenever times are tough, the first people to leave are those with whom the relationship is not good and communication is lacking. Communication is the key to strong and stable business.

> *Security does not come from money; it comes from relationships.*
> –Tim Hamilton

If you remove relationships from network marketing, it would just be Sales. Relationship is what makes this business so beautiful. Relationship is the glue that binds your team together. Use this business as an opportunity to develop this new skill of building and nurturing relationships.

Build genuine relationships with your teammates. In fact in many cases I have seen that first you develop the relationship and after that the person becomes your teammate. People are different and unique. They have their own set of values, experiences and challenges. They will not deliver their best till they trust you and share a good relationship with you.

Building relationships takes time and effort. It requires communication, trust, respect, sacrifice and all the qualities listed in this book about successful network marketers. Put people first; remember it is the people who move the products and not the other way.

> *Nobody cares how much you know, until they know how much you care.*
>
> –Theodore Roosevelt

Care for your people and nurture relationships. Be in constant touch with people. Visit their homes. Celebrate festivals together. Stand with them in their good and tough times. Handling a teammate is like a parent handling a child. Building a team mate is like growing a child in initial years and slowly this relationship will develop like that of a father and grown up son. Develop this ability to decide when to intervene and when to let go. Never hurt anyone's ego.

Maintain a Positive **Emotional Bank Account**: Every time you do a good deed one point gets credited in your emotional bank account and every time you do something bad 10 points are deducted from your emotional bank account. You should ensure that your bank account always stays positive with all of your key associates.

Lift people Up: Be an energy bank. Be an evangelist of hope and optimism. **Leave people better than you found them**. In network marketing business, our only resource are people and whatever we do, we are always with them. Every interaction with them is an opportunity to build their faith and to give hope, optimism and confidence. Every interaction is a chance for you to build their dreams and to help them sail through adversity and rejection. Whether it's a personal meeting or a phone call, rub off your positivity on people whom you interact with. Praise people on every possible occasion. Whenever dealing with people, do not judge; understand.

Also remember, building and nurturing relationships is a skill worth developing and it will serve you everywhere in life. Howsoever good you may be at this skill right now, there is always scope for betterment. Keep growing one relationship at a time.

If you keep judging people, you have no time to love them.
–Mother Teresa

Nobody is perfect not even you and me. Let's love people. Find something good in each one of them and celebrate it. Your life will be rich with money and relationships that will last a lifetime.

Relationships = Profit and Stability
I sponsored two guys on day one of my business and one of them was Gaurav Mehra. Having done MBA from a premier institute, Gaurav had been with me in the same company for almost a year. In our business he was doing everything he could but somehow his team didn't take off for almost two years. His turning point came when he realized the power of communicating with leaders at the bottom of the structure. He started interacting with everyone who was there in the team, irrespective of rank, location, profession, etc. and within next 6 months his business took off in such a way that he has never looked back again. Relationships are the key to any business.

13
Personal Sponsoring is a Game Changer

> *Everyone starts his or her network-marketing career by personal sponsoring. Those who make it to top 1% in the industry, continue doing it years after they had started.*
>
> –Deepak Bajaj

Personal sponsoring is getting new people started in the business from your own list. For personal sponsoring you need to approach people, show them the plan and ask for money. Since there is a risk of rejection and ridicule, many people are hesitant of personal sponsoring in the first place and those who do it initially just don't want to go through it again. So as soon as there are 2-6 people in the team, most distributors simply start managing their teams and become totally dependent on them. This dependence is really dangerous as you attempt to build your business on moods and fancies of your first 2-6 people. Also, you lose control of your business and it sets the wrong culture in the team.

> *When people start network marketing business, whole world is their team. When they have team of 4-5 people, this team becomes their world.*
>
> –Deepak Bajaj

If you want to make a strong, ever growing business that will continue to give you residual income generation after generation, you must develop the habit of continuous personal sponsoring. It's like bread and butter of your business. As a matter of fact less than 1% people are able to do this and they enjoy big income, status, respect and lifestyle. Just imagine if you can develop this one skill, you will automatically reach to the top position in your company. There are 8 key benefits of personal sponsoring:

1. It's highly profitable. Invariably in all income plans across the globe, there is extra profit in developing personal depth and width. All the new people that you sponsor can be placed strategically in such a way that it will give you extra income and rank enhancement.

2. It sets the right work culture in the team. In this business we are not creating followers; we are creating leaders. When you have created a leader, you should ideally withdraw yourself a little and let that leader lead his/her team. When you are not doing personal sponsoring, you will not have much work to do and you will overshadow your own people. When you are doing personal sponsoring regularly, you will be building new teams while give space and freedom to your old associates to develop into better leaders. So personal sponsoring sets the right work culture and keeps a person busy doing the right things.

3. You get stability in this business when you have multiple teams working together from different locations. Your personal sponsoring is the easiest and a sure shot way to develop new personal teams thereby making your business stable.

4. It gives momentum. When your personally sponsored team starts performing, it brings momentum in your entire team.

5. I am sure you are the best man in the team. When you personally sponsor someone and you develop that new person into a leader, he/she will duplicate you directly. If you can have direct effect of your personal charisma on more and more leaders in your depth and width it will build a highly productive and efficient organization.

6. Every time you are doing personal sponsoring, you are living the reality of a new distributor one more time. It keeps you connected to the grass root realities of the business. It gives you the pulse of the business. Every time you speak on the stage with this connection to the fieldwork, your words will have a magical impact on people. You will never be fearful of

anything in this business and it will give you a different level of confidence and optimism.

7. The best way to teach something to someone is to simply live it. When you are doing personal sponsoring yourself, you are setting in place a snowball effect through which everyone in your team will start doing personal sponsoring. It will set the right culture in your team and within weeks or months you will have unbelievable momentum throughout your organization.

8. Every new person brings along new energy and new hopes, so more the new people with us higher will be the level of energy and hope. You can train people only if there are people and personal sponsoring is the only way to get more people.

Personal sponsoring is all about your attitude and beliefs. Once you make a slight shift in your belief from selling to sharing and then from sharing to service, suddenly you will surprise yourself with what you can do.

–Deepak Bajaj

If you find personal sponsoring tough, trust me everyone finds it tough. That's why most of the people choose to stay away from it but top achievers do it anyways. It's just a matter of overcoming your fears and making it a habit. Like all other habits, personal sponsoring also is a learnable skill and once you do it for a few weeks, it will become a habit. Unlimited possibilities are available if you are personally sponsoring at least one new person every week or fortnight.

People who are first to quit this business are the ones who cannot do personal sponsoring.

–Deepak Bajaj

Any time you or anyone in your team is feeling stuck in the business or the business is going slow, increase personal sponsoring and you will be back on track sooner than you thought possible. It is almost addictive; once you start doing it, you can't stop it. Always have an eye for good people.

Leading means running fast enough to keep ahead of your people.

–SM Stirling

Go to next level by massive personal sponsoring. Have a month of personal sponsoring every 6 months where you sponsor 20-30 people during one month. Rest 5 months you can make these people achievers and teach them to duplicate you. Trust me personal sponsoring is the single most empowering and highly profitable habit to have in this business. Maintain it minimum for first 3 years and continue it as long as you can and be the undisputed king of this business.

> **Personal sponsoring is a mental game.**
> *At one point, my business was stable but my income was not growing due to lack of personal sponsoring. I went to a conference in Mumabi and had a discussion with a leader whom I always admired – Sankesh Wayal. I realized I was treating personal sponsoring as a punishment since my income was not growing but actually personal sponsoring was an opportunity to bring happiness and prosperity in someone's life. Now I believe if I am the best and I don't give opportunity to people to work with me, they will be forced to go to someone else who may not support them like I do, so it's my duty to give the best to people. Today I am a master at personal sponsoring and I personally sponsor and work with at least one new associate every week and I love it.*

14
Depth-Building

> *The height of any building is directly proportional to the depth and strength of its foundation.*

If you intend to build a tall and beautiful building, the first thing you need to do is to set up a strong and deep foundation. Likewise if you intend to set up a big business that will continue to give you and your family a stable and growing income generation after generation, you need to build it on the right foundation of strength and depth.

Depth-building is a process of planned business development wherein we create a set of leaders one below another in the same organization thereby developing a strong Line of Sponsorship in such a way that all of them work independently while staying connected to each other. All these leaders manage their own independent teams, while at the same time support each other to create a strong, stable and ever growing organization. Depth building aims to create multiple teams working below each other in such a way that all the team leaders are connected to each other as well as directly to you.

Depth building will give you 4 key benefits: Stability, momentum, security and right duplication.

- **Stability and Momentum:** The highest level of stability will come when you have multiple teams working below each other. These teams function as independent inter-connected organizations. When all these teams start performing together, what you get is group momentum. Since these teams are in the same line of sponsorship and are connected to each other, even if a few teams don't have momentum, they will soon catch it when they see others performing at peak. I have seen that every team will have its uptime and downtime. Whenever any particular team is performing slow, you can always pull them up with the help of group momentum going all around them. If you have built depth in the right way as prescribed in this book, you will have momentum all through the year in this business.

- **Security and Right Duplication:** Since you have personal touch with each of the teams, you are aware of their ground realities on a daily basis and you can take timely actions for development and growth of each individual team, which gives you good control and security. Since you are mentoring each of the teams and its top leaders personally, you can develop each one of them into a quality leader. They will have right culture because they all have your work ethic to copy directly. When these leaders develop more leaders in their individual teams, it will be a ripple effect giving you security, quality leadership and momentum.

How do you build depth the right way?

The moment someone starts with you, you start working with them on their list and help them sponsor some people as per the steps suggested in the success process. As you get some people sponsored through that person, now you guide these new people on the success process and help them take their first few appointments. At this stage you will have lot of work as your first distributor and his team will start setting up appointments simultaneously. While you give your equal support to everyone, a few of them will automatically emerge as leaders based on their different dreams, attitude and level of commitment. Based on all these qualities you identify 2-4 good leaders in first distributor's team and then start the same process with these people as you have followed with the first person. By this time you have already conducted 10-15 meetings with the first distributor and he is ready to show plans independently. While he is helping his team and building his set of leaders, you start developing more leaders in his depth.

> *Leaders are like eagles. They don't flock, you find them one at a time.*
>
> –Knute Rockne

Essentially what you are doing is that you work with one person and train that person to work independently. While you continue to mentor that person as he/she does what you have trained him/her to do, you start this same process with some other people in his/her team and directly train and develop the chosen distributors to become independent leaders. You follow this process till the time you have developed 8-10 independent leaders placed in the same line of sponsorship. There will be many distributors one below another in this line of sponsorship but you give your time, energy and commitment to the ones you have chosen based on their dreams, commitment and submission to you and to the system.

You will have to do this process simultaneously for your different branches. As you develop this business, you will automatically develop the ability to spot these leaders quickly and you will recognize signals from these leaders when they are ready and are fully independent. While it's your own judgment as to when do you call someone as an independent leader, you can check some of these parameters before you consider them as established independent leaders:

Some specific rank, minimum weekly/monthly income, full timers in the business, business in multiple locations, right attitude, own projector and laptop, car, teachability, 100% submission to the system, character, integrity, reputation with team and cross lines, ability to handle all types of prospects and to resolve all team issues at their own level, ability to plan appropriate programs for their teams and your relationship with them and their relationship with you and with key leaders in their team.

To get an ounce of gold, you need to remove tons of dirt.

Digging deeper to identify right leaders is important for one more critical reason—reaching out to right leaders. Network marketing is one business where everyone is welcome. In the best of my knowledge, we have the lowest entry and exit costs. Entry to network marketing is practically free and involves zero investment. No resume, no background check, no interviews, no certificates, whosoever wants to become a distributor is welcome. This is one of the key features of this industry and I personally love it also. But this same feature sometimes becomes a drawback of this business.

Generally people get their first set of 2-6 people and stop recruiting new people, expecting their associates to do the work now. Naturally some will and some won't. Sometimes all of these 2-6 people don't really work the way we want in first few weeks. Based on these first few associates, people start making their opinions about the business

We must remember, anyone can get into this business but everyone cannot be successful. This business doesn't require any financial investment, but it does require what a regular business needs: hard work, consistent working, commitment, sacrifice, etc. When you dig deeper and work through an organization, you will be able to spot good people with the right qualities that you are looking for. Sometimes such good people leave the business because of lack of attention by someone at the top. Once you have identified such people in depth, you can give your 100% time, energy and focus to these people and develop them into independent leaders.

One way to check your progress on depth building is to ask this question at every event, 'How many people are attending the event from different teams of same branch (A1 to A7)?' Keep building depth consistently for each of your branches and be at the top.

Some people will build business with you and some others will come into the business to introduce you to someone who will build business with you.

–Deepak Bajaj

Depth building = Stability

The biggest expert in my team in depth building is Gaurav Bajaj. He has a knack for spotting the right people and the moment he identifies the right person, he makes it his mission to develop that person into a great leader. He believes this business runs only on depth building. During depth building we repeatedly do what we have done with our first associate. He says if we follow the success process as given in this book, we can automatically build depth in our team. It's simple—recruit a person and make him/her an independent leader as soon as possible. It's the core activity and all those distributors who divert their actions away from this will be complaining about low income or non-performing teams.

I have seen the power of depth building with two of my good friends and great leaders in this industry Dhayalan TH and Rajesh Yadav. They both are getting stable incomes for years because they have several teams working all over India one below another.

15
Duplication – The Backbone of the Business

People will not do what you tell them to do; people will do what you do.

Duplication is the process of creating exact copies of someone or something. This is one of the fundamental principles of network marketing. What I love the most about network marketing business is that it does not work on leader to follower concept but it works on leader-to-leader concept. Whoever brought you into the business, will teach you everything he/she knows and a little bit more if possible. Creating leaders is not an option in this business; it's a necessity. In fact, network marketing without duplication is a job.

But we did not create this concept, God created it. Duplication is a part of human DNA and we are born with this skill called Duplication. Have you ever seen a child learning how to walk/ talk/ stand etc. No school, no language, no books but still the child learns effectively and solely with the principle of duplication. The child sees someone doing something and it just copies that. The child is curious and wants to try new things and the moment someone is doing something new, the child's instinct tells it, 'Hey. It must be fun. Let's try that out.' It's a very simplistic way of learning. Whatever you want to learn, just copy someone who is doing it well and you will master it over time. That's duplication.

You can get any desired behavior from people by just displaying that same behavior for long enough duration.

–Deepak Bajaj

Duplication is a very powerful tool available to a network-marketing leader. Time and again, every country or corporation or a political party behaves in certain predictable way because of their culture. When one person behaves in a particular way, it is called behavior and when entire organization behaves in one particular way, this is called culture. If you are smart, consistent, skilled and working hard alone you can reach up to a certain level but if a majority of the people in your organization become smart, consistent, skilled and start working hard, it will be a huge business. Leaders in every organization dream of such organizational culture but network marketers have the keys to this lock and we know how to create the right culture. The name of that key is duplication.

How duplication happens is very simple: whatever you will do, your team will simply copy that. Interestingly, whatsoever you may teach them, but ultimately they will do only what you are doing. So whatever you want your associates to do, you simply start doing that and if you are consistent and do it long enough; you will see your entire organization doing exactly the same thing. Your associates will copy everything: The way you walk, the way you talk, the choice of words, working habits, travelling patterns, spending patterns, choice of cars, etc.

Hence, the responsibility of good behavior lies essentially with the leader because the team at best is the copy of the leader. So if you want to change something, don't worry about changing your team, simply change yourself and you will see everyone else following the change.

Once there was this President of a billion dollar company, reading financial newspaper on a Sunday afternoon at his home. His 8-year-old son has been waiting for his father for last 2 weeks. Now since father was home, the child wanted to play with the father and was persistently asking father to play with him. Father was more interested in the news and wanted to make his son busy with something so that he can read the newspaper peacefully at least for next two hours. On one of the pages of newspaper there was a world map. He tore this map into many pieces and told his son to put this map together with a promise that he will start playing with the son as soon as he puts this map together. He was confident that nobody on earth can ever put this map together even in one full day and he went back to reading. To his surprise, the son came back with the map within 5 minutes. He was shocked. He crosschecked many times but found everything was in its place. He asked his son how he managed to put this complicated *map together in just a few minutes. The son's reply was simple, 'On the back side of this map, was the face of the man. **I fixed the man, world got fixed automatically.**'* I must have narrated this story a hundred times in my seminars and every time I end up inspiring myself to be the best I can be. Once you start improving yourself, your team will start improving automatically.

Don't worry if some people take longer than others to duplicate your behaviors. Duplication is another word for copying and our school system ingrained this belief in us that copying is bad. What the school considered unethical is actually called cooperation in the real world. Sometimes it is called teamwork. But because of their conditioning for decades, some people find it tough to copy but as they will see the benefits of it, they will start doing it. But it is easier for such people to follow instructions from an organization than from an individual. You make these people attend training programs organized by your seniors and when these people see the entire organization and all seniors talking about same guidelines, they will start following in an instant. Hence, a good upline and a strong and highly evolved success system of your organization will work as a winning combination for developing right work culture in your team.

One reason why some good people fail in our business is that they try their own brilliant ideas. These ideas need a certain level of competence that everyone may not have. These ideas may do wonders for these people but when their team tries those ideas, they cannot get the same result. This confuses people and they stop working. That's why we don't do great things in this business we simply do what is duplicable.

In spite of you doing everything right, there will definitely be some people who will behave differently. Don't start doubting the principles because of some people behaving differently some of the times. We are in people's business and people's behavior keeps changing with their own nature, attitude and circumstances. Learn the art of managing different kinds of people and keep moving forward doing what is right for the business.

A few good ideas for duplication in your team for big success:-

- ✓ I am the most hard-working person in my team.
- ✓ I work totally as per the success system of my organization.

- ✓ I do what I am supposed to do and a little bit more.
- ✓ I don't do what is good but I do what is duplicable.

Just remember duplication is a double-edged sword. If your good activities are duplicated, then so do bad practices. In fact your good work will be duplicated only 25-30% while anything bad you do will get duplicated with magnified intensity. People are watching you all the time: when you know it and even when you are not aware of it. People will listen to what you tell from the stage but before they start implementing it, they will observe you practicing it off the stage. In fact, your behaviors when you are not on stage have more chances of being duplicated and that too faster.

Sometimes at a photocopy machine, people complain about the bad quality of the photocopy. Remember if the photocopy is bad, there are chances the original itself was of the bad quality. You can never produce a good photocopy from a bad quality original and the best thing is that you always have absolute control over the original.

The three most important ways to lead people are: by example, by example and by example.

–Albert Schweitzer

Speed of the engine = speed of the train
Many people ask me how come my team is so fast. The answer is simple- it's because I am fast. One after the other I kept setting new records and my team kept on duplicating me. As a result, from a fastest man I became a fastest team. Even now, I get lot of new people every week who come to me for only one reason—they want to be fast achievers.

16
Edification – The Glue that Keeps the Team Together

We rise by lifting others.

–Robert Ingersoll

I never knew the word 'edification' existed before I came into network marketing and now I believe you cannot exist in network marketing if you don't live by edification. Edification is not a concept, it's a philosophy. It's a way of life. I learnt edification to make my business better but it slowly transformed my entire life in areas other than network marketing also. I highly recommend you also adopt edification as a guiding value of your life. It will open new doors, make new friends, bring lot of peace and happiness and also will build a business bigger than your wildest dreams.

Edify = Uplift, Enlighten and Encourage

Edification is lifting people up. Edification is giving respect, encouragement, love and affection to people around you, sometimes when they do a good work and some other times for no reason. We are in people business and people are our only resource. We are always dealing with people: personally, from the stage, on phone, on WhatsApp, through social media etc. What I recommend is that you use every possible interaction with people as an opportunity for lifting them up. Adopt one principle in life: *Leave people better than you find them.*

Strong people don't put others down; they lift them up.

–Michael P Watson

Look for something good in everyone and in every situation. Finding for good is also an attitude and I can guarantee you, if you look deep enough you will find lot of good. After you have spotted the good, make sure you communicate it to the other person. Give credit to people for all good things and take blame on you if something doesn't go right. Give them a little more credit than they deserve. Use uplifting and encouraging words. From the time you say hello and until you say bye, use words that lift their spirit. Build a new uplifting vocabulary.

Praise the slightest improvement and praise every improvement. Be hearty in your approbation and lavish in your praise.
–Dale Carnegie

Give respect to your upline, build him/her up. Your upline may not necessarily be more intelligent, older, more educated or wealthier than you, so are many parents vis-a-vis their children but your upline has seen the business a little longer than you and he/she is the one who brought you into this business. Show gratitude for your upline every time you get a chance to speak in any forum. Since ours is a business of duplication, you will get back what you give. You can never get respect from your downlines if you don't give respect to your upline. Interestingly you need to give it to only one person but you will get it from countless number of people. Also this edification and genuine gratitude for your upline should continue even after you achieve a higher rank or level than your upline.

Be an asset to your upline. Be someone whom every upline will be proud of. I even recommend that you should be someone who motivates his/her Upline.

Be an encourager, the world has enough critics already.

Edification is the easiest way to build relations and earn respect. Make edification your philosophy of life and you will be people's favorite. People will follow your suggestions, you will command respect, you will make more friends and you will be attracting the right people into your business. Keep edifying and keep flying higher in life.

Happiness is a perfume you cannot pour on others without getting a few drops on yourself.
–Ralph Waldo Emerson

> ***Give edification, get edification.***
> *Chintan Arora in my team is an expert at edification. On his last birthday, he got more wishes from his team than any other leader I know of. People were posting on Facebook and cutting his cake. I was wondering why it happened and I realized he is the one who does the same for his uplines. He is the one who edifies his uplines the most, gives them maximum respect and he gets it back from his team multiplied many times.*

17
No Accounts Policy

Lend money to an enemy, and thou will gain him, to a friend and thou will lose him.

–Benjamin Franklin

One unique feature of this business is that it's a no accounts business. There are no accounts receivables and payables in network marketing. You take something and you pay for it on the spot; you don't have to keep accounts. But a few people break this rule, giving some lame excuses. Seeing this business closely for more than a decade now, I have observed wherever upline and downline have got unsettled money transactions and accounts; it always ends up in a collapsed business. I have seen many promising business builders going out of business just because of this one habit of taking and giving credits for tools, products, program tickets or otherwise.

There can be hundreds of reasons for doing it and all of them may sound valid or reasonable to you at that point of time but I highly recommend that in any circumstances there should not be any money loans or credit transaction between upline and downline. Nobody in this business should have an accounts book. Everything has to be settled then and there.

No company gives products to any distributor on credit, then why should a distributor give credit to any of his/her teammates. All tools and program tickets come with a price that is paid in advance, then why should a distributor give tools or program tickets to associates on credit. What's the need? The worst part is that when it is done, it looks like a small, seemingly unnoticeable and non-damaging act but in no time this same act will set wrong expectations and breed a wrong culture in the entire organization. We are in a business of duplication and duplication of bad practices is ten times faster than good practices. Once this practice gets duplicated in your organization, it will crash your entire organization that you have built for years.

I highly recommend, don't give any program tickets/products/tools to any of your distributors on credit. The biggest loss would be the business that this person and his/her team has brought to you. So just work with only one financial principle: No accounts between downline and upline. Don't take credit and don't give credit. All products or tools or event tickets must be delivered only against payment received upfront.

> *When you loan money to an associate, you will loose both the money and the associate.*

Loan money and you will lose money, leader, team and all future business.
People call me the fastest leader. I am very fast in trusting people also and that is the reason I had liberally given loans to many of my teammates, particularly in the initial few years of my business. Every time, my intention was to help the person and to retain that person in the team. Interestingly, most of those people left the business and the loss was manifold—I lost my money, my team and all the future business that team could have done. I have learnt this lesson the hard way—never take money from your uplines and never loan money to your downlines.

18
Sponsor Many Choose Few

> *If you pick the right people and give them the opportunity to spread their wings, you almost do not have to manage them.*
> —Jack Welch

If you ask me one big blunder I have done in this business, which costed me millions of rupees and many wasted months/years, it is simply working with wrong people. Mind you, I am not saying bad people. I am absolutely not judging who is good or bad, I am just choosing with whom I would like to share a part of my life, and to whom I will give my precious time in this business. I may sound harsh but it is a fact that some people just do not have big dreams or commitment or the right attitude. A few others are full of ego and are not willing to surrender and work with a team spirit. So before I make a decision to give a part of my life to someone, I should make sure they are worthy of it.

> *While you can sponsor unlimited number of people, you can work only with a handful. Choose them wisely.*
> —Deepak Bajaj

Interestingly, before you can choose someone, people themselves quit or they give you enough signals that they are not the right ones. There is a clear difference when someone is doing this business like a hobby/interest and when someone is doing it like a business or when someone is really in submission or just acting. Differences are clearly visible if you just keep your eyes and ears open. You should extend your best support to everyone who starts with you, but gradually watch for the clues they give and invest your time with those who deserve it the most. Here are the signals we are looking for:-

- ✓ They have dreams and they are committed to work for those dreams.
- ✓ They are willing to learn and willing to follow your team's system.
- ✓ They are attending all events with team.
- ✓ They are working independently on all 9 core actions.
- ✓ They honour their words and do what they commit to do.
- ✓ They have made this business a priority and are ready to manage time for this business.
- ✓ They are committed to continue working for their dreams in spite of rejection and ridicule.
- ✓ Their 100% submission to the upline and to the system.
- ✓ Good relationship with team and upline.
- ✓ Good character and no accounts with anyone.

Working with wrong people is spending time, while working with right people is investing time that will give you best returns for years and decades to come.
–Deepak Bajaj

Now with the world's best book on network marketing in your hand, you can choose the best people to speedily build the business with. You just need to develop the ability to read the signals and this skill is worth developing, as it will save you months and years of hard work and lot of money.

I have seen many people quitting this business, but in almost all the cases signals for quitting came weeks before they quit. People may say something else but their actions show their real intentions. Every interaction they have with you and others will reveal more of them to you. You should observe the signals and give them the right counseling and right events.

If you don't value your time, neither will others. Stop giving away your time and talents—start charging for it.
–Kim Garst

Make every possible effort to help your teammates while reviewing the progress they make, but remember change happens only at events.

Make sure everyone attend events. Network marketing events are very powerful; they build faith and self-confidence. Every successful leader has one program after which things changed forever for him/her. Meet everyone in the events and always be willing to help everyone who is doing his or her part well. Encourage everyone but give your personal attention and focus to people who are repeatedly showing signals you are looking for.

Also, while you work with your selected leaders, keep your ears and eyes open to look for upcoming leaders. The more leaders you can personally mentor, the better it is for your organization. Work with several leaders at the same time, dividing your time judiciously.

> *Teach your team to earn your time. Train everyone in your team to prove they deserve your time the most.*
>
> –Deepak Bajaj

While you are looking for right people, remember you are a magnet. Only good people attract good people. Hence, work continuously for your own personal growth and become better than your best. Good leaders will come looking for you. Develop an eagle's eye and spot the diamonds. It's journey that you would cherish for life.

> *Everything we do in this business is aimed at reaching out to those few, who will take full charge of their lives and of this business.*
>
> –Deepak Bajaj

Stay connected to my social media channels to get best ideas on building a great team.

Success is planned rejection.
My great upline Mr Mubeen Muhammad always says, 'Think a 1000 times before selecting a person but once you have selected someone then do everything to make that person successful'. He has built a huge business with this principle. Thanks to him, I have also developed this quality now and every time a high dreaming person has come to me with a commitment to follow my system 100%, I have made that person a millionaire in few months.

19
Positive and Empowering Self-image

> *Our self-image, strongly held, essentially determines what we become.*
>
> –Maxwel Maltz

Three laborers were working on a construction site and someone asked each one of them, 'What are you doing.' The first one answered, 'I was jobless and this was the first job I got and started doing it'. The second one said, 'I work for a construction company and I am fulfilling my duty towards my job and company'. The third one answered, 'I am building a national monument'. They were doing the same job but the difference lay in how they viewed their job. Do you doubt who among these three would be doing an excellent job and at the same time would be getting maximum joy, rewards and satisfaction from the work he is doing.

Actually it's not what you do but your attitude towards your work that brings you the joy, satisfaction and excellence. How you view your work will determine your motivation level and the quality and quantity of efforts that you will put towards your goals. This will further determine your results and rewards.

> *If you have no confidence in self, you are twice defeated in the race of life.*
>
> –Marcus Garvey

Self image is a combination of what you think of yourself, your work, your contribution and the value you are adding by doing what you are doing. What others think of you or your business is not important, what really matters is how you view your business. People are different and so are their experiences and opinions. When you start meeting people for this business, you will hear different views about network marketing business. You may even come across people who don't consider network marketing as a business. When you hear such things particularly in the initial stages of your business, you may start doubting your business. Any unresolved doubts will lead to negative self-image, and you can never ever build a big business with a negative self-image.

I have seen many people struggle in this business with no results, in spite of doing meetings one after the other. In most of these cases, the problem does not lie with product, business knowledge or technique but with their self-image. In most of these cases, the problem lies not with product or business knowledge or with techniques but with their self-image. Please understand your results depend as much on your self-image and attitude as on your knowledge and skills.

> *It is not what you are that holds you back, it is what you think you are not.*
>
> *–Unknown*

What I highly recommend to everyone in this business is to work with a positive and empowering self-image. This is one business that provides equal opportunity to everyone to rise and to make a difference in own and other people's life. There are millions of success stories already about people who changed their lives through this business. Read relevant books, attend programs, meet seniors/uplines, and watch videos of successful people to build your faith and conviction. If so many people from different age, gender, profession, educational qualifications and economic background have already become successful in so many countries since so many decades, why not you. Have faith in yourself and your business. Go ahead confidently and build a life of your dreams.

You will definitely meet people who have different views and opinions. What I did from day one in this business is to understand the difference between an opinion and a fact. A fact is a general truth that is backed by data and reliable information, but opinion is purely someone's view about some person or business or about anything without any logical data or proofs. I strongly believe we should always take our decisions based on facts and not just opinions. What majority of people tell you about this business is purely their opinion and that is far from the truth. Listen to everyone but get your facts right before reaching to any conclusion.

You may find people who will say that they have been in this business and have failed or this business just doesn't work, etc. Please understand in a class of 100 students with same teacher, same books, same school, same syllabus and same question paper, everyone gets different marks. Everyone understands that along with all these things a person's marks depend on his/her own commitment, hard work and preparation. Likewise in network marketing or any other business the degree of success depends on individual's capability, efforts, commitment and willingness to work as per the system.

You should understand the business, master the principles and techniques of building the business and then honestly work with full faith along with your Upline as per the system. Remember you cannot promote something for which you don't feel good about. Excellence is possible only when you think high of yourself and your work. Build your business with positive self-image and see the magic.

You can perform up to your beliefs or underperform to your beliefs, but you can never outperform your beliefs.

—TT Rangarajan

Think high of your business.
We all top network marketers work with really high self image but I am highly impressed with 3 of my friends who have taken it to next level – Chanchal Rastogi, Durgesh Tripathi and Mohit Tandon. I have understood that whatever you think about your business doesn't stay inside you but it is reflected in your words and behavior in every meeting.

20
Growing Customer Base

> *While distributors give you growth, a consumer base gives you good stability and a pipeline of quality distributors.*
> —Deepak Bajaj

As per Wikipedia, 'a customer base is the group of customers who repeatedly purchase the goods or services of a business.' Bigger the customer base, higher is the income. Distributors may or may not be able to do new recruitment in some weeks/months, but if you have a big customer base, they will keep using your products and will give you consistent volume.

Every good and legal network marketing company will have good products or services that can be purchased repeatedly. In fact, if you find a company with products or services that don't give value equal to the amount you are taking from customers, stay away from it. Businesses that don't give value to customers are not sustainable. Your income will be stable when a good percentage of your business comes from repurchase of your existing distributors and customers.

Here are a few quick tips on how to develop a growing customer base:

1. Use all your products yourself. Whatever your company makes should be used in your home.
2. Get maximum knowledge possible about your products; more the knowledge greater will be the conviction.
3. Talk about it at every possible opportunity. Don't be a desperate sales person; rather behave like a satisfied customer.

4. Whenever you give a new product to a customer, give them all necessary information and send them brochure/video/testimony also. Knowledge will increase their faith in the product and when they use the product with faith it will have magical results.
5. Some products need to be taken as a course for a few weeks or months; give the complete course. Customer will not get the results if they don't complete the course and will blame you or the product.
6. Never over-commit or give a guarantee that you cannot honor later. Customers know everything, they are just testing you.
7. Give excellent service to your customers. Remind them for next orders, ask for feedbacks, ensure timely delivery, etc.
8. If you don't get positive feedback about some of the products, go and meet those customers personally. This is the time to win your customers for a lifetime. If they are outstation, arrange to send someone or do a video call.
9. Always be in touch with your customers irrespective of whether they are currently using the product or not.
10. Whenever you get a good product testimony, share it on all possible groups and platforms. It's an awesome practice. Let testimonials do the talking.
11. Ask for references from your existing customers. You will be surprised by how much sales you can generate only through references of your existing customers.
12. Give some discount or free gift or free products if your existing customers give you reference.
13. Every time you get a new product, share it with everyone in your circle and groups.
14. Use social media to promote your products.

Be the number one fan of your products/services and promote them with your maximum capability. Your customer base will give you consistent volume by self-use and by recommending your products to many more people. Also, your satisfied customers will gradually become your associates. Nurture your customer base while building your team of distributors, and build a stable and growing business.

If you are not taking care of your customer, your competitor will.
–Bob Hooey

> **Don't lose your repurchase volume.**
> *I have observed that many leaders focus only on recruitment of new associates. They teach only about recruitment in their trainings. I was also one of them. It's not bad and it's the core of our business. But if we do only recruitment, we lose volume at three places:-*
> *1. Everyone is not ready to do recruitment and when they feel this business is only about that, they leave the business.*
> *2. Repurchase can get us extra volume every time our teammates buy our company's products for their own consumption.*
> *3. Regular product usage will multiply the faith of our associates and their families. When people work with faith, results are much better.*
> *I am thankful to my dear friends – Vinod Solomon and Mohanan, who further strengthened my faith in the power of repurchasing during our discussion at Bali, Indonesia.*

SECTION-III

THE SUCCESS PROCESS

THE SUCCESS PROCESS

How does one become a butterfly? You must want to fly so much that you are willing to give up being a caterpillar.
–Trina Paulus

Success is a journey. It's a progressive movement towards the attainment of meaningful goals. You have a desire and you make a decision to work for the fulfilment of that desire. Once you start working, you learn a lot and change yourself in the process to become a better person. As you do more, you become more and you achieve more. Like in every other field, here in network marketing also, you set your goals and you work for the fulfilment of those goals, following a course of action. That is called the Success Process and everyone who has reached the top of this business has followed this same process.

Mastering this process is a journey. Be committed to work on this process and you will be a better network marketer with every passing day, achieving greater ranks and bigger income. The process explained here is the core of network marketing business. This process has been designed after studying the processes used by the best network marketing leaders across the world.

> *Success in business requires training and discipline and hard work. But if you are not frightened by these things, the opportunities are just as today as they ever were.*
> –David Rockefeller

I have always worked with this principle that there is no secret to success; there is a system to success. It really pains me to see thousands of people working in this business day in and day out without getting the success they deserve. They are motivated, hard working, have dreams and work consistently, but they are not able to get what they want because they don't know the right process. What I am presenting here is the exact same success process that has given me and thousands of other network marketers massive success for more than 11 years now. It's a definite shortcut to fulfill your dreams in network marketing. What a majority of people cannot do in 10 years, you can do in 2-5 years using this system.

You may already know some or all of these activities; you may also be doing some of, but the fact remains that since you are reading this book, you have a desire to grow in this business. The principles and activities explained in this section will build your skills in the core activities of network marketing business and will take your income and business to new heights.

If you keep doing what you have been doing, you will keep getting what you have always been getting.

What I intend to do here is to help you transform. Initially, some of the things recommended here may look difficult and some others may not appeal to you. You may not like to do some or all of them but if you are serious about your dreams, just go ahead and do as I propose here. You will surprise yourself with what you will achieve. Remember, every butterfly started as a caterpillar and looking at the caterpillar, nobody could believe that it would one day become a butterfly. But it quietly followed the process and the transformation was automatic.

Just when the caterpillar thought the world was over, it became a butterfly.

So, be excited about what you are going to become and what all dreams you will fulfill once you are successful in this business.

1
Let's Solve the Puzzle Called Selling

> *Selling is not something you do to someone; it's something you do for someone.*
>
> –Zig Ziglar

God made everyone a salesperson. Every person is a born sales person and selling comes naturally to all. It's a God gifted innate skill in every human being that just needs to be polished and used in more situations than where you have been using it currently. Everyone is selling all the time:-

- ✓ A boy proposing to a girl.
- ✓ A candidate at a job interview.
- ✓ A politician making a speech to get votes.
- ✓ A lawyer arguing his client's case.
- ✓ You convincing your wife for a lesser priced dress or a diamond.
- ✓ Your son convincing you for going to a party.
- ✓ Collecting funds for a religious program.
- ✓ You asking your kid to put things in the dustbin or keep his room clean.

It's all selling. Every interaction we have with someone and every activity we do has got selling in it. I strongly believe that Sales is the noblest profession in the world. Sales people generate revenue. Every other department takes money, but sales department brings in the money. Among all sales professionals, I admire commission salesmen the most because of their confidence and working philosophy, 'Pay me nothing if I don't produce sales'. Because of this, sales people are one of the highest paid people and selling is rated as #1 skill in the world of business.

The only problem is the perception we have made about sales people. Right now, when you think of selling, the images that come to your mind are those of people knocking doors, slamming your car windows or those pushy salesmen at the store counters. These images need to be changed to some other salesmen who are in fact bigger and better salesmen like Mahatma Gandhi, Narender Modi, Steve jobs or Jack Ma. They all are, in fact, the best salesmen in the world.

> *You cannot lead a battle if you think you look silly on a horse.*
> –Napoleon Bonaparte

When selling is so good, then why are some people scared of it? It's nothing but some wrong beliefs:

1. I am not good at sales. I have never done it.

Yes. You may not be good at sales right now, but sales is a learnable skill. Do you know anyone who was born as a salesperson? You can get better at it anytime you decide to do so. So many books, training programs and videos are available for the same. Actually, it's not your lack of selling ability but a lack of attitude to learn selling. Make a commitment to learn and do sales. Practice and persistence will make you proficient.

2. I cannot convince anybody.

It's a myth that you need to convince people. There is nothing called convincing. Your job is just to present and share your products/services in a pleasing and non-offending way. You just go with an attitude of solving their problems and helping them, the rest depends on the other person and his/her needs.

3. People are negative.

My 15 years of selling has taught me that sales depend more on the attitude of the sales person than that of the customer. A good sales professional is never ashamed of his/her profession and of what he/she is selling. Your role is that of a solution provider and soon the other people will be grateful that you proposed your product to them.

4. I don't know the tricks of selling.
There are actually no tricks. Learn the trade, don't worry about the tricks. Tricks are for short-term cheaters; while long-term players have solid fundamentals. Selling is just a transfer of faith and enthusiasm from the seller to the buyer. You should just know what you are talking about. If you have basic etiquettes, common sense and listening ability, you will do wonders.

5. I don't like sales.
When people tell me, 'I don't like sales', my question to them is – 'Do you do only what you like? Do you love your job? Do you love your boss? Do you like going to office every morning for the rest of your life? Do you like your lifestyle? Do you like the car you drive or the house you live in? Do you like the fact that you don't have financial security? Do you like making compromises and sacrifices every day?' Most of the people do what they don't like for most of their lives. It's not about what to do; it's about why we do what we do. If learning a new skill called selling can help you fulfill your dreams faster and give you better returns for your working hours, why not adopt it. What if this one new skill can give you such financial abundance that after a few years of doing it, you are free for rest of your life to do only what you like.

6. I am scared of a sales call.
Initial fear or hesitation is there every time we start doing anything new—driving a bike or car, first presentation, painting, playing any sport, learning a musical instrument, etc. So, it's normal that many people are scared of their first few sales calls and sometime even later too. Preparation, confidence and rewards are the antidotes to fear. Prepare well, keep your tools with you and just go ahead. Everyone you admire started the same way.

The best part about network marketing business is that you will get enough training for selling through a series of programs. Also, your Upline and all your seniors will personally support you in the field and hand-hold you till the time you become good at it. This dual support of training and ground working can make any one a master of selling.

Now, since you have started loving sales and your basic concerns have been resolved, let's explore our simple, time tested, proven and highly rewarding success process.

It involves 5 key activities to be done repeatedly:-
1. List building and selection
2. Approaching your list and securing appointments
3. Sharing the opportunity
4. Follow through and sales closing
5. Right takeoff for the new associate

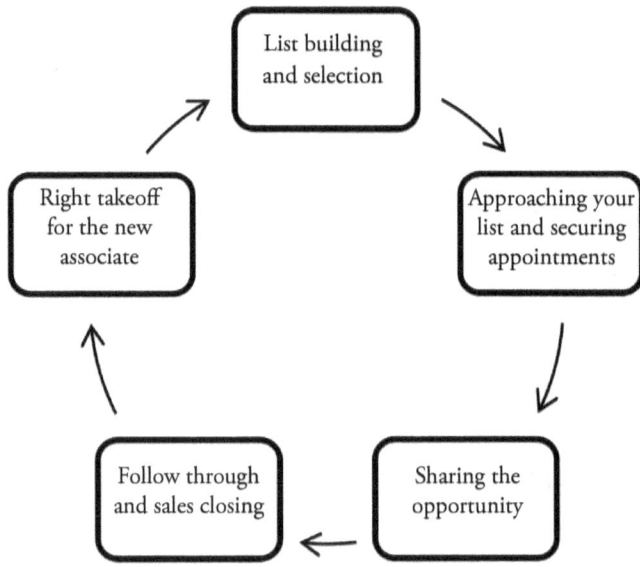

The only way to learn is by doing, and the only way to mastery is by doing it repeatedly.

–Deepak Bajaj

2
List Building and Selection

The first step towards building a strong network marketing business is definitely a big list of prospects. Your list is your biggest resource in this business.

List = Hope

List making is the simplest step in our business and takes hardly 30-60 minutes, but the irony is that 8 out of 10 people who start this business, never make a list. So, if you make a list, you are already in the top 20% people in network marketing and the best part is that you need not talk to anyone or even step out of your house to make a list. Whatsoever may be the result of your meetings or whatsoever others may tell you about you or your business, you will never quit this business as long as you have people on your list because you have hope that there are many more people whom you have not yet approached for the business.

So, quickly get on to making your list. Even if you decide to keep this book away for a while and make your list right now, I would be glad.

Benefits of making a list

- ✓ Your prospects will start business with you. If you don't write the names of your people on your list, chances are that some good potential associates will be left out. Looking at the massive growth this business is expecting in the coming years, there are chances that your prospects can be approached by some other person and there cannot be anything worse than seeing your friends working with a different company or a different team in the same company.
- ✓ The biggest benefit of having a big list is that you do not over react

to the negative reactions of people. Just imagine you approach your first set of 10 people and they all give a negative response. Some may even try to convince you to leave the business. Now, what will happen to you after these first few encounters does not depend on people's reaction, but on the size of your list. If your list is of 10-20 people, this reaction is nothing less than a tsunami, and chances are it will sweep away your business. In the same scenario, if your list is 300 or more prospects, then you will react to the same situation as if you have just warmed up because you still have an entire list of people to be approached.

People do not quit this business because of negative reactions from others, but because they have a small list.

- ✓ You get the leverage of selection. Once you have a big list, you can select the best prospects for your first few meetings and since you are meeting your best prospects, your chances of closing the sale will also be higher. Also, if you have the best people starting with you at an initial stage, it will give you a good head start in the business. Working in this business means giving a part of your life to someone that you just can't get back. Why not choose the right people to give your life to.
- ✓ A big list shows your seriousness and is a very effective tool at the time of follow-up. You can show it to people as evidence that you are serious about fulfilling your dreams with this business.
- ✓ A big list keeps your confidence high and keeps you going as you have a big resource with you.

When there are so many benefits, why are people so reluctant to make a list? It's simply because they don't have faith in the business. They are not confident that this business will really benefit them and their people. Some other people have this attitude that they know how to build this business and they don't need to follow any proven system. In all such cases, it is a good idea to make these people attend 1-3 events and then start the process of list making with them. You will be surprised at the change.

List making process for big success

What I present to you now is a simple, powerful and proven list building system. As you start working on your list, always remember my golden formula for developing a useful list: **The Best List.** Build a list, then expand your list, select the best people to approach from your list and train yourself to add more people daily to your list. Let's cover these four in detail now:-

The Best List	
1.	Build a list.
2.	Expand your list.
3.	Select from your list.
4.	Train yourself to add more people daily to your list.

1. Build a List

People whom you are skeptical of approaching today, will be thankful to you in a few months for putting their name in your list.

–Deepak Bajaj

✓ Make a list as big as you can and include everyone. It doesn't matter if you think they will start with you or not, or will they give an appointment or not. Just put all the names on your list. We may not contact everyone on the list, but we need people on the list. In our business, one contact can lead us to a series of contacts and we don't know where our star performers will come from.

✓ Change your perspective: When I started the business, I was also hesitant in making a list, but when I changed my attitude from selling to sharing and serving, I suddenly started remembering hundreds of people for this business. Since then, I have a never-ending list. In fact, now I believe everyone is my customer/associate.

✓ A few people will argue that they have a list in their mind and they don't need to put it down on paper. Why I recommend you to make your list in a diary is simple: When you empty your mind, your mind will automatically start working to fill in more names for you. You may even be surprised at how names will start popping up one after the other. The idea is to activate your brain to start adding names for you. Although writing names in a diary works wonders for me, you can make your list on your tablet or some mobile app also, if you want. Remember, the ultimate goal is to make a big list.

- ✓ Who should be on the list: Anyone who is alive and can give you 45-60 minutes for a business meeting is welcome. Friends, relatives, colleagues, neighbors, college mates, school mates, people you meet at different associations, your club mates, daily acquaintances etc.
- ✓ Look for people who are bigger dreamers than you. When these people will start business with you, they will take the business to levels beyond your imagination.
- ✓ You and your spouse should sit together to make the list. Involve your siblings or parents if you are single. They can give you clues that will help you remember more names and also they will have their own separate lists which can be added to your list. So, we will have a bigger family list.
- ✓ Do not prejudge people while making a list. We are looking for people who are looking, and we really don't know who is looking and for what. This business has practically something for everyone.
- ✓ An hour of power: Let me give you my secret formula called an hour of power. Set an hour aside exclusively for making your initial list. Sit with your wife or any one family member at a comfortable place in a resourceful state. Put your mobile to airplane mode, keep all distractions away and get on to noting down names quickly. Our mind remembers things and people in association. So, follow an order like starting from your birth to the current day, or the reverse order. Write names of people from all the companies you worked for, one by one. All schools and colleges you attended, one by one. Allow your brain a few seconds and it will start giving you a series of names. Don't analyze and argue. The agenda is just to pen down as many names as you can. Do this well and you will surprise yourself at the end of this exercise with a huge list. Don't look at the watch. Keep going as long as your mind is popping out names for you. Time invested in list making will save you months of frustration.
- ✓ I have seen people come up with 1000 plus names after this exercise, but I very strongly recommend you not to stop till you get some 300-500 names on your list. As per a survey done, an average 20-year-old person knows more than 2000 people by first name, so aim for 2000 names.

2. Expand your list

Prosperity is one contact away.

–Deepak Bajaj

- ✓ After making an initial list, quickly get on to expanding your list and I have a very strong belief and thousands of evidences that the real gold lies here. How do you do that?
- ✓ Have this attitude and belief that the whole world can be your team and you will be helping people by adding them to your list.
- ✓ We want to harness the amazing power of our mind for association. As you look at everyone in your list one by one, you will see their images. As you look at their images, you will also look at some more people whom they know. We want to add those names to our list now: The people who are known to the people whom we know. We now want to write down names of people who are generally seen with or around people who are there in our list. Don't worry about calling them and taking appointments from them now. We will probably never need it. Right now, just keep adding their names to your list. If your initial list was 500 and you just added 10 names of people they know, your list will grow to 5000.
- ✓ Like you did for building your initial list, set aside some exclusive time for expanding your list with your spouse, sibling or parents. Please ensure not to divert your attention to anything else. Don't start discussing relatives and what they do; stick to adding names in your list.
- ✓ You can use various resources for help like Facebook, LinkedIn, Instagram, WhatsApp group, phone book, old photos and albums etc., for clues to adding names.
- ✓ Help all your new associates in building their lists. Everyone who starts with you must make a list within one week of starting the business. Teach them the Best List formula you learnt just now.
- ✓ People resist making a list for a variety of non-significant reasons that can be handled easily. One major reason could be that they don't understand the power of building a list or the power of

following the system. Use your upline or upcoming training program to bring this orientation. Remember, the plan will work if you work as per the plan.

3. Selection

It doesn't matter who is giving the plan; what matters is who is taking the plan.

–Deepak Bajaj

Good selection is as important as making a big list. Right selection is half the work done. Selection is a very important part of our success process. Your initial few weeks in the business will be exciting and challenging. It's important to choose who will be with you as you begin the journey to your dreams. Select the best of the best people to start your business with. As soon as your list is ready, consult with your upline and both of you jointly select your first batch of people to approach and to share your business opportunity. My recommended guideline for selection of prospects is as below. Please sort your list into three categories: Hot, Warm and Cold.

- ✓ **Hot:** They are the people with whom you are in constant touch on a regular basis. You meet them often and you share a good rapport with them. You have a good relationship with them and since this proposal is coming from you, they will take it seriously. Everyone will have 20-30 people in this category.
- ✓ There are two reasons to keep them in your hot list: since these people are close to you there must be some common likings or thought processes between you two, so if you have liked something, chances are they will also like it. Secondly, network marketing is not new to people. Some other people might have also approached them in the past and they may have their own opinions about it. Since the proposal is coming from you, they will listen to it carefully and consider it seriously. We just want people to listen to our proposal with an open mind and people in the Hot category are the best for that.
- ✓ **Warm:** They are the people you know reasonably well and look suitable for your business. Generally, they are positive, high-dreaming, energetic people with a pleasant personality and a

good social image, but your relationship or rapport with them is not really strong. You meet them at family functions, at your kid's school, they may be your neighbors whom you recognize by face but don't really know, or many other people from different organizations whom you come in contact with now and then, but never interacted beyond work. Some of your social media friends can also come here.

- ✓ **Cold:** Everyone else is in the cold category. All those people whom you can't put in Hot or Warm category above, you should put them in the cold category. People who are relatives, friends of your relatives/friends, the people to whom you have never spoken, or a majority of your social media friends will fit here.

The above list has been made for people whom we would like to approach for our business opportunity; there may be a few people with whom you would like to share only the products. Keep such people in a separate list called product customers. They will use your products and recommend them. You should divide your product customers' list into three categories too, as per the same parameters: Hot, Warm and Cold.

4. Train yourself to add more people to your list daily

Remember, like all other skills, list building is purely a learnable skill that can be developed. Since we have chosen network marketing as our profession and we want to fulfill all our dreams through this business, we must master this skill of adding new names to our list regularly.

- ✓ After your initial list and associated additions, it's time to add strangers into your list. A big leap in your business will come from strangers—people whom you have not yet made friends with and they are a huge opportunity. Strangers are a gold mine and for many people, most of their strongest teams will be built with strangers. Personally, I was also introduced into this business by a stranger. So, the whole world is your market. Let's go out and tell everyone that we have a better and faster way to fulfill their dreams.

- ✓ Irrespective of your personality, experience, profession or background, I recommend you develop the skill of making new friends. Cultivate the art of starting conversations and building relationships. Isn't it exciting? Imagine someone asking you, 'What is your job in your business?' and your answer would be to make new friends. Be a little outgoing, talk to people while you are attending functions (parties, birthday, anniversary, club meetings, college reunions, local community events, etc.), parent teacher meets in school, sports events, festivals or while you are travelling and at every other possible opportunity.

- ✓ Trust me, it's all about who gives the first smile. Man is a social animal. In our DNA, we all have been originally programmed to socialize and work in association with others. Everyone craves human connection. No one will ever say I don't want one more friend. People just don't initiate the conversation because of ego, conditioning or wrong beliefs. You simply decide to be the one who gives the first smile and start the conversation, rest all will flow automatically. If in some cases, it doesn't flow, it was meant to be like that. Move forward.

- ✓ I strongly recommend you meet people to genuinely make friends and to get to know them; don't go with an agenda to recruit them. Don't worry about what will happen in the second meeting or about the future of this relationship. The agenda is just to know how wonderful the other individual is. The rule is simple: Make new friends and find a way to keep in touch. Now with social media and latest technology at your fingertips, it should be easy.

- ✓ Just remember not to pounce on people and start sharing your business plan in that very first interaction. We show the plan only when the time is right and only if it is required.

- ✓ Make sure you add a minimum of one name to your list every day. You can definitely add more, but keep one new name per day as your minimum standard. How long should you add names to the list? To be honest, as long as you want to grow. Or at least till the time you have 20 people in your organization earning half of what you are earning and that too in the right structure.

- ✓ Growing your list is your topmost priority in network marketing business. I am yet to come across a network marketing company where your income will not grow with your width and depth. So, when a growing list means growing income and stability, we have all the reasons to continuously grow our list. Go all out and find ways and means to reach out to people. Join associations, clubs, community services, RWA, social work organizations etc. or volunteer at events. Make it a priority to meet new people every single day and make new connections.

✓ Make it a practice to keep a small notepad in your pocket and whenever a name strikes you, make a note of it. I am doing this on a mobile app nowadays.

During my live event, Network Marketing Millionaires Academy, we do a lot of practical work on expanding our list and make strategies to create never ending pipeline of prospects.

Remember, in network marketing business, the person who wins is not the one with excellent selling skills or stage performance skills, but the one who has a big and growing list and one who approaches the maximum number of people for this business.

List = confidence and cheerfulness
I have seen two categories of people really happy and cheerful in our business—people who are making big money and people who have big lists. I know two guys in my team, whose lists are always growing - Debashish Khuntia and Nishant Chaudhary. They are always smiling and are two of the most optimistic people I know. The reason is big list and big income. Debashish is an engineer from Orissa and Nishant was working at a telecom store in karnal at a salary of Rs 11000 per month when he started business with us 3-4 years back. He now drives a premium car and makes 30 times more money than what he was getting in his job.

3
Approaching your List and Securing Appointments

When our list is ready and the selection has been done, the next immediate step is to approach people in that list. We approach people with either of the two objectives: To secure appointment for sharing our business plan now, or to prospect them for sharing our business plan with them in future.

There is absolutely no use of making a list and selection if we don't approach people immediately. When I started this business I had a list but I was hesitant in approaching people. I genuinely wanted to build a large team but I just couldn't make the call to seek appointment. It can be because of some of these reasons - the fear of rejection, the fear of losing my image/respect, the lack of confidence in the business/myself, or my ego/status/degree as I was a highly paid Regional manager with excellent credentials in an multi-national company. But whatever it was, it was stopping me from fulfilling my dreams.

Then one day in a training program, a statement hit me hard and it was the game changer for me. **'If God has chosen to bless you with a wonderful opportunity, you have absolutely no right to keep it to yourself.'** The trainer further emphasized that it would be selfish on my part if I don't share this wonderful opportunity with others. Slowly, this realization got so ingrained in me that **every time I shared this opportunity with someone, it felt as if I was doing God's work. During every plan presentation, I felt as if I am doing an act of social welfare by sharing this opportunity with the others**.

As you begin approaching your list, here is my guideline. Thousands of partners in my team and I have tried all sorts of combinations with different people and have realized every time that it is best to meet Hot category prospects first, followed by Warm. It is best to bring Cold category people to Warm category and only then we should share the opportunity with them. Here is our guideline:-

CATEGORY	ACTION
Hot	Call them right away and secure appointment using any of the 6 approaches suggested in this chapter.
Warm	Improve your relationship with them by having a meeting before meeting or a phone call. Don't share the business opportunity during this meeting/call. Once the above is done, Now call them and secure appointment using any of the 6 approaches suggested.
Cold	Start your interaction with them and improve your relationship. For people where relationship starts progressing and they move to warm category, seek an appointment for sharing your opportunity using any of the 6 approaches suggested. For those where relationship doesn't seem to be progressing, keep them parked in your list for next year.

People whom you have selected only for sharing your products, you can put them in Hot, Warm or Cold categories too and start sharing your products immediately with the Hot and Warm category prospects.

You can use any of the approaches suggested here for seeking an appointment from your Hot or Warm category prospects. If your Upline suggests some other approach, please feel free to follow that also. Experience is the best teacher. Experiment with all approaches and you can decide what works best for you. The ultimate objective is to secure appointment and that too in a way that increases the chances of our prospects becoming our partner.

Suggested approaches to secure appointments:-

1. The Direct Approach

This approach is used when you invite people by asking them to join you for working on a business opportunity. The message is very clear. It's an invitation to start the business. Possible scripts can be:-

- ✓ *'Would you be interested in looking at an opportunity to make some extra income without disturbing your current job/profession.'*
- ✓ *'I think I have found a way to solve all my financial challenges. Would you like to have a look and see if you too can solve your challenges with this?'*
- ✓ *'When you told me you (use any one - need more money, want to secure your family, want a better lifestyle, want to save more, hate your job, want a new home), were you serious or just kidding around? (Everyone says yes.) Awesome. I think I have found something that can get you (repeat what they had just told you)'*
- ✓ *'Are you still looking for a better job? I think I have found something so good that you will never have to look for a job again.'*
- ✓ *'Finally, I have found something where we both can partner together and live a life we always dreamt of.'*
- ✓ *'Everyone knows that we should have minimum two income sources. Would you like to set up a doable, time tested second income source for you?'*
- ✓ *'After a lot of research for many years, I have found an entrepreneurship opportunity where you can work part-time from your home, but can earn more than your current full time job/profession.'*

2. Opinion

This is a very powerful approach as it appeals directly to the ego of your prospects. Since you are asking for their opinion, advice or guidance, they would be glad to show up like a celebrity and offer their advice. This is particularly useful for young people when they are approaching older people or whenever anyone is approaching someone whom they consider senior or better in some regard.

- ✓ *'I have started working on something which I think can solve all my financial challenges. I really value your judgment. Can you please come and give me your opinion about it?'*

- ✓ *'I have found a way through which I can fulfill all my dreams faster, but before I get fully involved in it, I would like you to have a look at it and give me your expert advice.'*
- ✓ *'My dad always used to say that the best thing to do when starting a business is to take guidance from people I respect and admire. Would you be kind enough to give me your valuable advice if I share my new business idea with you?'*
- ✓ *'My company is expanding in your city. Would you please do me a favor? Can you please review our work and tell me if you think it would work in your area?'*
- ✓ *'I have found a proven, time tested and doable business to be rich and famous. Can you please guide me if this is right for me?'*

3. Suspense

As the name suggests, in this approach we are inviting our prospects for a meeting without telling what exactly we do. We are not telling them the name of the business, but we are telling the features and benefits of the business, like the way it typically happens in a majority of traditional advertising across the globe. But remember, you don't tell any lie whatsoever and don't make any false claims. Don't invite people in the name of a party or a friends' get-together. This approach works best with people who are your age or less than your age, or your colleagues and your subordinates.

- ✓ *'One of my friends has made a financial plan for me through which I can retire with a big ongoing monthly income in next 5 years. If you are interested I can share the same with you.'*
- ✓ *'I always thought entrepreneurship is risky and needs big money. But I was wrong. I have discovered an amazing, low investment and practically zero risk entrepreneurship opportunity with unbelievable returns. I am really excited. Let's meet up and let me show this to you too.'*
- ✓ *'Do you keep your career options open? (Wait for the answer. Everyone answers yes. When they say yes...) One of my very good friends have proposed some excellent career opportunity in one of the fastest growing industries. Why don't you also have a look and explore it?'*
- ✓ *'Do you plan on doing what you are doing right now for the rest of your life?' (Everyone wants growth and opportunities in this economy). One of my friends was telling me about a wonderful opportunity in*

one of the fastest growing industries. We are meeting next weekend, I can ask him if he is ok with you also attending the meeting.

- ✓ 'Isn't it risky in the current economy to live on one income source. Haven't you ever thought about diversifying your income?' (Generally, the answer is 'yes, I have been thinking', etc.) One of my very good friends in same job as yours has proposed a doable, time-tested and proven business for creating a good second income source. 'I am meeting him this weekend. Would you also like to have a look at it?'
- ✓ You can use words like 'organized retailing', 'private franchising', 'retailing', 'e-commerce', 'healthcare' or whatever industry your products or services belong to. 'I have stated an e-commerce business with my friend. There are huge growth opportunities and we are expanding. We are looking for a partner. Would you like to have a look at what we do and see if it suits you?'

So in this approach, we are not taking the name of our distribution model, but the name of the industry where our products or services belong. That's absolutely fine as long as you don't tell a lie.

What is network marketing fundamentally? It's a way of distribution. What is different between network marketing and other channels is just a way of distribution of products. Take for example a basic product like toothpaste.

If it is sold by a small store near your home, it is grocery/retail store sales.

If it is sold by a big retailer like More or Big Bazaar, we call it organized retailing.

If it is sold by a big distributor, it is called whole selling.

If it is sold by Amazon or Flipkart, it is called e-commerce.

If it is sold by us, it is called direct selling or network marketing.

So, a retail shop owner who sells toothpastes and other personal care products can introduce his business in any of these ways—I am a retail store owner or we are in personal care business or we are in distribution business. All these approaches are correct.

4. Expansion

This approach is pretty simple.

- ✓ 'The company I am working with is expanding in your area and we are looking for partnering with some ambitious and high dreaming people. If you think you are ambitious and open to explore some exciting opportunity, I can arrange a meeting for you with some right people. Let's see if something works out.'

✓ 'As you are aware I am successfully building an amazing business. I have some outrageously big plans for this year and I am looking forward to partnering with some right people. If you are high dreaming and want to make it big, we can do a no obligations meeting. Let's explore the possibilities together.'

5. Practice

This approach always works with close friends and relatives.

✓ 'I have just started a new business and I am nervous. Before I can talk to others, I need to practice on someone near and friendly. Would you mind if I practice with you?'

6. Reference and Recommendation

This approach is wonderful and works with a majority of people. It is very effective because it works at many psychological levels. In this approach, you tell the prospects that they are not the prospects and you are just looking for some people whom they know and who may be interested in doing this business.

✓ 'The business I am doing right now, may not be for you. What I am looking for is references of some ambitious and high dreaming people who will be excited about making some big money. But before you refer them to me, you should know what I do. Can I share with you what I do, so that you can refer the right people to me?'

✓ 'You may not need my business right now, but as per industry estimates, my business is one of the fastest growing businesses in the country. I am sure someone else will definitely come to you with a similar business proposal in near future or you may be inclined to start it. So, right now I just want to make you aware of my business model so that whenever you want, you can analyze and compare it properly and make the right decision at that time.'

✓ 'Whom do you know who is not happy with his/her job and is looking for a change?'

✓ 'Who all do you know who are looking for a business opportunity that

involves low risk and low investment which they can work on without affecting their current job or profession.'
- ✓ *'Who all do you know that are stuck with their current business and are looking for a way to diversify their income?'*
- ✓ *'Whom do you know who want to build a second income source along with their current profession?'*
- ✓ *'I work with a company that is expanding in this area and I am looking for some high dreaming, future oriented people who want to multiply their income and be the first movers of this area. Do you know someone who fits this description?'*

For any of the above 5 questions, irrespective of whether they say 'No' or everyone is like that these days or some names, you can say, *'Before I meet someone else (or tell their name), I want to quickly explain my business model to you. Can we meet Saturday evening around 6?'* (Suggest a day and time that is generally free for him/her.)

These are the suggested approaches that I have seen working for a majority of people. You can use any other approach also if that works for you. I approve of any creative approach, provided you don't tell a lie and have your upline's consent for the same.

Please remember, whichever way you approach them out of the above, when they come and you start the meeting, they will forget what you called them for and it will be like a regular meeting.

While some people will give you the appointment, some others will ask for more information. If you give all the information over phone or email or WhatsApp, there will be no reason for them to come and meet you personally. Our goal is to do a personal meeting, so we will give information that will arouse the curiosity to know more and help you get the appointment faster.

Be so confident and persuasive in your invitation that your prospect must come for the meeting. In case the other person is insisting for some information before coming for the meeting, ask your Uplines for some video links or some other tools that you can use for sending to the prospects at this stage.

The Right Process for taking Appointment

I have given several possible approaches for taking appointment; it's up to you to decide which approach works the best for you and for your different guests. Now you are ready to make the call, but to make sure you get the appointment, you need to follow the right process for taking the appointment. This process will guide you to give a quality invitation that will multiply the chances of getting an appointment and will ensure that the prospect comes for the meeting with the right frame of mind.

Here are the nine simple steps for securing quality appointments:-

1	Get into a positive and resourceful state
2	Make the call with a smile, maintaining the good state
3	Greetings and well being
4	Compliment the prospect
5	Make the invitation using any of the 6 approaches
6	Confirmation from the prospect
7	Commitment
8	Cut the phone with a smile
9	Send the information, if any

1. Get into a positive and resourceful state:- During my international Master NLP certification, I learnt that state is more important than content. So before every call and before every meeting, you ensure that you are in the best of state. When I say state, I mean the mental condition you have at any particular point of time. Your state is determined by your thoughts, internal dialogues and the emotions you are going through at any particular time. First comes the state and then the content.

Let go off all stupid emotions like fear, lack of confidence, doubt, anxiety or worry. It's not a life or death call. It's an invitation for a partnership that can change the life of the other person forever. This is a call to give something and not to take something. Shake your body, make some moves, listen to some good music, watch an uplifting video and bring yourself to a positive, optimistic and a happy state of mind.

It may be the first time you are hearing such stuff from someone, but this is coming from years of training and implementation with thousands of people over the years. You start using this and you will feel the difference from the very first call.

2. Make the call with a smile, maintaining the good state:- Now pick up the phone and make the call. Have your best smile and maintain the same resourceful state that you have just got into. Trust me, your smile can be seen over the phone also.

3. Greetings and well-being:- Start the call with regular greetings that you use and by asking about how are things at their end. Ask about their family and work and wait for the answer. If the person is going through a serious issue at work or home right now, this may not be the right time to start a new venture. Hold your approach for the next time and continue with your call as you generally do with that person.

4. Compliment the prospect:- Everyone likes a sincere compliment. It uplifts the spirit of the other person and energizes the air of the meeting. Find something good and give a short genuine compliment to the prospect.

5. Make the invitation:- Now, use any of the six approaches and invite the prospect for a meeting. After the first 4 steps are over, just say, 'I have called you today for something specific' and then use the appropriate approach lines for that person. After this, we would prefer to conclude the call within the next 2-3 minutes. So please follow the sequence suggested here.

If the first 4 steps are taking longer, that's okay as long as you make the invitation only during the last 3-5 minutes of the call. Maintain same resourceful state that you had in the beginning and give a quality invitation with the right posture.

Invitation can be for a one to one meeting or a group meeting or a hall meeting, depending on what is coming next for you and what is most appropriate for that person.

At this stage, the prospect may ask for some more information. Control yourself and avoid giving more information on the phone. Bring the conversation back to the personal meeting. If at all you have to give some information, only give that information which serves any one or both of these objectives: a. It helps you in getting the appointment faster; or b. It will set the prospect in the right frame of mind before coming to the meeting.

6. Confirmation from the prospect:- Now is the time to get a time commitment from that person. If it is a group meeting or a hall meeting, you need to give the time and get their confirmation. Even if it is an invitation for a one to one meeting, I prefer to give my time and day. Be a little flexible and give some options, but confirmation is most important.

7. Commitment:- Commitment is nothing but you summarizing the details of the appointment and fixing it affirmatively in the mind of your prospect. Possible script can be as below:

'Wonderful then. We are meeting on Saturday evening at 7 PM at my home (or whatever place you had decided). Please reach 10-15 minutes early if you can, and make sure you don't have any other engagement for the next one hour.'

8. Cut the phone:- Now is the time to disconnect the phone. Say bye with enthusiasm.

9. Send the Information, if any:- During your call if you have promised to give any information, please give the same immediately after the call or within a few hours of the call. Please check with your upline as to what all can you share with the prospect at this stage. Never mail the complete business presentation.

Please remember these guidelines below while taking appointment:-

Guidelines to follow while taking appointment

1. Always seek appointment over the phone. It's easier and faster.
2. Set an appointment; don't explain the plan. Follow the KISS principle—Keep it Short and Simple. Don't share more details over the phone; the more you tell on phone, the lesser will be your chances of getting an appointment for a meeting. I understand that times are changing and people have started using video conferencing or Skype in place of actual meetings, but I recommend you should first master the basics through one to one meetings and once you are an expert at it, go for whatever you want. Plus, it is a business of duplication, so do what can be duplicated easily.
3. You must emotionally detach yourself from the outcome of your calls. 100% people never say yes to anything. I know it is easier

said than done, but remember, we are not salesmen/saleswomen; we are working more as consultants who can guide and empower people to live a better life. Our job is not selling, but sharing. Also, in the initial stages, we are only looking for understanding and education. So, have fun and enjoy the experience irrespective of the outcome.

4. It's a numbers game. Don't analyze the initial few calls too much and arrive at wrong conclusions. If you make enough number of calls, you will definitely get required number of appointments.

5. Don't tell lies. Don't invite people for a birthday party or some other party and start sharing your opportunity with them there. It's the worst thing to do. They will consider you a cheat and no one wants to build their future with a cheater.

6. Be yourself. Don't act or imitate someone else. Your prospects know you and love you as you are. Admire people, learn from them, but don't copy someone else. Be the best you can be.

7. Work with a positive self-image. Be strong and confident. Through this business opportunity, you have a wonderful gift for everyone that can change their life forever. You have a better way and you should share it with faith and confidence.

8. Be in a hurry. Somehow people who are busy and who are moving fast towards their goals are considered successful. If you start your calls giving an impression that you are in a hurry, your calls will get completed faster with better results. You will secure more appointments with fewer questions. Even people will look forward to meeting with you.

Prospecting

Whatever we have covered so far on the subject of approaching people is meant for Hot and Warm category prospects from whom we want to secure appointment right now. But at the same time, we have a big list of people in the C category and there are countless strangers whom we will be adding in our list in future. Developing good relationship with these people and subsequently sharing the presentation with these people is the lifeline of network marketing business and can give us a never-ending pipeline of prospects. This is called prospecting and this will give you an edge in network marketing business.

As per dictionary definition, prospecting refers to 'a continuous set of activities performed to set up face-to-face meeting with potential customers'. It includes all those activities that are done to secure appointments. Fundamentally, it's about converting a stranger/acquaintance into a worthy prospect. Let's learn the best ways of prospecting:-

1. Gradually increase your interaction with C category people. Meeting them personally, an informal call, festival wishes, messages on WhatsApp or liking their social media posts can be a good starting point. Do it consistently and work on strengthening your relationship.

2. Look for opportunities to genuinely appreciate and compliment people.

3. Listen to people. Empathetic listening is by far the best way to build rapport with people.

4. Always work with an intention to genuinely help others. Develop this attitude of helping people wherever you possibly can. Give them references that can help their business, connect people to each other and gradually earn the reputation of a resourceful person who has solutions for everything. This will pull people towards you and will also build your credibility.

5. Every relationship is different and takes different time and shape. Ideally, the goal is to take your relationships to such a level that the person will recruit himself/herself. Keep doing it and you will have awesome partners and friends for life.

6. Will you be able to develop relationship with every person? Obviously not. So don't stress yourself if things don't move forward with some people. Our goal is to select people who are appropriate for sharing our business and please remember relationships will progress only when both the people involved are interested.

7. For those people where relationship starts progressing and they move to warm category, seek an appointment for sharing your opportunity using any of the 6 approaches suggested.

8. For those where relationship doesn't seem to be progressing, keep them parked in your list for next year. No need to show the plan on first meeting. Work on your relationship and when the time is right you can share the business opportunity.
9. Avoid negative people, especially in the first 6-9 months in the business. Everywhere there will be some people with whom nothing will work out and they always do a fantastic job of finding faults with everything. They can even find faults with God. Better to leave such people aside.
10. Have a prospecting attitude. Have an eye for spotting right people for the business. Cultivate the skill to start conversations and to check if people are ready to look at your opportunity. Make prospecting a way of life. Continuous prospecting can give you an ever-lasting pipeline of prospects.

4
Sharing the Opportunity

After you have secured the appointment, it's time to get ready, show up and share the opportunity. You can share the opportunity in any of the three ways:-

1. One to one Meeting

2. Group Meeting

3. Hall Meeting

All these ways are good and you can use any one of them depending on your prospect and your situation. Remember to bring yourself to your peak performance state whenever you are going to share your opportunity. Let's quickly explore what is good in each one of these and get going.

1. One to one Meeting

As the name suggests, one person alone or with their Upline shares the opportunity with the prospect. It's quick, personalized and can be done throughout the week in houses, offices, cafes or other convenient places. While hall meetings and group meetings will happen as per schedule, you are free to do as many one to ones as you like all through the week. Just take care of the following while conducting one to one meetings:

1. **Call prospect to your home or at a mutually convenient place like a café/restaurant etc.:**
   Never go to the prospect's office or house to share the opportunity. When the prospect comes to your place or a mutually agreed place, it's a clear indication of his/her interest in the opportunity,

the quality of invitation given by the sponsor and also about the good relationship between the sponsor and the prospect. In fact, calling the prospect out of his/her office or home itself is half the victory. Secondly, when you go to a prospect's house, you don't have any control on the environment of the meeting –TV, noises, pets, kids playing around, other distractions, who all will be sitting for the meeting, state of mind of the prospect, etc.

2. **Start showing your presentations by yourself:**

    Take your Upline with you for the first few one to one presentations, but quickly start showing the presentations by yourself. Follow the 5+5 plan: For the first 5 meetings your Upline will share the opportunity and you will observe. For next 5 meetings, you will share the opportunity and your Upline will observe. You can even start showing your presentations before the first 5 meetings are over. After these 5+5 meetings, you should show all your plans yourself, consulting with the Upline only in special situations. This business will become your business only once you start showing your own presentations.

3. **Control the environment:**

    Make sure there are no distractions at your meeting venue, like, TV music, kids, mobile phones, people moving around, unnecessary noise or loud music, etc. It's the primary responsibility of the sponsor to set the environment right, but if you have gone as an Upline and your associate has not taken care of these things, you should set the environment right before you begin sharing the presentation.

4. **Appropriate edification of the upline and the prospect:**

    Proper edification sets the prospect and the presenter in the right frame of mind. If the Upline is present in the meeting, it's the sponsor's job to edify both the Upline and the prospect before the business presentation begins.

5. **Excitement is way more important than knowledge:**

    Many new people are hesitant to show the opportunity by themselves, feeling they don't know adequately about products or the income plan. Trust me, your excitement is way more important than your knowledge about the income plan and products. If it was only about products and plan knowledge, we could just send a mail or give the presentation through a video. We are doing a personal meeting to convey our faith and excitement. Remember, you have a life transforming opportunity that can change their life forever. Just go ahead and share it confidently.

6. **Never go without appointment:**

    It's a disaster. It never works. In fact, what you have spoken during taking appointment is more important than what you talk during the meeting. Always go with an appointment for a 45-60 mins meeting.

7. **Be punctual and smartly dressed:**

    Since it is a one to one meeting, the entire focus is on you. You are representing the company and you are the business. Reach 5 minutes before the meeting time. Dress smartly. Your dress up helps the other person to connect with you. Your dress up will be different when you go to meet your own uncle at his house and when you are meeting a relatively new guitarist friend at a café. The simple rule is to be dressed like you expect someone to be dressed when they come to share some big business opportunity with you.

8. **Prepare well for the meeting:**

    Rehearse your presentation. Keep all the tools with you – forms, brochures, magazines, product testimonies and different kinds of videos: company profile, big events' videos, success stories, products, product testimonies, etc. Keep your passion, energy and faith at its peak.

Right conduct during the meeting

There are two types of meetings: one, where you will be sharing the plan yourself with your prospect; and the other one, where you will go with your upline. Although the below steps have been presented for the setting where sponsor and upline are going together, in either of the cases, all these steps should be followed. If you are going with your new teammates, it's always good to brief them about these steps before going for the meeting.

1. **Get to your best and resourceful state:**

    This meeting can get you the right person you have always been looking for. Get ready to give your best shot. Prepare well before the meeting. Even if something is left out, don't worry; just go for it with faith and confidence.

2. **A firm and friendly handshake:**

   A handshake is the beginning of a relationship. Give a firm and friendly handshake. Don't be dominating or submissive; exert just the right amount of pressure. Same gender handshake is good, while in some communities, opposite gender handshakes are not encouraged. Avoid it there.

3. **Smile:**

   Wear your best smile all the time; it always helps.

4. **Compliment the prospect:**

   Everyone loves a heartfelt compliment. Develop the art of finding good in other people, places and situations. If you look deep enough, you will find a lot to compliment. Sincerely compliment the prospect.

5. **Create the right meeting ambiance:**

   In a café, choose a table with less noise and less distraction. When sitting around the table, sit in a way that the prospect is facing you and the wall. Switch off the TV and manage the kids if the meeting is happening at home. Ensure that the mobile is put to silent mode or switched off. Just say something like, 'We all value and respect our time and each other's time. Let's keep our mobiles to silent mode for next few minutes till the meeting is finished.' Then be the first one to switch off your mobile. Create a positive energy and a feel-good ambiance for the meeting.

6. **Introduction and edification of the upline:**

   Sponsor should give a short introduction of the upline, followed by the right edification. The right time for the same is actually before the meeting when your upline is not present. In any case, do a quick edification of your upline again at the time of starting the meeting. If you can find some similarities between the upline and the prospect, you can point out the same here.

7. **Introduction and edification of prospect:**

   Now you should introduce your prospect, especially highlighting your relationship with the prospect and the prospect's qualities that are helpful for starting the business using phrases like the person is open minded, willing to experiment with new ideas, trusts me completely, always makes his/her decisions himself/herself, financially well off to start right now, has always supported me in the past also, very positive, high dreamer, always takes my suggestions seriously, etc.

8. **Quickly prime your prospect for the opportunity (TSD):**
   (a) Start by saying, *'Before we tell you what we do, I want to quickly tell you why we do what we do. Here is a list of reasons why people do network marketing.'* Present the list of Top Success Drivers (TSD) now on your visiting card or on mobile or on your laptop or through a printed TSD card. TSD Chart is available in the Tools section of this book and you can also download it from my website www.deepakbajaj.biz

   (b) Then say, *'I am curious to know what are your top 3 success drivers from this list. What is most important for you to achieve in life?'* and let the prospect answer.

   (c) Then ask, *'Why are these three important to you?'* and let your prospect answer.

   (d) Conclude by saying, *'After working with several people in this business, I am sure if you look deep enough with an open mind, you will find how this business can help you accomplish these 3 in a better and faster way.'*

9. **Share the business opportunity:**
   Now share your business opportunity yourself with full excitement or gracefully request your upline to share the same. If you have some short introductory video, magazine or any other tool showing information that makes your company, product, opportunity or team unique and better than the others, share it now.

10. **Share your Story:**
    After the business opportunity presentation, share your story. This is the most important part of the entire meeting and this is where the decision would be made. Whatever we have done so far in the meeting can be copied, but your story is what makes all the

difference. Remember, people don't join a company or product; people join people. Learn the art of story-telling.

All great network marketers are great storytellers.

–Deepak Bajaj

These are the 7 components of a good story and in this same order:-

(a) What were you doing before starting this business?

(b) What was your condition? What was good and what was bothering you?

(c) What was your first reaction to this business presentation?

(d) What convinced you to get started and what mind blocks did you remove?

(e) Your achievements and journey so far.

(f) What are your long term and short-term goals with this business?

(g) Your commitment for the best possible and personal support for the prospect!

You can learn how to master your story in the Tools for Excellence section of this book. The same is available on my website also. You can listen to my story for your reference in several videos available on my website www.deepakbajaj.biz or my YouTube channel.

11. **Time to say Bye:**

Most of the people know when to start the meeting, what they don't know is when to end the meeting. 60 minutes is a good amount of time. Set a reminder if you have to, but get out of the meeting 5 minutes before your prospects wants you to leave. It gives an impression that you care for their time and it's also a good practice for your team to duplicate.

To further enhance the quality of your meeting and to multiply your chances of sales conversion, read a chapter titled 'Power Connectors' in the 'Tools for Excellence' section of this book. It's also available on my website.

The primary objective for this meeting is to get the person started in your team right now. Some may start now and some may start later.

But my 11 years of experience has taught me something even more powerful and life changing.

'Conduct the meeting in such a way that it leaves such a positive and powerful impact on people that whenever some other person approaches them for similar business or products, they should first call you to consult about this business. Every business presentation you do should sow the seeds that will result in a good harvest in future.'

2. Group Meeting

This is my personal favorite. Group meeting, as the name suggests, is a meeting where we meet more than 2 prospects in the same meeting. We generally have 3-30 people in a group meeting and it is conducted in homes, restaurant, some institution or at any other convenient place where several distributors get their prospects for business presentation. There are several advantages of a group meeting:-

- ✓ You can conduct meeting for several prospects at the same time multiplying your number of meetings and saving you a lot of time.
- ✓ Sometimes one to one appointments gets cancelled at last minute, resulting in a wastage of time. When you invite several people together, some of them will turn up and some won't, but your meeting will definitely happen.
- ✓ Since it's not a big hall or hotel meeting, it's shorter in duration, environment is family like and inviting people is easier.
- ✓ It's a good platform for developing leaders. You can give the chance for presentation and experience sharing to new associates who are either shy of public speaking or don't get a chance at big meetings due to their beginner ranks.
- ✓ Regular weekly group meetings bring consistency and stability to the business. People get used to a meeting schedule.
- ✓ As a new distributor, if you can establish 2-3 group meetings every week in your team, it will give you incredible speed.

A team that has a culture of group meetings grows bigger, faster and has a stable business. If you are doing it at home or at a restaurant, don't indulge in too much of hospitality. Finish the meeting in 90 minutes or less. You may serve tea/coffee/water etc. with cookies, but don't get into snacks or food.

3. Hall Meeting

This is a larger version of a group meeting that is conducted in hotels, auditoriums or seminar halls with a bigger audience and larger number of leaders available to share their experience. This is also very effective and offers several advantages:-

- ✓ This is a system driven meeting. The best part about a hall meeting is that it is regular and it can run without you. This is where the business really starts. This is the place for duplication and multiplication. Once your team starts attending hall meetings regularly, your business will grow bigger and faster.
- ✓ Group energy and peer pressure helps in quick conversion. Many people take the decision to start right there.
- ✓ Prospects get more faith when they see so many people with different profiles, professions, gender, age, etc working and succeeding together
- ✓ In the hall meeting, many achievers share their success story from the stage, so there is very high possibility that your guest will connect with someone or the other and will come out positive and determined about the business.
- ✓ You can invite all those people with whom you have shared the opportunity in a one-to-one or group meeting, but they have not yet started the business with you. This meeting will serve as a follow up meeting for all of them.
- ✓ A lot of senior business leaders and your uplines will be available to meet your guests and to answer all their queries.

To make a hall meeting successful, just take care of the following:-

- ✓ Give a strong invitation with confirmation and commitment.
- ✓ Remind your prospects a day in advance about the meeting.
- ✓ If you have a team of people with you already, get the names of their guests a day in advance.
- ✓ Don't forget to do the follow up immediately after the meeting in the hall itself. Make sure all the questions of your guests are answered. Close the meeting by either collecting an advance or getting a date for follow up meeting within the next 4 days.

- ✓ For excellent results hall meeting should be conducted every week and all leaders connected to that meeting must personally promote the meeting aggressively.
- ✓ All leaders of a particular hall meeting must ensure that meeting attendance is increasing week after week.

Whenever you work in a location, where a hall meeting is already happening and accessible, start attending hall meetings with your new associates and their guests as soon as possible. Work all through the week and make sure all your associates attend hall meeting with maximum guests. If anyone is not able to bring guests along, they should come alone.

Whenever you start a new team in a new location where there is no hall meeting, start with one-to-ones, move to group meetings within 2-4 weeks and once you have a team size of 20+ associates, move to a small hall and start hall meetings.

> ***Hall meetings are best for multiplication.***
> *Personally I also enjoyed the real taste of business multiplication after I started hall meetings in my team. My faith in hall meetings is so strong that when I do coaching for senior leaders I ask them only two questions – How many weekly hall meetings are you operating in your team and do you know your weekly hall meeting numbers for last three months? I have some great friends in Mumbai and I learn a lot from them every time I meet them—Mrinal Phalsankar, Harish Shettigar, Babu Thomas, Sunil Sagvekar, Badresh Chauhan, DH Kadam, Kishor Ahire and many more dear ones. They all further strengthen my faith in the power of hall meetings.*

5
Follow Through and Sales Closing

> *Selling is simple. It's the transfer of your conviction and feelings to the other person.*
>
> –Deepak Bajaj

Here comes the time to convert our efforts into cash. It's time now to add new partners to our family. Follow though is a series of meetings conducted after business opportunity presentation and before the sale closing. *In our industry, we are not paid for list making or showing the plans; we are paid only when we close the sales.* Everything that we do from list making to sharing the plan is just a milestone towards closing the sale. Here are the keys to an effective follow through:-

- ✓ Follow up meetings are an essential part of the sales process. Sales closing always happens in follow up meetings. This is where you ask for money and invite your prospects to be your partner. Remember, you never get it if you don't ask for it. Never assume that your prospect will say, 'I am ready.' We need to ask for the money. There is absolutely no point in showing the plan if you cannot do a follow up meeting within one week of sharing the plan.
- ✓ A follow up meeting is not just a quick meeting to ask a yes or no from your prospects. It is even more critical than the business opportunity presentation, because here your prospect will also ask you questions and make a decision to start your business. So conduct this meeting seriously
- ✓ First follow-up should be done immediately after sharing the plan. After the presentation, simply ask them for anything they want to clarify and once their points are discussed, ask them to start right away. Ask for money.

- ✓ Second follow-up should happen within the next 2-4 days. If you are a weekend person, then also I suggest you do the follow up meeting within the next 4 days. If you cannot manage it, make sure you have a follow up meeting on the immediate weekend. If any more meeting is required, do it within the next 4-7 days.
- ✓ **The basic thumb rule in follow through is that every meeting should either end with money collection or a confirmed appointment for the next meeting.**
- ✓ Have patience. It generally takes 2-5 meetings for anyone to start. It's a process. Every meeting is multiplying the faith and knowledge of your prospect and every meeting is bringing you closer to sales closing. When you do it enough number of times, you develop the intuition to decide how long to continue this process, but I recommend you keep it on for 5 meetings.
- ✓ Preparation is the key to success. Always carry your business kit. Everything that the prospect may ask for and everything that can help in building his or her faith, should be handy and readily available with you in your kit as well as in your mobile/laptop/tablet.
- ✓ Use tools throughout the follow up process. Handover some literature, magazines or other tools for them to review in every meeting. You can forward them videos, newspaper clippings, articles, testimonies or some other important information that can help them in making a decision faster. **Let tools do the work for you when you are not with your prospects.**
- ✓ Follow up meetings should be done personally and not over phone. Phone or chat should be used only to take an appointment for the meeting. If the prospect is in a different city, we should schedule a video call and then do follow up through video calling.
- ✓ Remember, people don't join a company or plan; people join people. They will take a decision to start only because of you. So you should be at your best and you must give your **full personal assurance** for providing your best possible support to them in building this business.
- ✓ Your excitement and faith is more important than the product or plan knowledge. Our main product is not the product or services

that we sell, but the opportunity to fulfill dreams with a proven and doable system.

- ✓ Never commit to what you cannot do. Never say they don't have to do anything or any other statement that you cannot honor later. Make their role very clear and be honest and transparent in your dealings. Truth prevails.
- ✓ Don't ask stupid questions like *how did you find it, what do you think,* etc. Ask the right questions. Ask questions that move the discussion towards sales closing. Help your prospects in making a decision.
- ✓ All through the process, maintain a good rapport with your prospects. Our goal is not to win an argument, but to transfer our understanding and knowledge. When you talk from the heart and with an intention to help and empower the other person, your point quickly reaches their heart.
- ✓ Be a good listener and have patience. Don't listen just to give a reply; listen to understand the other person and his/her beliefs. Prospects themselves do the sales closing if you listen to them and ask the right questions.
- ✓ Some people will say no. Don't take it personally. They are not saying no to you, but to your proposal and if they have said no today, this doesn't mean they will never start in the future. Time is not right for them right now. Put such cases aside and follow them up after 6 months. No simply means next opportunity.
- ✓ Emotionally detach yourself from the outcome. We are looking for people who are looking. If they decide to come into business, it's best; otherwise, next. Keep moving forward.

Follow up and sales closing is a very dynamic area and tools and techniques keep changing with time. Stay connected on my social media channels and on my website www.deepakbajaj.biz to get latest cutting edge tools and strategies for multiplying your sales conversion.

Handling FAQs (Frequently Asked Questions)

Like in every sales situation, once you complete your business presentation, the prospect will ask you many questions and this is where the real work begins. Business presentation is the same in every meeting, what makes it exciting is the questions and discussion.

Remember, questions are a good sign. Questions show the interest of the prospect. Prospects open up and speak their heart out through questions.

You may not like some of the questions and the way these questions are asked but never get offended by questions or the person asking them. Questions are not about you or your business, but they tell you a lot about the mindset and the attitude of the person asking the questions. Never argue with the prospect. You are not here to win the argument you are there to win the person. Wordings of questions may differ but fundamentally, questions arise because a prospect doesn't believe in any of these two things: 1. Network marketing is such an amazing business and it is a better way to fulfill your dreams or 2. The prospect will be able to do the work required to be successful in this business.

There are broadly two types of questions asked:-

1. Data driven questions–questions that ask for specific information, like when was this company established? How many years have you been in this business? etc.

2. Emotion driven questions–All other questions fall in this category.

While the exact language of your answers may be different for every person and situation, I am giving you few fundamentals to handle FAQs:-

- Start your answer with your best smile and a compliment like, 'That's a very intelligent question or I totally agree with you or you are absolutely right or I was just waiting for this question or Thanks for asking this question. I was about to address this, etc.' The prospect was expecting you to fight back, but your smile and acceptance puts him/her off balance. The best thing that you have done here is to be on the same side as your prospect by accepting what he/she is saying. Now whatever you say will have more chances of acceptance. This approach works for both data driven and emotion driven questions.

- Use the *feel felt found* technique. This is a powerful old concept that every sales person knows or uses. But interestingly, it works for less than 10% of the people and falls flat for the other 90%. I found the answer to this puzzle during my international NLP certification program at Bangkok. This technique is perfect, but it works only when you are in good rapport with the prospect and you have been able to establish trust and credibility with the prospect so far in the meeting. This concept works with emotion driven questions.

This concept says that whatever question the other person may ask, reply to it by using the words feel, felt and found. For example, the prospect asked – *'I have not seen anyone being successful in this business.'* You may answer to it like – *'I know what you **feel**, when I was approached for this business I also **felt** the same that no one gets success in such businesses, but when I attended several events, researched the business model in depth and met some leaders in the business, I **found** out that my opinion about this business was wrong. After I found this truth, I decided to build this business seriously and now I am determined to fulfill all my dreams through this business.'* You can use this same format for almost all questions.

- Answer question with questions. This is also a *wonderful approach wherein we help our prospect find the best answers to his/her questions by asking some more questions. Also sometimes, the question that the other person is asking is not the real question, and we can find out the real question through this approach.*

- You can say something like, *'Wonderful question. Are you seriously looking for an answer for this question? (The immediate answer would be yes). Then I recommend you must attend our next week's event and it will give you the best solution to this. Or we have a special session covering this question in our next weekend event. Why don't you join us and get the answer to this?'*

Don't just answer questions, engage with your prospects and explore. Let them talk more. Answer questions with questions. The goal is not to get money today itself, the goal is education and understanding. Use tools and events during follow through. It may take 2-5 meetings. Gradually, many of them will realize that this is a good business model and it will help them reach their goals or solve some of their problems and then they will start business with you. These follow up meetings will develop your relationship with them and many of them will be your lifetime partners.

Sales Closing

Now is the time to close the sale. You must get the payment now and complete the registration. Once you have answered all the questions, you can summarize the discussion towards sales closing using the following process.

- I know what you are feeling right now and what all questions are going in your head. I have felt the same and I also had similar doubts. But when I met few people and did my research on this opportunity, I realized that the facts were different from my opinions and feelings. I have attended a few meetings and met a couple of seniors. After my thorough research, I can assure you:-

    1. *It's a wonderful business opportunity and now is the best time to start this business in India. This is an amazing company with proven track records, excellent income plan, amazing products and wonderful support system. This is definitely the best option available in the industry.* (You should tell your reasons for choosing this company.)

    2. *I have been watching such businesses for quite a long time/I have been looking for a business opportunity for quite some time/I have already invested money in 2-3 similar looking opportunities earlier also (say your truth here in terms of your own experience about network marketing), but I never worked on this seriously. Now I have decided I will do this business seriously and will be super successful in this. I have already started working on it and I will reach a monthly income of Rs._____ in the next _____ months.* (Say your real goal here.)

    3. Seeing is believing. Show your prospect your list of names and your workbook. Show them how prepared and serious you are about your goals in this business. Confidently tell your prospect – *'I am serious for my life and come what may, I will achieve _____ income/lifestyle/car, etc. through

this business in _____ days/weeks/months. I have understood the basics of the business and I commit to give you all possible support in this business. Together we will build a big business.'

Saying these lines is important, but even more important is the faith and conviction with which you say these lines. Remember, it is not just the content, but the state and congruency with which you say these lines that will determine the results.

- ✓ Talk with an assumption that they have already decided to start the business. Confidently ask for documents or money. A confirmation without money does not mean anything.
- ✓ Get their signature on the form if your team uses some forms.
- ✓ Take some advance if they can't transfer or handover the full amount.
- ✓ Have patience. Try to close sale in every meeting, but have patience. It takes some time. People have heard and seen a lot about network marketing business and they have their own set of opinions about the business. It takes patience and compassion on your part to allow them to change their opinions. Our role is to provide them all the relevant information that will help them understand the business in the right way.
- ✓ Power of Five: It may take up to five meetings to establish a good relationship and to finally close the sale. A majority of people don't do more than two meetings. If the sale is closed in the fifth meeting, were the first four meetings a waste? No, it's all work in progress. It takes time for someone to understand you and your business. Every meeting is vital. If you adopt this philosophy of five today, you will be way ahead of everyone else in your organization. It works everywhere in life.
- ✓ Remember the acronym that is taught everywhere SWSWSWSW. Some Will, Some Won't, So What? Someone is Waiting.
- ✓ Remember to put some heart into your sales presentations and conversations. It works like magic. Offer them your genuine heartfelt support and they will understand.

Yes or no is part of the process.
In 2007, when I started the business, I used to do minimum 4 meetings a day even after the busiest of my days at my job. Imagine doing daily four meetings for five continuous days and when the 20th person says no to you, sometimes you start doubting yourself, your company, upline or business. But that's the trap most losers fall into. That's not the time to quit, that's the time to show more plans. That's the time to do more follow-up meetings with extra passion. As per law of average, your chances of getting a 'yes' actually increase after every no you hear.

6
Right Takeoff for New Associates

It takes a lot of time and effort to get a new distributor in the business. But 60-80% of new distributors leave the business within 4 weeks of starting it. In a majority of cases, the reason is negligence on the part of the sponsor. Most of the distributors are very aggressive till the time the sale is closed but get non-serious after the person has signed up. But the top income earners in network marketing have mastered the basics of giving the right takeoff to new associates.

Your work as a network-marketing professional doesn't stop at getting the sale; it actually starts after you get the sale. In fact this is what differentiates network marketing from selling.

–Deepak Bajaj

If we can master the science of the right takeoff for new associates, we can reach the desired income levels in record time. Here are 3 key activities we should conduct with new associates for their right takeoff.

Conduct a **Welcome Meeting** at their home within one week of starting the business and do these 3 activities:-

1. Provide tools and information:

(a) Tell your million dollar story again with faith and passion. Introduce your industry, company, team and upline using diary/manual/website/video or any other tool.

(b) Collect any pending documents required for registration (if any).

(c) Ensure that they have received all products/services. Explain to them the products and services and get them to start using them.

(d) Get them a copy of tools—any welcome kit or other tools available. If the tools come with the registration, get it for them or if it has to be purchased, then make them buy it.

(e) Discuss the income plan broadly and answer if they need any clarifications on the same.

(f) Get them added to the WhatsApp or other online groups so that they get all the information.

(g) Recommend them books, audios and videos that they should start on right now. The list is available on my website and in the Tools section of this book.

(h) Never discuss politics or religion in this meeting.

(i) If you feel this book can benefit your new associates, you can lend/give them a copy of this book or make them buy it. Lot of free useful information and tools for network marketing are available on my website www.deepakbajaj.biz, my YouTube channel, Instagram page, Facebook page and other social media channels.

2. Define their dreams and set goals:

(a) Build their dream. That's the most important exercise. Take out the Top Success Drivers (TSD) sheet and arrive at their top 3 reasons for starting this business.

(b) Set their Goals from this business by writing answers to these 2 major questions:-

  (i) How much income do you expect to earn in the next 1 month/3 months/6 months/1 year/5 years?

  (ii) What all dreams do you want to fulfill from this business in next the 3 months /6 months/1 year/5 years?

(c) Explain to them any product promotions or contests going on currently.

(d) Update them on the next ranks and do a goal setting for them for the next level.

3. Business development actions:

(a) Plan a business opening ceremony at their house within the next one week with their family members, close friends and neighbors. The objective of this event is to showcase products and to announce to their family and friends that they have started a business. Simple invitation, anyone is welcome and we will not show our formal business opportunity. We can check the interest of people and can share the opportunity with the selected ones at a later date. Build the excitement of having starting a life changing business.

(b) Make their list of prospects with them.

(c) Select the first batch of prospects for the immediate meetings.

(d) Empower them to make the first set of calls and set up first set of appointments. You should encourage them to make calls in your presence.

(e) Confirm them for the next event. (We want new associates to see a minimum of 3 events as fast as possible. Make sure that one of them is a big event.)

Developing a new distributor in our business is like planting and nurturing a tree. Once done properly and if you take enough care in the initial few weeks/months, this tree will take care of you and your future generations.

Remember **the power of five**. It will take five events and five personal meetings for the new distributor to really start developing faith in this business and in their own self. After this, the new distributor will start considering this venture as a serious business. So you should make sure you complete this with the new associates as soon as possible and be in active communication with all of them till this time.

You don't really have a new person till the time you get them to sponsor someone.

> ***Right orientation in first 2-4 weeks does wonders.***
> We have always followed this culture in our team that we must do a welcome meet for all new associates within 2-4 weeks of starting the business. There is new excitement and motivation within 2-4 weeks of starting anything new. When we do a welcome meet at new associate's house within 4 weeks his/her chances of survival in the business multiplies 20 times. One of my loving teammates Saurabh Mehra has built a big and ever growing business with this. Saurabh did his hotel management course followed by a job in Australia. Started this business with us while he was on holidays here and left his Australia career for this business. Today he has touched top income level in the company and is enjoying his success.

7
The Triangle of Massive Success

> *It's not the system; it's the intensity of your faith on the system that brings extra ordinary results.*
>
> –Deepak Bajaj

All these principles above will work only when you execute them with absolute faith and in the right state of mind.

Faith does the magic. It gives power to everything you say and do. Your faith on what this business can do for you and your prospects is the magic ingredient in all your meetings. Faith is what moves the heart and the heart takes the decision.

You say more with your mental state and body language than with your words. Make sure to get into a happy and resourceful state every time you go for meetings/phone calls/video conferencing. State gets transferred fast and does wonders.

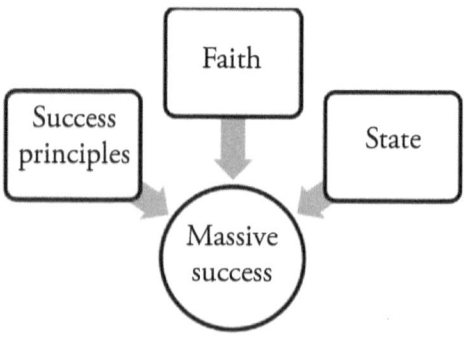

Success principles + Faith + State = Massive success

Every business has its own set of principles. The same goes for this business. These principles have been tried and tested by thousands of distributors with millions of people for more than a decade. Follow them and you will reach your goals fasters, saving yourself years of effort and big money.

I have met thousands of people who want to build this business, but without telling anyone about it. These people will tell you they have dreams and they will do whatever it takes for their dreams etc., but for some stupid self-created reasons, they will not tell anyone that they are into this life changing business. Such people do everything half-heartedly with doubts and with their own ideas, and ultimately leave the business feeling frustrated and blaming the company, industry, uplines, etc. for their failures.

One major expense for any company is advertising where they shout and tell the maximum number of people what they do. When any business looks for a showroom or a premise, they pay premium for a location where more and more people can see them. No business runs by hiding. It's simple. We hide what is bad, immoral or illegal and we promote and flaunt what we are proud of or what is precious/valuable.

Your attitude towards this business is an indicator of your faith on this business. You simply can't give what you don't have. So fix your convictions first. First work on yourself and then start working with others.

If it is worth doing, it is worth doing the right way. Quit if you feel this business is not right, but if you make a decision to do it, then do it the right way. Also, the more you do it, the better you will get at doing it. You cannot learn swimming by sitting on the sides. You need to be prepared to get wet.

So have absolute faith, be in the best of your mental state and win your way to the top using these principles.

SECTION-IV
SUCCESS ACCELERATORS

SUCCESS ACCELERATORS

Principles and Techniques to Put your Business on Fast Track

To enjoy what only 1% of the people have, simply do what only 1% of the people do.

–Deepak Bajaj

There is only one reason why people get into this business and there is only one category of people who make it big in this business. The reason is their big non-negotiable dreams that they have not been able to fulfill from what they have been doing. The people who make it big in this business are the ones who are hungry, insatiable and who are committed to work till they accomplish what they want. People choose this business to get the life they want, and that too much faster than it is possible in any other profession.

This section is written especially for the above set of people who will do whatever it takes to fulfill their dreams faster. The next few pages contain the distilled wisdom of 11 years of creating thousands of fast achievers in this business. Once you decide to follow these principles and techniques, you will see your business sky rocketing, giving you in just a few months what people take years or decades to achieve.

It matters how big you dream, but what is even more important is how long you can keep those dreams alive.

–Deepak Bajaj

Please remember, the contents of this section are not for everyone, because everyone is not willing to devote the level of commitment that is required for legendary success. It's simple: no pain, no gain. You are the owner of your business and you are the only one who will decide how you want to build your business. You have total and absolute control to decide the goal, the speed and the methodology of building your business. But still, I would highly recommend that since you have decided to do this business, why not do it in the best possible way. Why not achieve in 2-3 years what a regular network marketer would take 10-20 years to do.

If not your whole life, use this accelerated success methodology for the first few months and then use all or parts of it whenever you need to skyrocket your business.

Why wait for a lifetime to get something that can be earned right now?

–Deepak Bajaj

So, fasten your seat belts and get ready for the big take off. Here are your success accelerators. Work on these 11 success accelerators with one principle: No rest till I become the best.

Eleven Success Accelerators:-

1. Work with big dreams
2. Get MAD (Massive Action Daily)
3. Convert individuals into teams faster
4. Power shots
5. Make your team a leaders' creation factory
6. Create speed in your organization
7. Develop business in multiple locations
8. Reinvestment
9. Build your Brand – Your most valuable asset
10. Contests: Be a winner, create winners
11. Social media – Turbo charger for your business

Let's master each one of these accelerators now.

1
Work with Big Dreams

Dreams are not what you see in sleep; dreams are those that do not let you sleep.
–Dr A P J Abdul Kalam

There is a great leverage in working with big dreams. I believe there is a reserved power in every human being that is unleashed only when you operate with big dreams or a big mission. When you work with big dreams, you become a different person—an untiring and undefeatable superhero with a magical energy and enthusiasm.

The future belongs to those who believe in the beauty of their dreams.
–Eleanor Roosevelt

Don't just have dreams, have big dreams. Ask for the best things in life. The best thing about achieving big dreams is not what you get but what you become in the process of accomplishing those dreams. You stretch your limits and create a new you.

Also, big dreams mean big income and a big income is possible only when a big number of people in your team earn big money. Long term stability and growth in network marketing is possible only if you have a strong lineup of leaders who are giving their 100% every day. Your team members will remain committed to this business only when their goals are getting accomplished. The achievement of your big goals is followed by many achievements of your next levels of associates. So, when you decide to do big business, people in your team will also achieve new ranks and dream incomes. Your big dreams will produce a ripple effect in your team and create a momentum all across your team.

Like attracts like. When you dream big, you tend to attract more high dreamers in your team. You become a magnet for people who will build great business empires with you.

Every business goes through challenges every day. When you have big dreams, you don't really get disappointed by petty issues, non-performing or complaining people and recurring challenges.

You don't have a boss in this business. You are accountable only to yourself. Many people who are used to working under a boss would perish if they don't have dreams. Dreams keep us going forward.

Work with goals, not hope.

Make dream setting a practice in your team. Enable everyone to write their dreams, work with their dreams and review their dreams at least once in a month. Be a high dreamer and build an army of high dreamers with you.

If you can dream it, you can do it.

–Walt Disney

Keep surprising the world.
When I told people I would win Thailand trip in 2 weeks, people laughed at me. I did that and set a new goal to touch top income level in 3 months. People laughed again but I did it. Then I set a goal to be the 1st Mercedes Benz achiever in entire North India and achieved that. Then we became the 1st team to hold an international convention on a cruise. I even did a conference with my team in Burj-Al-Arab, Dubai. I had to do a Facebook live from my diplomatic suite at 44th floor to make people believe it. That video went viral on social media and people were again surprised. Trust me, I enjoyed every bit of hard work and stretching I did for these goals and working for these goals was the happiest period of my life. Now I have made it my life philosophy and I love surprising myself and the world again and again. We all have hidden powers inside us. Bring them out with big dreams.

2
Get MAD (Massive Action Daily)

The path to success is to take massive, determined action.
—Tony Robbins

Be a man/woman of action. Speed is not possible without massive action. Average action will give you an average income, massive action will give you a big income and massive success. It's simple. If you want an extra ordinary income, lifestyle, cars, vacations, house and fame, then you need to put in extra ordinary efforts. Life simply works on the principle of cause and effect. All the success and achievement is the effect, while daily hard work is the root cause. Everyone wants the effect/rewards, but no one wants to take the journey and pay the price. ***You must commit to be the most hardworking person in your team.***

Network marketing is one of the few professions available to an ordinary person where you pay once and if you do it right, the rewards will last a lifetime. Commit to get MAD and take massive action towards your dreams every day, day after day.

Big 6 of Network Marketing
Formula for being Fast and unstoppable
1. Show more plans
2. Close more sales
3. Learn more & faster
4. Get more people to events
5. Create more leaders
6. Prospect more people

Do the right things and do them fast.
—Deepak Bajaj

It is important to work hard, but it is equally important to ensure that you are doing the right things. With my experience of building a team of lacs of people in a record time, I can tell you 6 activities which, if you do daily, you will become a legend in the business: Show more plans, close more sales, learn more and faster, get more people into events, create more leaders and prospect more people. Make sure that 80% of your time goes into these activities which I call the big 6 of Network marketing. Develop laser like focus and don't waste your time. Daily focused action on these big six for a few months will create huge a momentum in your team.

Do whatever you need to do and then do a little bit more.
—Deepak Bajaj

Develop the attitude and a life value to do a little more than asked for. Don't do just enough to manage, but do enough to excel. During my initial years when I was a corporate employee, I realized that a job slowly teaches a person that instead of working hard, it is considered smarter to just manage by doing only what is good enough. In a book by Robert Kiyosaki, I read that an employee will work only so much that he/she is not fired and an employer will pay only that much so the employee doesn't leave. If you are a new entrepreneur, I urge you to quickly develop this habit of doing more than what is required. When you do more, you learn more and when you learn more, you be more. And that's all that matters.

How do I know if you are on MAD? Simple – Do you have a calendar full of appointments?

Don't wait until you are ready to take action. Instead, take action to be ready.
—Jensen Siaw

> ***Pain is temporary, pride is forever.***
> *Today when people see me coming out a chauffeur driven Mercedes benz and having a huge fan following everywhere, some of them feel as if all this came in my welcome kit when I started in 2007. No! If you want this lifestyle, you need to adopt a work style that leads to this lifestyle. I started off my business in an Tata Indica car. I had kept my pillow and blanket permanently in my car itself. I had roasted grams and peanuts in my car for anytime food. People carry water bottles in their car, I had a 10 liter water jug.*
>
> *For many months I survived on unlimited parathas* and galloons of tea from roadside dhabas*. Many nights I slept in my car parked on roadside dhabas because I couldn't drive any more. I listened to every piece of mockery and ridicule. I saw my friends turning into my biggest critics. But every moment I knew it was not permanent; it was only a temporary phase. Every moment I believed I would soon get what I had come for and I got more that that. Bigger the dream, the greater is the amount of MADness required.*

---

* A paratha is a North Indian Preparation made with wheat and a dhaba is a small road side restaurant. Many of them are open for 24 hours.

3
Convert Individuals to Teams Faster

> *Your job is not to just sponsor a person. Your job is to convert a person into a team.*
>
> —Deepak Bajaj

When you sponsor someone, you only get one circle added in your structure. That circle becomes a person when he/she sponsors someone. So, you have not really sponsored a person till the time this person has sponsored at least one person. After that, you need to make that person an active distributor and gradually build a team with him/her.

> *Sponsoring a person is the starting point in our business, what you do after that will determine how far will you go in this business.*
>
> —Deepak Bajaj

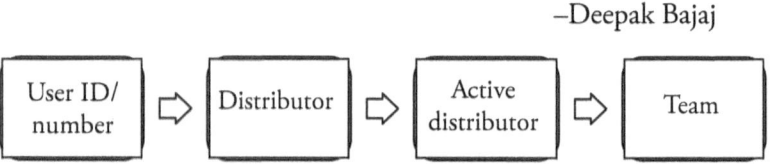

As soon as you sponsor a new person, do a welcome meet with him/her and get him/her to attend an event within one week. Help him/her secure 8-10 appointments and close their first 2-3 sales within the first two weeks of starting. You can learn the detailed steps of how to get a new distributor started in the business in 'The Success Process' section of this book.

That's the beginning of their team and a team always has more chances of surviving and thriving than a single individual. Now, train this team on the right practices, give them your best possible support and make sure they attend all the events. A team that is connected to events stays longer and performs better.

This is the fundamental process we need to follow with every new person who starts with us. Your efficiency in doing this faster and with more and more people will give you excellent speed. Repeat this process with more and more people and empower them to do it with their people in turn. The goal is to have several independent teams working with each other. This will ensure speed and stability.

Everyone starts with excitement. Get them some achievement before this excitement comes down.

–Deepak Bajaj

At every event, ask yourself, 'How many different teams of yours are attending this event?' and multiply your business by multiplying the number of teams you have.

> **TEAM = *Together Everyone Achieves More.***
> *Both me and Gaurav are first time entrepreneurs. We were introverts and excellent individual players. But few months into the business, our incomes were not growing beyond one level. We burned out because of doing everything by ourselves. Our turning point came when we realized network marketing is a team sport. We then started working on developing a team for every active distributor. Slowly we had hundreds of small teams working together producing much bigger and stable volume. I have some very good friends who are excellent at creating teams and we keep sharing ideas—Sheejan Nair, Uttam Chetia and Vijay Teterwal.*

4
Power Shots

Ours is a business of excitement and achievements. There are times this spark and excitement is missing, even though all activities are happening smoothly. Some other times, your current teams are doing good but you need to add a new personal team directly to multiply your income or to achieve a new rank. Sometimes you need to drive momentum in one team by creating fire at the bottom, or sometimes there is a foreign trip or some other contest that you need to qualify in record time. What you need in all these situations is a power shot.

I define Power Shot as a series of focused and result driven actions, which produce massive results in a short duration of time. We commit ourselves to a period of 60-90 days of power shot to recharge the whole team and to ignite excitement, passion and fire in people, along with an increase in income, ranks, rewards, free trips, etc.

In this 90 days period, you devote the first 30 days to mass recruitment—recruit people in bunches and recruit 20-30 new associates in the first 30 days. Make sure they attend events as soon as they start. Over the next 15 days, train and empower them to duplicate this same massive level of activity. In the next 45 days, this entire new team should be on a mission to achieve some new rank and earn big incomes. We may choose to conduct a big event at the end of these 90 days for the recognition of new achievers and to give them the energy to carry on this momentum by themselves.

Looking at your lists will not make you rich and famous; converting your lists into meetings and partners will do it.

–Deepak Bajaj

Massive sponsoring drive

The first step in a power shot is massive personal sponsoring. While everyone is sponsoring people in network marketing, if you want to make it really big and fast in this business you must get into massive personal sponsoring. Be a sponsoring factory. Exhaust your lists and then make new ones. Talk to everyone. Get moving. Set more appointments. You can get a lot of strategies for expanding your lists in this book, on my website and in several of my free videos available online.

Like Allan Pease said, *'For massive results, meet the next week's prospects this week itself. Meet the next month's prospects this month itself. You must complete in 3-4 weeks what an average person takes 5-6 months to complete.'*

So, a Power Shot is simple: Recruit people in bunches, empower them and make them achievers, multiply the success and do a celebration event after 90 days.

Power shot your way to the top.
I could resign my high paying job at the peak of my career only because of power shot. Within 90 days of starting the business I was a full timer and within 98 days of starting I touched the top income level. These 90 days I worked with Gaurav Mehra and Gaurav Bajaj exactly on the same plan as I had just explained in this book. Later on many leaders in my team duplicated that especially Vikas Singla and Manik Kaura and we created the fastest growing organization.

5
Make your Team a Leaders' Creation Factory

> *Leadership is about making others better as a result of your presence and making sure that impact lasts in your absence.*
> —Sheryl Sandberg

Have you ever wondered why some people who are very successful in their respective professions are not successful when it comes to network marketing business? A very successful sales person who has created records in his industry, sometimes finds it tough to break through in network marketing, while at the same time, an average person with a humble beginning and absolutely no sales experience exceeds everyone's expectations in terms of performance. This is essentially because network marketing is more of a team sport than an individual game.

> *Lead from the back and let others believe they are in front.*
> —Nelson Mandela

A successful and growing Network Marketing team functions primarily as a leaders creation factory. When you start the network marketing business, you do everything by yourself and your primary job is to build a team and sell products. As you grow in the business while these two primary tasks remain the same, multiplication in your income comes from increasing the number of people in your organization who will be doing these two primary tasks of building a team and selling products. If you want to build a big, stable and ever growing passive income stream in the business, your job fundamentally is to create more and more people who can successfully do what you do. While building my own large and thriving network marketing team with thousands of people working in hundreds of villages, towns, cities and metros, I have identified a few practices that can quickly and successfully turn your team into an ever growing leaders creation factory, and these are as follows:-

1. First and foremost, you must prepare your teammates to stand on their own. The biggest help you can do for your teammates is to equip them with the knowledge and skills required to run their business completely by themselves. Like no plant can grow under the shade of a big tree, no competent leader can emerge under an upline who is constantly overshadowing his or her team. It's a thoughtful balance between when to intervene and when to let go, and all great leaders in this business have mastered it. Leaving people to stand on their own feet is not an option but a cardinal principle and pre-requisite for success in this business.

   It's as simple as raising a child. If you continue spoon-feeding the child after a certain period, you will be ruining the child instead of helping him/her. So have faith in your teammates and let them learn and grow as they implement your team's systems. Some teammates will grab the opportunity themselves while you need to push some others, but whatever be the case, fulfill your duty of empowering your distributors at the right time.

2. Have patience and make allowances for mistakes. You were not perfect either when you started. Enough repetitions under the right mentoring will make all your distributors better over a period of time. Also remember, during presentations or programs, it is not the word-to-word copying of the content that creates the impact, but the enthusiasm, spark in the eyes, confidence level and absolute faith in what one is talking about. Let your associates learn from their own experiences.

3. It is also good to tell new distributors in the beginning that very soon they will have to take charge of their business and show plans for themselves. Right expectations set in the beginning will make your task easier. In spite of all this, if some people expect you to keep showing the plans for them for their whole life, take them to training programs or arrange for a counseling with your upline. When they hear everyone in the organization talking the

same language, they will also accept it and start following the system.

4. Your biggest aide in empowering your new associates to be independent leaders will be your conversations, especially the words you use. Words have immense power and can make or break a person. Have a vocabulary rich in empowering and uplifting words and make it your second nature to use these words repeatedly. Practice it so much that it becomes a part of you. Regular conversations with your new distributors should make them confident and eager to take initiatives. Use stories and anecdotes from your experience wherein people who had taken initiatives, learnt the basics and quickly took charge of the business reached different heights altogether. Practiced effectively, you will have your new associates coming and asking for an opportunity to do it themselves. That's real empowerment and the best multiplication strategy for the business.

5. While giving business presentations for your teammates, please teach them to observe the presentation with a clear objective of learning and mastering the art of showing the presentation, because after 3-6 presentations they will be doing their own presentations. I recommend 5 + 5 model for business presentations as given in The Success Process section of this book.

6. Being an upline, it is your responsibility to provide appropriate growth opportunities to your teammates. Encourage your teammates to take initiatives and support them as they take up new challenges for the first few times. Make them part of committees and put new people with old distributors while organizing meetings and events.

7. Provide all requisite tools to your teammates for their smooth functioning in the field: presentations, videos, brochures, testimonies, demo kits if required, etc. Tools give a lot of confidence to a new distributor and ensure that all necessary information is passed on to the prospects.

8. Train all your teammates to attend all the programs and follow the system 100%. Programs impart such a level of conviction and confidence that can never be built in one to one counseling and presentations. When your teammates attend programs

and are working as per the established system, they will not go wrong in the first place and even if they do, the system takes care of it. Everyone in the organization, irrespective of level, rank, qualification or experience in the business, must use the same presentation. Be very strict about it. No one is allowed to change the business presentation at any circumstance.

9. Home meetings are the actual leader creation factories that serve as an excellent training ground for all future leaders. A home meeting is a non-threatening and easy platform for a new distributor to try his or her presentation, objection handling, program organizing and public speaking skills. It's a home setting and comfortable for both the presenter and audience. It's a small meeting and serves as a stepping-stone for bigger events. It's the perfect learning opportunity and preparation ground for leaders. Encourage your teammates to organize and participate in home meetings and gradually give them different roles and responsibilities.

Leaders are not born, they are made. And they are made just like anything else, through hard work.

–Vince Lombardi

Create leaders and not followers. **Teach your people to deserve your time. Give your time to those who deserve it and not to those who need it.** Bigger the dream, the more important is the team. What good leaders can do to your business is awesome. Leaders will simply take you and your business to levels beyond your imagination. Since they are in your team, their dreams, faith and confidence will get added to yours.

Some people ask me: Are leaders created or found?

My answer is that leaders are always created. We can find good people who are doing well in their current jobs or profession or studies, but these good people need someone to influence them and some system/institution to fine-tune their mind-sets and attitude. They need to be developed, groomed and converted into great leaders through the right influence and a powerful system.

When people are ready, they should take up this business as full timers. Anyone who has achieved a certain level of income, achievement and right structure, should become a full timer in the business. You need to give your full time to the business to change gears and to go to the next level. Becoming a full timer in the business magically multiplies the faith of your team and the outsiders, in you and in your business. Please make a plan with your upline for taking up the business full time.

> *Everything we do in this business is aimed at reaching out to those few who will take full charge of their lives and of this business.*
>
> –Deepak Bajaj

Creating leaders is an attitude.

In my team Gaurav Bajaj is an expert in making leaders out of ordinary people. He told me, 'Creating leaders is an attitude and when we work with an intention to serve and empower people, they start taking up greater responsibilities and become leaders. Also we need to give them confidence that we are always there for them. We have learnt this a lot from a legendary leader from USA—Bill Britt.'

6
Creating and Sustaining Speed in your Entire Team

An army of sheep led by a lion can defeat an army of lions led by a sheep.

–African Proverb

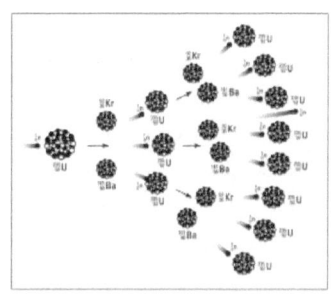

You can create good speed once in a while, but if you want to sustain your speed and accelerate it beyond imagination, then this speed must spread across the entire length and breadth of your team. Most people in the network marketing business don't attain speed, and a majority of those who pick up speed are not able to really spread it through their teams. You must aim to attain the ranks of those rare few who attain speed and then successfully spread the same speed in their team also. This is where you get the biggest income and recognition, and for much longer periods of time too.

My aim for you is to empower you to start a nuclear reaction that will continue to grow bigger and bigger. I want your success to lead to a self-amplifying series of successes throughout your team.

So here are the keys to creating and sustaining speed in your entire team:-

1. There is only one way to attain speed: Massive action done in a short span of time. 100 plans shown in 1 month or 100 plans shown in 6 months will have totally different and surprising

results. So select a period of 45-60 days and let everyone in your team give their best in this period. This will start creating speed in your team.

2. Make a lot of noise and action during this period: Let this be the period of maximum activity—home meetings, celebrations, recognitions, group meetings, promotions and events. Involve maximum people.

3. Your own continuous speed: Speed of the train is the speed of the engine. You give your best every day and work with passion and urgency during this period. It may take some time before it catches fire but work with the commitment to put in more effort today than yesterday.

4. Make a mission for the whole team and attach everyone to that mission: People connect first to a mission than to a person. The mission may be an event coming within 45-60 days, a new rank, new benchmark, new product, company's international convention, etc. It can be anything, but the idea is to ensure that everyone is participating and giving their best. The idea is to have one goal, one language, and one common action all across the organisation.

5. Make special core teams for this mission: When people are called to be a part of a core team for a mission, they feel special and needed. They will surprise you and themselves with what great things they can do. You can make a core team at your end and then all your team members can make their teams. Sometimes, it's a good idea to create a healthy competition among the teams.

6. Promote a contest: I have seen contests give new hope and automatically set an exciting short term goal for everyone. All companies give international trips or some special promotions from time to time. You can give small contests for your own team too. It does not have to be a trip or a monetary benefit all the time. A chance to be recognized in the next big event also works equally well. The key in contest is not what the reward is, but how passionately you are able to promote it and make maximum people connect to it.

7. Communication is the key to transfer speed to different sections of your team: Every good news, every achievement and every

progress must be broadcasted to the entire team. Very few people have the guts to start a race, but everyone loves to join the race. Communication is actually the key to spreading speed in the entire team. Use WhatsApp and every possible social media tool that is popular in your team to spread awareness about a successful movement on your mission.

8. Simple duplicable actions: Don't give people a lot of things to do, give them one or two actions to be repeated everyday. Simple and easy to do activities are the only ones that will be duplicated in the team. The whole team should follow 2-3 simple daily/weekly actions e.g. 2 new plans every day, 4 new guests in the Sunday open meetings, etc. Follow the KISS principle—Keep it Short and Simple.

9. Monitor your events numbers: Through your core team and communication channels, monitor the number of associates attending the different events. If the events numbers are growing, speed will increase for sure. Promote all events aggressively. Ensure that maximum number of programs are organized and there is maximum participation in every program.

10. To ensure a guaranteed success, we should prepare well in advance and select a few associates who will personally ensure to produce breakthrough results. Let everyone in the team be on FIRE.

FIRE = Focused Ignited Right actions done with Excitement

During this period, sales conversion simply doubles or triples and many people who are seemingly slow also produce unbelievable results. The benefits are phenomenal: Bigger incomes, faster rank promotions and extra achievements. The biggest benefit is a faster recruitment of people. Whoever was supposed to join in 6 months, will be with us in 6 weeks. Also, it helps in the identification of potential leaders.

It takes some time but when executed correctly, it can spread like wild-fire and give big rewards to everyone.

> ***Speed is the key.***
> *We have come to this business for only one reason—to achieve our dreams faster. Speed is the key. My upline used to tell me that an aircraft will take off only when it attains a minimum speed. I understood this fact and started teaching to everyone in my team. We used everything that I have given in this chapter and we created a speeding organization. Two of my good friends from Koltaka—Prasenjit Mondal and Tarun Kumar Pradhan once told me that you don't need extra talent to build speed; you need a dream and commitment to do it.*

7
Developing Business in Multiple Locations

Consistency in volume generated in your team is directly proportional to the number of locations where you do business.
—Deepak Bajaj

I have seen this formula work every time. The more the number of locations where you do business, the higher and the more consistent will be the volume generated in your organization. So as your business grows, I urge you to start travelling and start building business in different cities one by one. You can choose to personally sponsor people from different locations or you can work with the prospects of some of your associates in other locations.

When you start the business, build it in your own area. Slowly start expanding within a 50 km radius. As your current business gets established and you start developing leaders locally, start exploring the nearby towns and cities for business.

Starting in a new location comes with the responsibility to serve them regularly. So, start with locations which are close to your current location so that you can easily and frequently visit those locations. If you are a full timer, then building business in multiple locations is not an option; it's an absolute necessity. You must travel and develop business in new locations regularly. Pick up those locations first where your team/company is already doing regular events and you have the basic support available for a new team.

As we have discussed repeatedly in this book, ours is a business of developing leaders and ultimately the person with the maximum number of independent leaders will win in this business. When you build business in a new location, you generally work one or two days with your new location associates; the rest of the time, they need to work by themselves. They can't ask you to come every day for every small matter and you would also expect them to do few things on their own after you leave. This automatically makes them good independent leaders. Working at different locations serves as a beautiful filtering mechanism too because only those people will survive this arrangement who are willing to do their part. Weak leaders will quit the business and you will be left with only the good quality leaders.

Also, when you are not available at your home location for more than 2-3 days in a week, your associates at your home location, who are used to having you around them all the time, will now have to work by themselves while you are away. This will help them stand on their feet too. People tend to respect and value what is not easily accessible, so when you are accessible selectively, you shall command good respect from your associates.

Thus, your travel will help all your associates, both at the home location and at the new location, to become independent leaders. Very soon, these people will lead their own teams, generate huge volume and will help you attain the necessary speed you want.

Also, travelling is good for your own intellectual and business development. To grow bigger and faster, make it a top priority to develop your business in new locations.

Travel brings power and love back in your life.

–Rumi

> **More the locations greater is the profit.**
> *I have seen Gaurav Bajaj do it. He is hungry for working at new locations and creating achievers from new locations. Majority of his growth has come from working in locations where there was zero business earlier. He has mastered this art and every time I speak to him, he has a new location where he is going to build business.*

8
Reinvestment

> *If you are a business owner, at the first sign of profit, rather than spending that, you should try to put it back into your business and better the quality. If you reinvest your profit, you in turn enable growth for your business.*
> —Warren Buffet in warrenbuffet.com on 14th January, 2017 in an article - *Buffet on Reinvesting*

Reinvestment is simple: Whatever you earn from the business, invest all or a part of it for the development of the business. During the initial days, it may be all of your earnings, but as you grow in the business, it will only be a part of your earnings. In network marketing, you are the business. We don't have an office, staff or other infrastructure, so most of the reinvestment essentially will be utilized for your own development. Every business needs reinvestment all the time. In our business, reinvestment means:-

- ✓ Attending training programs for your own self-development.
- ✓ Purchasing books and other tools for your own personal development.
- ✓ Keeping a stock of books or tools to circulate among your team mates.
- ✓ Sometimes organizing events for your team or contributing in organizing events.
- ✓ Giving some contests or incentives to your team for multiplying your business.
- ✓ Occasional travel arrangements for taking new teammates to events.

- ✓ Keeping some stocks for immediate delivery to product customers.
- ✓ Making expenses on expanding the business in a new city.
- ✓ Business travels and several other expenses for building and motivating the team.

Remember, program tickets are not an expense but an investment for the business. All the money that you spend in your own development is not an expense you are doing for someone else, but an investment for your own development that will give you a big return and will stay with you forever. Few people have this attitude that first I will earn and then I will attend training, but the truth is that first you attend the training, then only you will be able to earn fast. So, invest in your own development and the development of your teammates; your business will multiply and you will enjoy the highest return on your investment.

Reinvestment in your business lead to huge growth. Reinvestment is the best way to build wealth. Reinvestment is crucial to your business' continued growth and success.
  –Brenton Hayden's article titled, *'Warren Buffett Knows It'*
  in Entrepreneur.com.

Outside success is a reflection of inside growth.
I believe our primary job is to develop ourselves along with developing our business and we can do it through books, audio-video programs, training events, association of right people and implementation of what we learn. I have realized this only after coming to this business. I now have a library with 1800+ books and audio-video programs. I have spent more than five millions rupees in last few years to attend best trainings in the world from world's best trainers like Tony Robbins, Antano Solar John, Robert Kiyosaki, Les Brown, Shiv Khera, Jack Canfield, Brain Tracy and many more. This has already made me the best in what I do and will soon take me on world stage. I believe training never stops. I am excited about learning more from the world's best and delivering the same to my readers and to the participants of my training programs.

9
Build Your Brand: Your Most Valuable Asset

> *Your brand is the single most important investment you can make in your business.*
>
> —Steve Forbes

Build your brand. What I have understood is, *'A brand is simply a set of values and attributes people attach to your name by observing your repeated words, actions and behaviors.'* What you repeatedly do and say becomes your brand. First, you create your brand and then your brand creates you. Being a leader, you are constantly being observed. How fast and how far you will go in this business is determined by your reputation or brand. Brands are both good and bad. It's basically a label that once stuck, will stay for quite a long time. So build a good and positive brand for yourself and enjoy the benefits. Few of the benefits of building a good brand are:-

- ✓ Retention of people is easier. Since they know that they are with a good leader, they feel secure, stay loyal and don't leave your team.
- ✓ Your leadership is established and people listen to what you say. When people respect you and follow your plan, your whole team works with a single plan of action and the results are multiplied.
- ✓ You attract good quality prospects and can grow bigger faster.
- ✓ Your sales conversion is better. You get better results.
- ✓ You get big fame and recognition. Goodness is always rewarded.
- ✓ It is easier to multiply your income through personal sponsoring in width and depth.

✓ It multiplies the impact of our speech and training. Your words carry more weightage.

All things equal, people will do business with and refer business to people they know, trust and like.

–Bob Burg

Your brand value is determined by two key activities:-

1. Your character and personality
2. Your speed and achievements in the business

Your Character and Personality

Your character is made up of your moral values and behavior. If you have the basic moral values like giving respect, truthfulness, honesty, integrity, punctuality, loyalty etc. people will see and experience the goodness in you. People will flock around you and would like to stay connected with you.

Your personality is made up of several traits like your language while talking to people, your demeanour, personal hygiene, mastery of business concepts, confidence when dealing with other people, your smile, your stage performance, etc.

Gradually, people will start noticing all these virtues on and off stage and will start making a judgment about you. That's the creation of your brand. Trust me, there are millions of people who are looking for a good sponsor or upline to start business with. Like in any other industry, there are many people but very few who have a good reputation of values, character and personality. Build a positive brand for yourself and sooner than later, people will come looking for you.

I have dedicated an entire section in this book on qualities required to be a successful network-marketer. You evaluate yourself on those qualities and work towards making yourself better on all of them. Gradually, you will build a wonderful brand for yourself.

Your Speed and Achievements in the Business

Momentum is a network marketer's best friend. Use it to establish your charisma and leadership.

–Deepak Bajaj

There are millions of people doing this business, but only a small percentage do this business with speed and those are the few who get name, fame and become a brand. Why not you also make a decision to do this business with speed and be a brand? When you pick up speed, you get the same results in weeks, which many people take months or years to achieve. Everyone around you will idolize you and you will get recognition and compliments in every event. People will start asking you how you did this and you will start developing a fan following. Now you can build further speed on the strength of this brand of yours and grow bigger faster.

> *When you are successful, that is exactly the time to do more of what brought you here. Then, you become a legend.*
> –Deepak Bajaj

Your fast achievement will do two great things for you in this business.

- ✓ **You will have more leaders in your team.** Most of the people who start network marketing business are not sure about their success in this business. They don't have enough faith in themselves or their business. Out of 20 people who start, generally 4 will be ready to start working immediately (Now), 4 will say they will never work on it (Never), and rest 12 will not be sure about what they want to do (Not Sure). All 20 of them have dreams, that's why they have started with you in the first place, but they want to see your success before they can imagine theirs. When you work with speed and urgency, you create good results and start building a team in a short time. This builds faith and conviction among your teammates. Looking at your progress, these 16 people in the Not Sure and Never categories will also move to the Now category and start working actively with you. This is what we need the most: A majority of those who start with

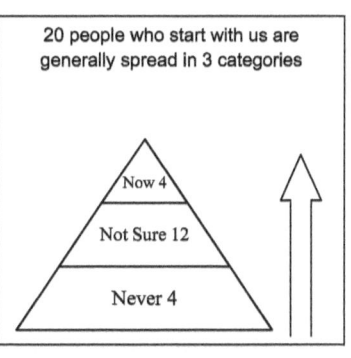

20 people who start with us are generally spread in 3 categories

Now 4
Not Sure 12
Never 4

you should work actively and fulfill their dreams. Also remember, if you are slow, even the Now and Not Sure categories of people will move to the Never category.

- ✓ **People will listen to your advice.** Many a times, people come to me and ask me this question, 'My team doesn't listen to me. What do I do?' I answer back with a question: 'What all have you done to earn the privilege of their listening?' People listen to leaders, and leadership is not given, it is earned. When you do business with speed and urgency, you prove that you are a champion. People will listen to your advice because only a champion can create another champion. If you are a fast achiever, you need not chase people, rather people will chase you for helping them become as successful as you are.

Anything worth doing is worth doing well. So, if you have chosen to do the business of network marketing, then you should do this business with speed and urgency. Create a brand for yourself and enjoy amazing rewards.

Your brand is what people say about you when you are not in the room.

–Jeff Bejos

Build your brand; it pays.
As soon as I started the business, I achieved an ongoing Thailand contest in 2 weeks becoming the fastest achiever. Next 12 weeks I touched top income level in our company. After 9 weeks I became fastest Singapore achiever in North India. These back-to-back achievements branded me as 'Speed Machine, Record breaking machine, history creator, etc.' and made me the first Mercedes Benz achiever and I achieved another prestigious rank in 29 months. This branding gave me an edge throughout my journey.

10
Contests: Be a Winner, Create Winners

A contest works like a triple dose of motivation. It gives maximum return on time and effort invested in the business.

Contests are my personal favorite. Achieving every contest is how I created my personal brand and big wealth in this business. In the beginning, my focus was to achieve a contest myself and I always achieved it faster than everyone else. Most of the times, I was among the first few achievers in the entire company. As my team's size grew along with my own achievement, I worked on creating maximum achievers in my team during every contest.

A contest is an extra incentive given on achieving a specific target in a predefined period. Contests can be given both by the company or the team. Many a times, contests are given for free international trips. If promoted well, contests can multiply your business. Contests can give you a lot of benefits—multiply your income, multiply the income of your teammates, retention of your teammates, establish you as a winner/leader, special recognition as a contest achiever, puts everyone in the team in action mode, free rewards or trips, creation of new leaders, new centers, team momentum, etc.

If you love contests, here are some key strategies that can help you multiply your contest results:-

- ✓ Promotion matters. Don't think that contests will work automatically. You'll need to promote it as if your life depends on it. Use all tools like videos, brochures, stickers, etc. in all possible forums. Make special campaigns for WhatsApp, Facebook etc.
- ✓ Start early. Building momentum takes time. Start as soon as the contest in announced.

- ✓ Massive activity during the contest period is critical for success. Plan special recognitions, events, promotion meetings, etc.
- ✓ Conduct a key leaders' meet immediately after the contest announcement, and your entire team should talk one language—be an achiever, create achievers.
- ✓ Be an achiever fast. Only a champion can create another champion. Achieve your contest first and then it will be easier to encourage your teammates to be achievers too.
- ✓ Avoid bad practices. I have seen some people engaging in practices like bulk volume or wrong selling etc. to achieve the contest. Never do something today that can have bad consequences in the long run. Also, ours is a business of duplication and you don't want your team to indulge in any wrong practices. Also keep a check on your team for the same.

If executed well, a contest can fast forward your journey in the network marketing business. What you generally achieve in one year can be achieved in 2-3 months with a contest.

Contests can do magic.
Most of the leaders in my business achieved their top level income during some contests. Two leaders in my team take full use of contests—Amit Battan and Chanchal Vats. They even design their own contests and always keep their teams active. You can earn 3-10 times of your regular income during contests. Be smart and use contests to propel your business. I keep learning a lot about contests from my very good friends, a dynamic couple—Sanjay Agarwal and Indu Agarwal.

11
Social Media – Turbo Charger for your Business

> *We don't have a choice on whether we do social media; the question is how well we do it.*
>
> –Erik Qualman

When I started this business in 2007 in India, there were no smart phones, no WhatsApp, no Facebook and the only means of communication was phone and sms. FaceTime, YouTube, Skype, Instagram, Twitter, video conferencing and many of such latest technologies were just not in practice. There was nothing called social media. We had sms groups, where we used to send sms to many people together in one shot and we were proud of that. So, all the prospecting was essentially done on phone or by meeting people personally. Contacting strangers was possible only by meeting them face-to-face or on the phone. Even when I was a star performer of my company and I wanted to tell the world how good the business has been for me, I could do it only by meeting people personally and to that extent our reach was very limited. Starting business in new cities was a herculean task.

These new technology frontiers have opened possibilities that never existed before and if utilized judiciously, they can give you unprecedented speed and growth in the business. Social media has made our communication and reach faster like never before in two key areas of our business:

1. Communication with our team and keeping them updated on all the good work and achievements in our team.
2. Communication with people who are not there in our team:

strangers and people whom we know but who have not yet started business with us.

Let's explore how we can take benefit from social media in both these areas:-

Communication with our team:

Network marketing is a people's business and for people to stay motivated and to keep performing, they need to feel like they are a part of a growing and evolving organization. They should feel connected to other people in the organization and with the organization as a whole because with connection comes the security and drive to perform. In network marketing business, we don't have an office, a formal hierarchy or official relationships. Here, people are connected to each other by means of informal relationships and to that extent it becomes a challenge to keep people connected to other people and to the team.

This connection was definitely managed through various programs, but social media if utilized well can take this connectivity to another level altogether. With Facebook, WhatsApp and other social media tools, everyone in the organization gets real time updates on what is happening in the organization. When people see activities, achievements, programs and a lot of communication, they feel secure and connected with the organization.

When people are working in the field, they get some success as well as some rejections and disappointments. You and your associates meet people who encourage you and also people who try to pull you down. Sometimes you need hope that things will work out for you soon, and the best hope comes from success stories of others who are on the same journey as you are.

Social media can play a key role in spreading the good news. When you share success stories or product testimonials, you can transfer the good vibes and momentum from one team to another, from one city to another, and from one distributor to another. I have also observed that sometimes people are not as motivated by their upline as they are by the success of their cross lines or associates in other lines. Social media is virtually a free tool to gain momentum for your entire group and multiply the good results.

Communication with people who are not there in our team:

In network marketing business, we are always looking for new people. Howsoever strong our structure has been, we always have a vacancy for one more new person. This task of reaching out to new people can be done much faster now with social media. Social media can be used to prospect for new people who may be interested in your business. You can post your activities, achievements and lifestyle and build credibility and reputation for yourself. Location and distance is no bar, you can communicate with the whole world with one single post on your WhatsApp, Facebook, LinkedIn, Twitter account etc.

You can even put up posts seeking people who are looking for what your business has to offer. The best part is that social media is accessible to all and costs very little. Of course we are not discussing massive campaigns here that include paid promotions and advertisements. Not only will you connect with the right people on social media, but also when people come to meet you, they'll know what you are doing and why they are meeting you. Since you have already established your credibility through social media, the people who will come to meet you will be good quality prospects for you. They are coming to you almost ready to join you.

So, I highly recommend using social media to communicate the good work you are doing and to build a never-ending pipeline of prospects.

Everything you post on social medial impacts your personal brand. How do you want to be known?

–Lisa Horn

When you are going on social media, please follow these basic etiquettes or guidelines:

- ✓ Be careful about what you put on social media because once anything goes on social media, it can never be taken back.
- ✓ On and off posts are okay if you are just causally playing around on social media, but if you want to build a good reputation for yourself and if you want good business from social media, then you must be regular on it. Make sure you put appropriate content regularly.

- ✓ It would be a good idea to work with a social media expert or consultant. Also be prepared to invest time and money on it.
- ✓ If your objective is not to get professional benefit from social media, I recommend you to restrict your time on this. I have seen people who will go to Facebook to casually check one post and will spend 2 hours on it without even realizing it.
- ✓ A word of caution: Be careful about whom you follow and whom you choose to be friends with. Anyone can put virtually anything on social media. Don't interact too much with cross-lines. Don't follow everyone blindly particularly those who don't have any interest in your good. Think thoroughly before implementing everything that is available on social media. Don't look for fancy things, look for authentic and proven information from reliable sources. Follow the advise of those who have actually implemented what they preach and have got a proven track record. Try new ideas yourself first and then gradually take it to your team. Many a people have lost focus and spoilt the momentum of their teams by implementing everything new that comes up.
- ✓ Handle negative comments carefully. Never ever indulge in a fight on social media. If you get a negative message, just acknowledge it, apologize if there is any mistake and tell the person you are willing to do your best for the matter. Tell the person to send you a personal message.

Now, the question is when and how you should start your social media efforts for this business. I am sure most of the people who are reading this book must already be there on several social media platforms, so when I refer to social media efforts here, it simply means social media efforts to seriously promote and develop your network marketing business. I have tried a couple of strategies and seen others trying different things. Based on my experience, what I recommend is that first, you start your network marketing business. Attend some programs, counsel with active Uplines, get knowledge of the basic principles and then start action on social media. Follow the success accelerators given in this book and get some initial success. You can use the system given in this book to give you a very good take off too. Master the principles, apply them and teach them to your associates. Once you start getting some success and your business has taken off, that is the right time to seriously start your social media efforts for your business multiplication.

The objective of social media efforts would not be to start your network marketing business, but to take your network marketing business to another level altogether. It will be done to build momentum in your existing network and to build a pipeline of quality prospects. Also, when you start with social media, don't start with all the platforms at the same time. Start with any one which you find the most appropriate at that time and then within 3-4 weeks, build another one and so on.

Why I recommend you to first build a base and then go for social media is because social media is free and is very cluttered. The important thing here is not to just make noise, but to be heard. When you have achievements and a decent track record, you will be noticed by the people. Also, you will need regular time for social media. When your business has started moving, you will be able to devote some time to social media too. People would be curious to know what you do and how you do it. Most of the people are aware of network marketing, what they are looking for is someone who is authentic and successful. So, build some success and multiply it with social media.

Go to social media with preparation. Do it daily and plan it well in advance. Your primary business is to build leaders and you already have a lot of work to do in your business. Once you decide to start your social media efforts and want to build a reputation for yourself online, you'll need to be consistent. You will need to be present on all major social media platforms with regular frequency. Be careful of your content. You cannot target everyone. Decide your target audience and put content that will appeal the most to your target audience. Social media is a different journey altogether, but a highly rewarding one. Use it to your favor and be the star of your business.

> *Why use social media? Marketing is no longer about the stuff that you make but about the stories you tell.*
> –Seth Godin

> ***Social Media is an awesome tool.***
> *My life mission is to empower people to live better lives. I want to positively impact millions of lives across the globe. In my encounters with social media in last few years I am convinced that this can help me multiply my impact in much lesser time. I have studied some great leaders like Ray Higdon, Frazor, John Melton, Rob Sperry etc. I am sure I will be able to add greater value to my readers and followers using this tool.*

12
Clarity and Focus

Clarity is power. You cannot hit a goal that you cannot see.

You can get the fastest car but you cannot drive fast if you have fog or dust on your windscreen. So the question is not about the car, the question is, can you clearly see the road ahead? If you can't see clearly, you just can't move forward.

Likewise, if you are not clear about what you want in your life or what you want from this business, you can't really make any progress. You will still continue the business, you will still come to meetings, you will still make some amount of income but you cannot really build a big business empire and fulfill big dreams if you are not clear about why are you doing this business.

Clarity brings passion, speed and enthusiasm. Clarity gives you strength. Speed is just impossible without clarity. When you know why you are doing this business, there is flow in your daily working and that brings greater and faster results.

The successful warrior is the average man with laser-like focus.
—Bruce Lee

Once you are clear about why you want to do this business and what all activities will help you accomplish your goal, then all your need is the focus to keep doing those activities day after day.

Whatever you focus on, will start growing. One big reason why many people are not successful in network marketing is that they don't really focus on the business. Some are not sure why they are doing it, some are not sure if this is a good business model, some are doubtful if will last, some always have endless questions, some are analyzing, some are too busy at their current jobs or profession, some have family issues, whatever may be the reason or excuse they offer, but the fact remains that this business will grow only when you focus on this business.

The movement your focus shifts, your productivity and your performance will start going down bringing down your results also. As your results go down your focus will further go down and this cycle will make you quit the business.

Generally people start network marketing business part-time with some other job, profession, business venture or studies. This keeps them busy and makes it even tougher for them to focus on this business.

So if you want to be successful in network marketing, you need to focus on it. You can't focus on something else and expect to be successful here. Ask yourself some fundamental questions; get all your doubts clarified by your seniors and focus all your energies on doing activities that will propel you closer to your goals.

FOCUS = Follow One Course Until Successful

Also remember that you can very well focus on this business while doing it part time also. Most of the successful Network marketers built their business part-time in the initial days.

Your life is controlled by what you focus on.

–Tony Robbins

Every extra-ordinary achievement begins with clarity and focus.

Everyone around me was surprised when my YouTube channel, Deepak Bajaj, grew from 1000 to 100000 subscribers in just 63 days. My book became a bestseller within few days of its launch and as I am writing the revised edition of this book now, this book continues to be among top 3 Bestsellers in all business self-help books on Amazon even after eight months of its launch.

This extra-ordinary growth came from absolute clarity on how I wanted to serve the people with my videos and book. Genuine intention to help people fulfill their dreams and focus on delivering the best knowledge, tools and strategies in every single video and every chapter I wrote gave incredible results to people.

SECTION-V
QUALITIES OF A SUCCESSFUL NETWORK MARKETER

QUALITIES OF A SUCCESSFUL NETWORK MARKETER

Leaders are made, they are not born. They are made by hard effort, which is the price which all of us must pay to achieve any goal that is worthwhile.

–Vince Lombardi

In every training program or a seminar, people ask me what does it take to be a great network marketer. What are the essential qualities of a successful network marketer? Every time, I tell people that you need to be a good human being with absolute faith in the system and unconditional commitment to learn and grow. If you have these fundamentals in place, you can develop the other things on the way. The best thing about being a successful network marketer is the journey to be successful. Trust me, this will be the most rewarding and highly transformational journey you would have ever taken, and you will become a completely different person at the end of this journey.

This section covers the essential qualities that you need to develop to become a successful network marketer. Interestingly, all of us have already got some or all of these qualities in varying degree; all I urge you to do now is to evaluate yourself on each of these qualities, determine the growth areas and improve them. As you develop these qualities, your business will also multiply.

Remember, every great network marketer was once an amateur. Everyone starts at the bottom when they start this business. Those who understand what they need to change and work on it, get massive success. It's not where you start but how you end it. Use this section as a guide to your personal transformation and fulfill all your dreams. Congratulate yourself on what all qualities you already have and start developing the rest.

It's not the will to win that matters. Everyone has that. It's the will to prepare to win that matters.

—Bear Bryant

1
Burning Desire

> *When you want to succeed as bad as you want to breathe, then you will be successful.*
>
> *–Eric Thomas*

Actually, you can have anything you want, if you want it bad enough. There has to be something that you want to achieve so badly that you can't be at peace till the time you get it. Something that drives you to work hardest untiringly every single day. Yes you can call it a dream but I propose to take you one step ahead of a dream. You need to move from dream to a burning desire. It's a fire burning inside you that propel you to keep moving forward. I am sure you already have a burning desire inside you, that's why you are reading this book.

All great success begins with a desire, a burning and pulsating desire. You must keep your desire alive by keeping it in front of you as often as you can. Paste pictures on your work desk, make wallpapers on your laptop/mobile, announce your goal at every possible forum, keep it with you on 3x5 cards and read it often during the day.

> *There is nothing that a belief plus a burning desire cannot make real.*
>
> *–Napoleon Hill*

Remember, as you start pursuing your dreams, you will come across many people who will try to steal your dreams. These self-proclaimed philosophers will tell you to be satisfied with what you have and not to work hard for your dreams. They will give you a lot of examples to prove this business doesn't work and dreams become a reality only in movies. In all those moments, just hold on to your dreams even stronger and keep moving ahead.

> *Whatever is your excuse for not doing it, the same thing can be your reason for doing it.*

Wherever we are today, everything that we are enjoying and all the development that mankind has witnessed is only because of one reason: someone had a burning desire and that person was not ready to quit on his/her desire. If everyone would have been satisfied with the situation in which they were born, we would have been living naked in jungles today, jumping over trees like monkeys. Evolution of mankind is a living proof of the burning desire of a few individuals and they are the ones whose names we remember even centuries after they are gone. I strongly believe that the desire for growth is what makes us different from other animals.

> *Satisfaction is an excuse given by failures.*
> —Deepak Bajaj

The most spiritual thing you can do in life is to have a burning desire for growth. It's divine. It's the most humane thing you can do, because you can't lift yourself in isolation and once you decide to grow, you uplift many others around you too.

> *Be content with what you have while constantly working for what you want.*
> —Deepak Bajaj

Keep your desires burning till you achieve them. You have chosen the world's best business that will fulfill every desire of yours.

It starts with a burning desire.
Behind every accomplishment I have, there was a burning desire to make it happen. When you have a burning desire you stay focused, you never complain and you keep moving in spite of all obstacles and setbacks. I got my inspiration from an American leader, Dexter Yager. When I looked at the resources from which he built his network marketing empire in last 4 decades, I know it was clearly his burning desire in action.

2
Integrity and Reputation

> *Integrity is doing the right thing when no one is watching.*
> —CS Lewis

As per the dictionary, 'Integrity is the quality of being honest and having strong moral principles that you refuse to change.' It's the way you will conduct your life. Integrity is a set of principles that you strongly believe are right and you live your life by them, come what may. The greatest quality you should develop for yourself is to live a remarkable life and be a person of integrity.

It is fundamentally about being a good human being before being a good businessman. As a matter of fact, it takes a good person to build a good team. Only a great person can build a great business. In a world where people are running around to change everyone and everything else, what I recommend is you work on making yourself better and everything in the world will automatically fall in place.

> *Your outside world is a reflection of your inside world. What goes on in the inside shows on the outside.*
> —Bob Proctor

People are watching you all the time: times when you are aware, and even the times when you are not aware of being watched. People listen to what you say from the stage and what you say off stage. In fact, people not only listen to you, they carefully match your actions with what you say. If what you say and what you do are in alignment, you earn the reputation of being a person of integrity.

A person of integrity is the one who is the same in every situation and with every person. Be a person of integrity and you will attract many right people into your life and business, because people feel safe and secure with a person of integrity. Once you establish your integrity, you will have unlimited number of followers and earn an ever-growing credibility and trust.

Trust is not given; it's earned.

–Deepak Bajaj

While integrity is your internal quality, your reputation is what others think about you. Reputation is your most valuable asset; you must build it and then guard it at any cost. Simple ways to build your reputation are:-

1. Honor your words. Nobody needs to record what you say. Walk the talk.
2. Never cancel a meeting/appointment. Never be late for a meeting.
3. Never mess up with anyone's money/products/spouse. No accounts with anyone.
4. Be the most hard-working and the most trust-worthy person of your team.
5. Display an attitude and behavior that people would love to follow.
6. Live your life with a good character and moral values.
7. Be honest and transparent in all your dealings.

Talent and ability will get you to the top, but it takes character to keep you there.

–John Wooden

I have also come across a few people in this business who grew very fast, but their business crashed after a while. A few stayed in the same company with low income, while some moved to other network marketing companies. Why did this happen to them? The reason is simple. Network marketing is a team-based business. Many a times, people with low integrity or low capability also rise in the business because of a great upline, committed downlines or a powerful system. But many of these high risers do not develop the character and integrity required to stay at the top. Then they do a few wrong things and slide down to where they had started. Those who learn from their mistakes rebuild it to the top and the rest of them quit, blaming the Upline, the team, the company and the whole world except themselves. It's okay not to have a few skills or qualities in the beginning, but develop your skills and integrity as you move up the ranks in the business. This is essential, not only to have a big network marketing business, but also to have a good life.

> *There is something wrong with your character if opportunities controls your loyalty.*
>
> —Unknown

I come across a lot of leaders in this industry who have got everything it takes to make it big, but they lacked one simple thing called loyalty and it killed their reputation and career forever. You will also come across such people who will come out with a new revolutionary company every time you meet them, and every time they will claim that now they have found the best one. They are in a never-ending quest to find the best company on earth. What such people don't realize is that it's not about the company; it's about you.

Such people don't follow the system 100% and are moving from company to company, or from upline to upline. I can understand if you got into a wrong company and you realized it after few months and shifted to a different company. I can understand if it happens 1-2 times, but beyond that, it's not about the company anymore, it's about your nature and character. Falling down once from your moral standards is tough. Second time is easier and after that, it becomes normal for you.

What does this movement do? It finishes your reputation to zero. Rather, it earns you bad reputation. Every time people meet you, they will ask you, 'So, which company are you associated with these days?' However smart and competent you may be, you will never be able to attract the right people with this reputation. So I highly recommend that you find a good company and stick to it. Build your reputation with loyalty and it will give you exponential growth after 5-10 years.

> *You don't earn loyalty in a day. You earn loyalty day-by-day.*
>
> —Jeffrey Gitomer

Once you have the right reputation, multiplying your business is just a matter of weeks or months. Also a word of caution, good reputation once built is not forever, it's like a plant that you need to water and nurture every day.

> *It takes 20 years to build a reputation and 5 minutes to ruin it. If you think about that, you will do things differently.*
>
> —Warren Buffet

Good reputation gives you an edge.
Gaurav and me recruited more than 300 people from our personal list in the first 4 months of the business. We did this without any experience in network marketing or product selling. Gaurav was in fact a software engineer. How could we achieve this impossible feat—the reputation we had earned in our personal and professional lives. Even the reputation that we have earned in this business is so incredible that people come looking for us to start business with us. Thanks to our character and integrity. When you recruit people with good reputation, they can do the business with great speed.

3
Attitude of Service and Gratitude

> *Life's most persistent and urgent question is—what are you doing for others.*
>
> —Martin Luther King Jr

Living this business closely for over a decade now, I firmly believe that only good people can do good network marketing business. Time and again I have observed two vital personal qualities in every good human being and every good network marketer: The attitude of serving others and the attitude of gratitude.

> *They only live, who live for others.*
>
> —Swami Vivekananda

A genuine desire to serve your team and to be of help to them is essential for big success in this business. Network Marketing is purely a team sport. Your success in this business depends a lot on the contribution of others. While this is true for every business, but in a typical business set up, everyone is paid a salary to do the work, there is a corporate hierarchy and the fear of losing the job. But in network marketing, you work with a set of partners called associates and your income is the result of the cumulative efforts of everyone.

People in network marketing business are attached to each other only through mutual respect and trust. *People will trust you only when you prove that you are standing with them and standing for them.* Before people do anything for you, you need to do something for them. This business works on a principle of people helping people and starts from you giving maximum help to all your teammates and setting the right example.

You can have everything you want, if you will just help enough other people get what they want.

—Zig Ziglar

People ask me what are the rules of helping others. My answer is simple: once you sponsor a person and that person is committed to do his or her part, then you must do everything possible to help him/her achieve his/her goals. While I suggest giving maximum help to people in your team, I never advise anyone to do something for people that they should do themselves. We want them to stand on their feet and take full responsibility of their business. God also helps those who help themselves. Always invest your time with the right people and on the right activities.

Gratitude is the healthiest of all human emotions. The more you express gratitude for what you have, the more likely you will have even more to express gratitude for.

—Zig Ziglar

While we all are busy chasing a lot of things that we want, we sometimes tend to overlook so many good things we already have. Develop this attitude of gratitude for everything good happening in your life right now and it will start multiplying. Interestingly, if we put our mind to it, we will realize there is more to feel grateful for than what we notice and realize. Our team and our actions may not be giving the results we want right now, but definitely they are moving us closer to our dreams; be thankful for that. When you work with this attitude, you will have peace and you will do better.

Attitude of service and gratitude go hand in hand. In this business, we are interacting with people all the time and different people are going through different emotions at any point of time. People may talk and behave differently from what we expect. If we start judging and analyzing people, we will loose our peace of mind and will also not be able to work whole-heartedly with other people. Gratitude is one emotion that will help you ease your burden and will empower you to serve each one of your teammates in the best way.

At times, you may expect some qualities from people that they may not have, but this expectation will blind you from seeing many qualities that they do have. They may not be doing those specific activities that you want them to do, but they are definitely doing some other activities that are helping you and your organization in some way. If you don't acknowledge and appreciate them and their good work, they will stop doing that and it's a loss. When you start acknowledging these seemingly small victories and start giving gratitude for the same, you will build deep connections with people.

Make it a practice to appreciate and give gratitude for the following:-

1. Small victories that anyone gets every day.
2. Good things each person is doing and the contribution everyone is bringing to the team.
3. Good qualities of each and every person.
4. Improvement, movement and growth anywhere in you and your team.

Everyone is an independent distributor in network marketing and has absolute freedom to choose how he or she wants to build his or her business. No one is taking salary from you. Be grateful that these people are working hand in hand with you.

The struggle ends when gratitude begins.
—Neale Donald Walsch

I have found my life balance by working on this principle—*Be grateful for whatever you have, while you continue working for whatever you want.* Be the greatest server in your team and your daily little acts of service will build your dream team. When you are as happy about the success of others as you are for yourself, you definitely have the attitude of service. Thank God for giving you the opportunity not only to serve others, but also to find the deepest joy and pleasure in serving others.

Always be grateful and loyal to your upline. Yes, you have reached great heights with your hard work, but remember the day you started and how your uplines helped you stand on your feet. It's a long-term business. Stay loyal to your team and your company. Don't keep changing your upline and company. Work on yourself and on building a great team with sincere hard work and commitment. If you keep changing companies, you will end up spoiling your own reputation.

Do network marketing business with your heart and you will realize that this is the most spiritually and emotionally uplifting experiences of your life.

> **Service wins hearts.**
> *I always tell people in my leadership training sessions that a leader is a great server. You can be a great leader only if you can genuinely and happily serve people. People may forget your achievements but they will never get what you did for them. I get unbelievable love from all my fans not because of my achievements but simply because of my love and affection for them. It's because I want to genuinely add value to their lives. When I started building my business in Mumbai, a great leader helped me a lot that I will never forget—Shailash Singh. I will ever be grateful to him.*

4
Leadership

Everything rises and falls on leadership.

—John C Maxwell

The number one role that a successful network marketer is expected to play is that of a leader. Although every human being on earth is a leader, for this business, the moment you sponsor one person in the business, you officially become a leader. While leadership is a life skill and it is required everywhere, but for network marketers, it is an indispensable quality. The greater the size of your leadership, the bigger will be your rank and income.

Contrary to popular belief, leadership is not a rank or a title, but a responsibility. Leadership is not a position, but behavior and accountability.

If your actions inspire others to dream more, learn more, do more and become more, you are a leader.

—John Quincy Adams

Leadership is simple—be the role model. You are the same on stage and off stage. People need not record what you say. Your audio matches your video. You have a value system and you stick to it. You have high standards for yourself and you live them day in and day out. If you are struggling to become better, it is absolutely alright. Never be ashamed of struggles. We all have our own set of struggles and thank God for our struggles, because struggles mean we are trying.

Leadership in this business essentially means having all the 14 qualities that I have explained in this book and totally following the success system of your team, or as suggested in this book. But it's not about talking about these qualities and activities, but demonstrating them every waking hour of the day: living them, breathing them, eating with them and sleeping with them. You practice these qualities and behaviors in such a way that they become your second nature.

My proposal for developing your leadership is, simply become a live demonstration of how a successful network marketer should be. Display every quality and behavior that you believe makes a great network marketer. Practice it so much that if someone asks a question to another person, 'How do I become successful in this business, or what is the secret of becoming a big success in this business?' That person should immediately tell your name and reply, 'Don't do anything else. Just be like this person and success will all be yours.'

Leadership is not about titles, positions or flowcharts. It is about one life influencing another.

–John C Maxwell

I asked my son what he meant by a leader. He quickly replied, 'A leader is the one who has someone walking behind him.' Simply put, a leader is the one who has followers. There are two key advantages of being a leader in our business:-

1. You can build a big and growing business only when you have lot of performing leaders in your team. If you display leadership, you will see many people in your team rising up and taking up leadership. You will have greater influence and your team will generate big business by following your strategies. This means more and more new people starting the business and more and more people rising up to be leaders.

2. In network marketing, what keeps the business going is a constant flow of new people. You need a lot of new people starting with you, and not just any person but the right kind of person. You attract what you are. When you act and behave like a real leader, you attract the right kind of people to you that will further strengthen your team and keep the momentum going.

To summarize, when you become a true leader, you set on fire a chain reaction wherein your existing associates keep performing great and you constantly add new leaders to your team in the right structure.

A leader is one who knows the way, goes the way and shows the way.

–John C Maxwell

After living this business for a decade now, I genuinely believe network marketing is the most spiritual business I know. People don't choose network marketing, God chooses people for network marketing. I have a firm belief that network marketers are God sent angels who are out there to help people fulfill their dreams and make this world a better and happier place. Getting a person sponsored in this business is a responsibility. By sponsoring someone into this business, you are giving wings to their dreams and you are accepting a responsibility to be with them in this journey to achieve their dreams.

This definitely is a big responsibility and God will give you only that much responsibility that He believes you can handle. God will give you only that many people to lead who you can take care of. If you want a big team, you must grow your leadership ability. Keep growing your leadership ability and your business will continue growing.

God could not help everyone, so he sent Network Marketers.

–Deepak Bajaj

Leadership with a smile.
I have seen leaders all through my career and have seen a great example of the same with my friends Suranjan Das and CN Patel.

5
Enthusiasm

> *Nothing great was ever achieved without enthusiasm.*
> —Ralph Waldo Emerson

As per the English dictionary, 'Enthusiasm is a feeling of energetic interest in a particular subject or activity and an eagerness to be involved in it.' Based on my 11 years of personal field experience of working with thousands of people in Network Marketing, I firmly believe this one quality far outweighs all other qualities in a person.

Winston Churchill said, *Success is going from one failure to another without loss of enthusiasm.*

For this business, I would say that big success is going from one meeting to another without a loss of enthusiasm.

Be more enthusiastic than the most enthusiastic person you have ever seen. Be the power bank of your team. Be the living example of hope and optimism in action. Everyone loves to be around an enthusiastic person. Also, enthusiasm is contagious. If you are an enthusiastic person, gradually it will spread to your entire team and yours will be an enthusiastic team giving you big income and fulfilling all your dreams. Also remember, if you feel your team is not enthusiastic enough, it is time for you to cheer yourself up and be more enthusiastic.

Yes, there are times when you will be low. That is just a part of being human. I have also felt the same many a times. But success lies not in never falling, but in standing up every time you fall, and every time you stand up, you stand up stronger than ever before. Every time you feel low or you seem to be bogged down by rejection and adversity, try any one or both of these techniques and you will snap out of the bad state instantly:

1. During a live training with Tony Robbins in USA, I learnt that motion creates emotion. Change your breathing, make some move. Jump, dance, run, change your place, shake your body and it will change your state.

2. Change your focus with an activity I call 'Future Gazing'. Sit in a comfortable place, close your eyes and just imagine all your dreams coming true through this business - your dream cars, mansion, luxury international holidays with your family, being an inspiration to millions of people, luxury lifestyle, people lined up for your photo and autograph and everything else you have dreamt for yourself. Do this for 3-5 minutes and you will be ready for the next meeting with more enthusiasm than ever before.

Why not be happy and thankful to God that you have got a phenomenal business that can make all your dreams a reality? Wish you an enthusiastic journey to your dreams.

A salesman minus the enthusiasm is just another clerk.
–Harry F Banks

Enthusiasm is hallmark of a leader.
In my quest to learn secrets of outstanding success and learning from successful people I found two very enthusiastic leaders Mr. Surender Vats and Mr. Siddharth Singh. I really admire how these simple men are leading great teams.

6
Always Ready to Learn and Change

> *If you keep doing what you have been doing, you will keep getting what you have been getting.*
>
> –Stephan R Covey

Every profession requires a different set of values, tools, methodology and skills. A doctor, lawyer, engineer or a chartered accountant, all go through a specialized training for several years to be eligible to join that profession and later to excel in their profession. Likewise, a network marketer also needs a specialized set of skills, mindset, values and tools to be successful. The good news is that all of these are learnable and can be developed. Every good network marketing company and team has several ongoing training programs for everyone to learn, change and succeed in this business.

So, if you are serious about building a strong and highly profitable network marketing business, just keep your qualifications, certifications, experiences, profile etc. aside and become a student of Network Marketing. Like every other business, network marketing business is built on some proven and time-tested principles. The sooner you are able to adapt to these principles and practices, the easier and faster will it be for you to succeed in this business.

> *Far too many people are looking for the right person, instead of trying to be the right person.*
>
> –Gloria Steinem

In fact, the best value that a network marketing business gives to any person is the life changing education that makes a person better; money is just a byproduct. Be open to this education and new way of living. I highly recommend when you choose a network marketing company for yourself, just make sure you choose a company or team that has got a proven system of training and development.

After you have learnt what it takes to be successful in this business, immediately get onto the field and apply all that you have learnt. **There is only one-way to make learning permanent and innate in you: Practice, practice and some more practice.** How long to practice? Till the time it becomes a habit. Also remember, when you are learning any new skill, you are starting from scratch and your initial performance and results may not be up to your expectation. It may be unfulfilling, disappointing and frustrating in the initial few days, but that's the only way to build a new skill or capability. Just keep on practicing.

All change is hard at first, messy in the middle and gorgeous at the end.

–Robin Sharma

So learn the right system from your active Upline, apply it in the field, get the desired results and then it is time for you to train people in your team on these same principles. Teaching is not just for others, but for you also. When you teach a certain principle to someone, you reinforce the same for yourself also.

Follow the LDT Principle – Learn, Do, Teach. Also, never try to teach others what you have not practiced yourself in the field.

If you are not willing to learn, no one can help you. If you are determined to learn, no one can stop you.

–Unknown

Learning = Growing

Learning from each other is the most amazing thing in this business. I always love interacting with two of my good friends Kamran Mujawar and Sachin Raikar. We always talk about ways to make our associates more powerful and productive.

7
Drive for Action

One small action is better than a thousand noble intentions.

A majority of people are suffering, not because they don't know the solution, but because of their inability to take action. Knowledge is not power, only the knowledge that is acted upon is powerful. If you can develop this one quality, you can quickly stand out as a champion in this sea of network marketers. Have a drive for action. Act fast. It's not the person with ideas that wins, but the one with a greater speed for execution.

Be the most hardworking person in the team. When you become a man/woman of action, it will set the right culture for your team, and within weeks you will see the ripple effects of the same in your entire team. When your team sees you in action, they respect you more, they listen to you and most importantly, they start doing the same and you get rewards far more than your expectations.

> *The real decision is measured by the fact that you have taken a new action. If there is no action, you haven't truly decided.*
> —Tony Robbins

Also choose actions that give you maximum results and that build the right culture in your team.

Three key daily actions for building a strong network marketing business include:-
1. Continually expand your list and prospect new people.
2. Show maximum business opportunity presentations and do timely follow-ups.

3. Promote events.

Why people do not take action?

1. They don't have faith in the company/business plan/products.
2. They are not sure if they will stick to the business or will be successful in the business.
3. Lack of a burning desire.
4. Fear of rejection and ridicule.
5. Lack of confidence due to a lack of knowledge or practice.

Whatever be the reason for you or your teammates, I highly recommend an immediate personal counseling with the Upline and attending events. Remember the rule of five: It takes up to five meetings and five events for developing the required understanding and faith in the business.

Remember, no meeting is a perfect meeting. We are not dealing with machines or robots, we are dealing with humans and every human being is unique. Every meeting is different and there is no way to measure which is a good meeting or a bad meeting. The only thing we can measure is a meeting or no meeting.

In your initial days, if you feel your presentation is not as good as that of your Upline or other old leaders, just don't worry because they have had their share of practice and now it's your time to put in your hours of practice. Remember, repetition is the mother of all skill. Just stick to the process and with enough repetitions you will be an expert sooner than expected.

Just make it a habit to act and to act now. Act on your dreams.

Results are rewarded; efforts are not.
—Shiv Khera

While daily action is critical, have a fortnightly or monthly review meeting with your Upline. Do not do activities just to keep yourself busy, do activities to get the desired results. If the results are not coming, it may be because of any of the reasons listed below or any other reason altogether.

1. Not selecting the right prospects for showing the opportunity presentation.

2. Not showing presentation at all or not showing enough number of presentations.
3. Improper follow-ups.
4. Showing plans without the right attitude and preparation.
5. Missing out on some core activity or doing it wrongly.

Whatever may be the reason, address it with your Upline immediately. Make corrections and get going.

Remember, wherever you get stuck in the business, just show some more presentations. Showing the business opportunity presentation to more and more people is the sure shot way to get out of any problem you are facing in this business.

Actions speak louder than words. Act now and let your bank balance do the talking.

Action = Success
I have seen this drive in one of my teammates, Varun. He is one of those guys who will talk about his ideas after he has done it. He not only takes actions but keep on innovating to find new actions if the old ones are not working. This drive for action made him a top income earner in our company.

8
Discipline and Consistency

> *Discipline is doing what is right, when it is right, irrespective of whether you like it or not.*
>
> –Deepak Bajaj

Motivation can get you started in this business, but you need discipline to sustain the work and to be successful in this business. Actually, to be successful in this business, you need not do some big fancy activity, but a few simple activities daily.

Be committed to the activities which have been taught to you by your active Upline and which are given in the Training System followed by your team. Sometimes, we are tempted to try out different activities one after the other, but they only lead to frustration in ourselves and confusion in our downlines. **Follow one system 100% and do it daily.**

> *Discipline is the bridge between goals and accomplishments.*
>
> –Jim Rohn

Develop the discipline to perform the right actions and the consistency of doing them daily over a long period of time. Continue doing all the actions that are recommended by the system, even though you may not enjoy doing some of them. Gradually, the results will become visible. Yes, practicing new behaviors will take some time and will definitely be uncomfortable in the beginning, but the rewards of this new learning will be beyond your imagination.

Once you do these specific activities every day, they will slowly become your second nature and then you will start doing them without even your conscious effort and attention. That's how habits are formed. We choose what we do each day and those daily choices executed over a period of time become habits. Habits repeated over time become talent that leads to massive success. It will take around 60 days to establish a new habit, but going through this journey is worth it.

We first make our habits and then our habits make us.
—John Dryden

When you make the right choices every single day over a period of time, it activates the Compound Effect. The principle of compounding states that our daily behaviors accumulated over a period of time result in massive achievement. Sometimes these daily choices don't show any different results in the first few weeks or months, but when continued overtime, they give you such a big edge that you become a legend in the industry. One extra meeting everyday will add up to 365 extra meetings in one year. 5 extra calls every day will accumulate to 1825 extra calls at the end of one year. To be successful in this business or in any field of your choice, activate compound effect in your favor as soon as possible. **Have the discipline to practice the right things and then the consistency to repeat them till they becomes a habit.**

Excellence is a journey. Discipline is the vehicle.

Right actions over time = Success

Gaurav Bajaj once told me how he built so many new centers. Every time he chose a new city, he had to take up many different roles at the same time. Reaching an hour in advance, ensure hall set up with chairs, sound, projector, lighting, mike, etc., then returning in a suit and tie. He became the host, the plan presenter and the top leader together in one meeting. For every event, he took ownership of booking the hall, printing of tickets, mementos, making all arrangements of sound, light, projector, chairs, etc. He did everything that was required for his business at that stage without complaints and that's what gave him an ever growing business empire.

9
Perseverance

It does not matter how slowly you go as long as you do not stop.
—Confucius

As per the dictionary, 'Perseverance is persistence in doing something, despite the difficulty or delay in achieving success.' Perseverance simply means to begin with a commitment that you will not quit till you reach your goal; every other quality and skill can be developed on the way. If millions of people have fulfilled their dreams through this business worldwide, why will you not fulfill your dreams? But you will fulfill your dreams only if you stay with it and do not quit, because 'winners never quit and quitters never win'.

Rejections and ridicules are part of the business. Adversity and disappointments are expected and are normal. Be immune to NO. Consider NO as the Next Opportunity. Also, do not get stuck with some particular people. It is a numbers game and if one person is not ready, quickly move on to the next. Nobody is good or bad; it's not their time yet. In fact, you should start approaching and working with many people together and build a pipeline. In due course of time, several good people will start following the system one by one.

Persistence is the hard work you do after you get tired of doing the hard work you already did.
—Newt Gingrich

There will definitely be moments when you feel like quitting, I also had such moments. I say this in my trainings that before you make it really big in the business, there will be at least 5 such moments when you would have almost quit and you would have felt that this is not going to work for you. I realized that there are 3 vaccines which will help you continue in the face of adversities: Be in constant communication with your active upline, attend all events (even if no one is attending from your team), and read the recommended books every day for 15-30 minutes (preferably in the night, just before going to bed or early morning. The rest of the day, particularly evenings, is the time for doing meetings).

Have patience. If a big stone was broken on the 41st hammer stroke, it does not mean the first 40 strokes were a waste. Some seeds just take more time to sprout than others. Even the growth of every kid is different. An aircraft takes far more time and an elaborate set up to take off than a helicopter, but once the take off is done, there is no comparison of what an aircraft can achieve vis-à-vis a helicopter.

Just keep going and you will discover strengths and talents in you that you believed never existed in you.

> *If you can't fly, then run. If you can't run, then walk. If you can't walk, then crawl, but whatever you do, you have to keep moving forward.*
>
> –Martin Luther King Jr

Let me tell you from experience that network marketing is simple, but not easy. It will test you hard and it should. The amount of money, freedom and lifestyle that most of the people can't get by working for their whole lives, people want the same in just 3-5 years of working in network marketing and that too without any major investment, staff, premises, working capital, etc. Definitely, it is going to be demanding.

It will challenge you, both physically and emotionally. It will exhaust you. It will test you. But as you start moving ahead with absolute faith, destiny will manifest itself. Faith will not reduce your struggles, setbacks or disappointments, but faith will give you the strength to move through them. Just make a decision to work every single day till you achieve your dreams and move forward with faith.

> *Perseverance is not a long race; it is many short races one after the other.*
>
> –Walter Elliot

4 times my income crashed to zero and I had to rebuild it.
Few people in my team left for no fault of mine. But each time the reason was different and so was the learning. I cried, I protested and I asked God, Why me? It took me some time to accept it and start all over again. But it was worth it and every time, I took lesser time to bounce back. Actually these mistakes have made me whatever I am today, standing with an unshakable business with a solid foundation.

In the initial months, there were moments when it was tough. My relatives bet on my failure when I resigned job. I handled hundreds of No Shows. I booked halls where people didn't come. First day after resigning my job I had planned an event costing me Rs 2 Lac. My sponsor and team promised they would contribute. Actual Expense came to Rs 3 Lac and total collection was 33000. I have handled events in Delhi in extreme summers where ac suddenly stopped working. I have delivered seminar to 500 people for 3 hours without a mike. There was no office in our city so we had to travel 250 km every week and collect products when I was building business part-time.

But we accepted all of it and did the best we could do. We didn't even realize that those were challenges and created records that are tough to beat even after so many years.

10
Committed for Continuous Personal Growth

> *Give me six hours to chop down a tree and I will spend the first four sharpening the axe.*
>
> —Abraham Lincoln

Being a lifelong student of network marketing industry, I have seen one clearly distinctive quality in people who grow fastest through the ranks in network marketing: They are hungry for growth. They are hungry for growth in them as well as in their business. They are always looking for opportunities to learn and grow. I have always seen them sitting in the front row in every training program. They will always be talking to the best in the industry. They have made daily improvement their passion and life value. This attitude makes them better at what they do and they simply excel.

> *Growing old is mandatory, growing up is optional.*
>
> —Chili Davis

Only a true leader can create leaders. Leadership is a journey: a journey to be better every single day. One thing that should drive you above everything else is that you should be better today than you were yesterday. My benchmark for personal growth is simple—people who are meeting you today after 6 or 12 months must feel you have become better.

Work every day with an **excellence mindset**. This book has clearly listed down everything you need to become a top achiever in this business. Evaluate yourself, identify the growth areas and consciously work on your growth areas until you become excellent in each of these areas. While you are pursuing excellence, your business will automatically grow with your own growth.

> *We are what we repeatedly do. Excellence, then, is not an act, but a habit.*
> —Aristotle

In business terms, how does your personal growth translate to profit? Once you make continuous growth and excellence your daily habit, you **become a magnet**. You will radiate success, leadership, growth and excellence, and will start attracting the right kind of people in your life and in your business. Once you have the right people with you, your business will definitely grow in leaps and bounds.

So, don't be comfortable with your current success. Quickly put yourself on the path of continuous personal growth. Focus on getting better, and see the magic working for you.

> *If you focus on success, you will have stress. But if you pursue excellence, success will be guaranteed.*
> —Deepak Chopra

Constant Learning = Constant Growth

This business has given me a brother and best friend—Gaurav Mehra. In my organization, I have seen him always hungry for growth and always looking for things to enhance productivity of our teammates. I keep interacting with some other growth oriented leaders like Anand Bansal, Vinay Mishra, Sudesh Malik, GC Upadhyay, Jagdeep, Abhay Mishra, Mahender Singh, Nisha Bharti, Ravinder Singh, Sunil Ramawat, Binod Kumar, Mukesh Singh and many more.

11
Pleasing Personality and Dress Up for Success

A man without a smiling face must not open a shop.
—Chinese Proverb

Everything else being the same, we love to do business with people whom we like and the first condition for liking someone is their pleasing personality. To me, a pleasing personality is a simple accumulation of a few basic human traits and behaviors such as smiling, giving respect to others, genuinely listening to the others, kindness, honesty, generosity, hospitality and a display of good etiquettes.

Remember, it's more about you and less about your company, products or income plan. In sales terms, a person decides to start business with you or buy from you much before you have started talking. In the first five minutes. a person can make more than 50 judgments and inferences about you. Fundamentally, he/she makes up his/her mind about purchasing your product or services in the first five minutes; the rest of the meeting is about validating those inferences. In simple words, people first love the person and then what the person has to offer. One of my mentors used to tell me, *it starts much before it starts.*

> *Your smile is your logo, your personality is your business card, how you leave others feeling after having an experience with you is your trademark.*
>
> —Jay Danzie

The good news is that a pleasing personality is learnable and wherever you are right now, you can infinitely improve yourself and keep getting better.

I am not telling you to please everyone you meet, I am telling you to develop yourself into such a human being that whenever you are with people, you naturally look pleasing and everyone loves to be around you, or to have you around them. Many people started business with me by telling me explicitly that they did not need the business or the products, but just wanted to continue their association with me.

Also, you attract what you are and not what you want. So, if you want people with a pleasing personality to be there in your team, then you must develop a pleasing personality yourself.

Dress Up for Success

Your pleasing personality will get a chance to do wonders only if your attire opens up the doors.

—Deepak Bajaj

Yes, your pleasing personality will definitely win the person and assure you the sale, but what gets things started is simply how well dressed you are for the meeting. Your dress up gives the first impression.

So, it is highly recommended to be dressed up for success and to make the right first impression.

A few keys for dressing up for success:-

- ✓ When going for meetings, always be dressed in formals. Smart causals are also okay.
- ✓ For men, shirts give a better impression than t-shirts. Likewise for women, appropriate clothing is advisable. You should look sharp, confident and ready for success.
- ✓ Be well groomed. For men, nicely cut hair, clean shaved or a well-groomed beard. A nice perfume in moderation is recommended. Likewise for women.
- ✓ Wear well-polished shoes with clean socks.
- ✓ If you fear a bad breath or odour, use a mouthwash and deodorant.
- ✓ Always wear your smile. That's a sure shot accessory to win hearts.

First impression is the last impression and you don't get a second chance to make a first impression.

I am not advising you to blow away all your money on clothes and accessories, but the thumb rule is that if you are talking about success, you should look successful. If you are talking about lifestyle, you better show it. The idea is to look like someone whom people would love to associate with. Just be at your best every time, every day.

Smile often, be genuine and look like your role model. The whole world will be queuing up to be in your team.

> ***Pleasing personality opens all doors.***
> *On the first day of my business, I was lucky to meet a legend who is my Godfather in the business and he is the first man I go to every time I need any help or guidance—Mr. Pravin Chandan. He told me two things: 1. Build this business like your own business and 2. When dealing with people keep sugar on your tongue and ice on your head. These two learning have shaped my personality in such a way that I have always got tremendous love and respect from people everywhere.*
> *Dress up like you are a top performer of your company.*

12
Punctual and Prepared

Be on time if you cannot be early.

Being punctual is the easiest way to be liked by people: be it your teammates or new prospects. Everyone loves to do business with people who care for them and the easiest and the first way to tell them that you care is by being on time for the meetings. Make it a habit to reach at least 5-10 minutes before the meeting. Being punctual sometimes may not be appreciated, but being late is guaranteed to kill your business. Also, it is important to start and finish all meetings on time.

The good news is that being early or being late is just a habit that can be changed. So, work on developing punctuality.

The will to win means nothing without the will to prepare.
–Juma Ikangaa

Sooner or later, the person who wins in life and in business is not the one who is lucky, but the one who devotes the time and energy into its preparation. Most of the people who get into network marketing are new to this industry and are sometimes doubtful if they will be successful in this business. But everything becomes easy if you have the desire and discipline to prepare for the same. It really does not matter what you did before you came into this business; the only thing that matters is what you are willing to do once you start.

Be Prepared for your Moment

1. Start your day with a belief that today you will find your champion. Remember, today is the first day of the rest of your life.

2. Meet people with an intention to help them. Intentions matter.
3. Never leave your house without your best smile. Always dress like a successful person.
4. Carry your complete business kit with you. Have product videos, testimonies, success stories, program photos, product brochures, business presentation etc. ready in your phone, laptop or mobile.
5. Always carry a writing pad/notebook and a pen. Never ask for pens or paper from your guests.
6. Make sure you know about products and business plans, and you have done enough practice.

Preparation is antidote to fear.

–Deepak Bajaj

Your confidence is your best friend and it comes with preparation. With enough preparation, you will come out as a winner in every meeting.

> ***Reach 10 min in advance for all meetings.***
> *Never cancel a meeting and reach 10 min in advance for every meeting. I understood early in my career that your first few minutes in the meeting determine the output of the meeting. Reaching on time is a victory and creates a positive first impression. When you are late, you start your meeting with a sorry and that's the worst opening for any meeting. Reaching early is a habit. I have seen it in a very senior leader Mr. Ashwini Sharma who is always on time in every program. In terms of preparation I really admire three of my teammates—Sahil Garg, Harvinder Singh, Pradeep Chaudhary and Subhash Chander. They are always prepared for every meeting and program.*

13
Ability to Lead a Balanced Life

We are our choices.

–JP Sartre

When this business comes into your life, you are already managing 4 keys areas of your life – you, your family, current profession, and social obligations. To happily build this business for your dream life, you need to fit this business in the already busy schedule of things. You need to make time for this business on a daily basis. Like in any other business, the first few months in this business may be more challenging because it will take a lot of time and the income may look quite small compared to the effort you put in.

Remember, no pain, no gain. Life is all about choices. Just decide what you want in life and do the actions and behaviors that will move you closer to your goals.

Action expresses priorities.

—Mahatma Gandhi

Here are my recommendations for a better handling of your four key life areas:-

You: Take care of your health. You can't enjoy wealth if you are not in good health. Devote a minimum of 60 minutes a day for exercise. Carefully choose what you eat. Network marketers tend to travel a lot which disturbs what we eat and when we eat. Avoid junk food, eat meals on time, carry homemade food on travels, eat balanced nutritious foods and exercise daily. You will be able to enjoy your income, status and fame along with incredible health.

Read books and watch videos for your intellectual and emotional growth. Spend time with right people. Spend quality time with your family. Do some meditation and strengthen your faith in God. Listening to some good music also works like meditation. Always be happy and full of joy. Give thanks to God for giving you so much and for giving you attitude and capability to work for your dreams. You are lucky to get network marketing business also. Take care of your physical, emotional, intellectual and spiritual growth while building your business.

Family: You must get your family on your side. Initially, the time you will devote to this business will be the hours after your work and the weekends. This time was meant for friends and family earlier. They will be ready to sacrifice this if you show them the vision and what lies 2-5 years ahead. Have a communication with your family on why you are doing this business and what you expect to get in the months to come. Attend a few business events with your family and arrange some meetings with your Uplines and their families. Be committed to produce good results in the first few months and your family will be your biggest support.

Current job/Profession: Whatever you are doing currently in terms of your job or other profession, keep doing it smartly with better time management. You need that job or profession for the next few months or years, so do whatever is essential to maintain that job/profession. Be more efficient and take out the maximum time possible for building your network marketing business everyday. Utilize all your weekends and holidays effectively. Attend events with your team and connect your teammates to events so that they are not solely dependent on you. As this business starts gaining momentum, consult your active Uplines and decide when to take this as a full time business.

Friends/Social obligations: Just reduce this to the bare minimum, at least for the first 12-24 months, attending whatever is absolutely essential. At the same time, social functions can help you in adding new names to your list and prospecting people.

Essentially, for first twelve to twenty four months of starting the business, keep your network marketing business at the center and manage the other things accordingly. Will it be easy? No. Will it be worth it? Yes. You will be glad you made these choices. Network Marketing is not only going to give you millions of rupees, but also an excellent training in time management and setting your priorities right. Enjoy the journey.

If it is important to you, you will find a way. If not, you will find an excuse.

–Ryan Blair

Be happy, healthy and successful.
Learning from the best masters in the world, I have realized that real success comes from a combination of health, growth, family, happiness and career. Luckily this business can give all of it. I do my priming and meditation at 5.30 am. Have quality time with family everyday. Gym or sports all 7 days. Quality work whole day in peak state. I read daily and learn a new sport or something every six months. I take a short holiday every month and a long holiday every 3-4 months. I have learnt a lot about food, meditation and balanced life from my beloved friend, Vimal Sarin. Everytime we meet, we talk about evolving higher in our spiritual enlightenment. I keep learning from my friends, Harshvardhan Jain and Sanjay Sharma in this area.

14
Financial Discipline

> *Any good businessperson applies financial discipline to everything they do.*
>
> —Paula Wagner

Why I decided to keep financial discipline as a separate quality for success in network marketing is because I have seen many good careers collapse due to the lack of financial discipline. This is the make or break area and if not handled well, it can jeopardize your business.

> *Do not save what is left after spending, but spend what is left after saving.*
>
> —Warren Buffet

Since most of the people who come to network marketing are not from a business background, it is vital that we understand the importance of this skill and master it. A good degree of financial discipline will be required at every stage of the business. Here are a few recommendations for better financial management:-

1. **Income in the first few months:** Initially, when you are building this business part time along with your current job or profession, whatever money you will earn in this business will be extra because you are already managing your current expenses with your current income. Yes, there will be some business expenses, but the rest of the amount you must save and create a fund that will be of great help to you when you decide to take this profession as a full time career.

2. **Programs:** One of the expenses in our business is training

programs for your own development. This is an investment you do to become a better person. These programs will prepare you for big success in the business and have got multi-fold advantages. Although these programs are optional, they are essential for your development. When you look at a program, don't look at it as an expense, but as an investment that will give you the highest return on investment in days to come. Once in a while, attend programs from trainers outside the network marketing industry also. You will learn a lot and will also meet a lot of new growth-oriented people in these training events.

A program is not an expense; it's an investment.
–Deepak Bajaj

3. **Revenue vs. Profit:** What you earn in this business, treat it as revenue and not profit. Don't' start spending everything you earn. As a smart and visionary businessman, you should first meet the business expenses from your income, then invest in business development (your own training and development), then keep aside some amount for future contingency, and now whatever is left is profit and can be utilized by you as you want. Even a smart shopkeeper first pays rent and the other expenses of the shop, then takes home some profit. Develop a businessman attitude.

4. **Planning programs and events:** As your business grows, your role in the business will change from a participant to an organizer of events. If you are attached to a professional team with a good training and development system, they will organize most of the events, but still as you grow in this business, you will have to organize different events for faster multiplication of your business. Finance is one major area to look at when organizing an event. While planning an event, have a meeting with your active uplines and take into account all possible expenses plus some contingency. Any program should not result in a financial setback for anyone. Also a word of caution, for every event, make an organizing committee. Never collect money alone and share the program accounts with all concerned immediately after the event. You don't want to risk losing your credibility and millions of rupees in royalty for a few thousand bucks.

5. **Travelling, team meetings and other business expenses:** In the initial days, build your business in your town or city. Gradually, as you gain experience and develop a good team in your local area, go out to develop your team in outside locations also. When you travel, it will be a business expense and for the first few weeks, travelling and other expenses in building a new team in a new city will cost you more than what you get as return from there. Please don't stop building outside business because of this reason. This, again, is a business investment. Also, there will be times and situations when you will have to spend some money on your team—coffee, lunches, travelling etc. It's a business expense and it is important for business development.

6. **Buying a car or other luxuries:** If you talk about money and success, you need to show it. At the same time, if you spend more than your income or more than what you can handle, you may get into a difficult situation. Don't buy a car or any other costly item without a discussion with your active upline. Plan it well and plan it based on your back up funds, the past 3-6 months of income track record and the structure of your team. Always do it with proper planning.

7. **Loans:** At any stage in this business, avoid two types of loans—loans for luxuries/unnecessary personal consumption and loans at a very high rate of interest. Plan your purchases well in advance. In the initial stages when business is building up and is unstable, please be realistic in your projections and consult your active upline while planning a loan. Your business needs your 100% commitment physically and mentally. Any bad financial decision will take away your time and attention into unnecessary things. Principally, stay away from loans in the initial few years.

8. **Invest when you start making big money:** When your business is growing big and you are making more money, you should buy a car or other luxuries, but at the same time don't forget to save money and invest it. Keep a good portion of your income aside from your weekly or monthly income for investment. Consult your financial advisor (choose a financial advisor carefully) and build a good portfolio of investments. Let your money also work for you while you enjoy the big passive income from your network marketing business.

A big part of financial freedom is having your heart and mind free from worry about the what-ifs of life.

—Suze Orman

We are doing this business to achieve the ultimate financial freedom. We want to set this business in such a way that once it is established, it will continue to give us money even when we are having fun and go on holidays with our family and loved ones. You have chosen the right business and you will definitely achieve financial freedom from this business faster than in any other business I know of. However, it will take some time and till you arrive there, work on these 8 invaluable principles of financial discipline that I have mentioned above to have a smooth journey to the top. Keep building your network marketing business with your heart and soul, and you will enjoy financial abundance that the whole world just dreams of.

> *Control your finances.*
> *I have my friend and finance expert in my team who teaches me a lot about money—Sanjay Jindal. I have now mastered the basics of money multiplication and have made some great investments from my network marketing income. I always tell people that everyone must do whatever it takes to maintain a positive cash flow every month. Plan things in advance and never allow a negative financial situation in your life.*

15
Building and Nurturing Relationships

> *Business is all about relationships. How well you build them determines how well they build your business.*
>
> —Brad Sugars

Network marketing is entirely different from a traditional business. Traditional business operates with a boss, a formal structure, authority and penalties. On the other hand the network marketing runs purely on goodwill and relationships. Running a successful network marketing business is like running a family and the principles of running this business are exactly the same that runs a family. Hence, a person who can develop and nurture relationships is the best suited for network marketing business. Some people come with this virtue and others develop it as they start building their business.

Relationship + Sales = Network marketing

Please understand that selling products is only one part of Network Marketing, the actual business is built on relationships. Relationships are anyway necessary in every business but in network marketing, relationships are the backbone of the business. People are your only resource here and people will stay with you for decades to come on the basis of your relationships with them. I can anticipate a time in the near future when only friends will come into the business and distributors who are friends will stay in the business.

> *Business, after all is nothing more than a bunch of human relationships.*
>
> —Lee Iacocca

If building and nurturing relationships doesn't come naturally to you, please remember it's a learnable skill and an attribute that can slowly be developed as a part of your personality. Be a person of sound character, integrity and morals and your business will continue growing for the generations to come. Keep developing the below mentioned virtues till they become your second nature:

- Always respect people irrespective of their performance in the business.
- Appreciate others at every opportunity.
- Never put people down.
- Never mess up with people's ego, money and family.
- Put team's interest before your own personal interest.
- Always be on time.
- Have a pleasing personality.
- Work with an attitude of gratitude.
- Always give more than what you get.
- Be a problem solver and not fault finder.
- Demonstrate good manners and courtesy.
- Honor your words.
- Be honest and transparent in your dealings.

Value people and put relationships above short-term gains. This is a long-term business and your emphasis on nurturing relationships will give you a stable and ever growing business.

> *People do business with people because they choose to not because they have to. We can always find others doing the same thing or selling the same product, it's the personal connection that makes the difference.*
>
> –Anon

Genuinely love and care for people before anything else.
When I launched my new training and consulting company, more than 1000 people showed up from every part of the India and Australia for my first live event – Launch Your Dream Life. The event was sold out much before the event date and we had to request people to come for the next event. People had never seen 1000 participants for the first-ever training program of any trainer but this happened because of the relationship I had developed with people and the value I had added to their lives in the past. Most of those participants signed up for our next events and have been regularly to us. For all my training events, I always follow 10x principle: We must deliver 10 times value/benefit than what every participant has paid. This philosophy of adding value, gratitude, service and valuing people has been the core of massive success of my books, videos and training events.

16
Emotional Resilience

> *We all need resilience to live a fulfilling life. With resilience, you will be more prepared to take on challenges, to develop your talents, skills, and abilities so that you can live with more purpose and more joy.*
>
> –Eric Greitens

Emotional resilience is the capacity to recover quickly from difficulties and setbacks. When you and your teams are working in the field, everyday there will be situations when things will not work out as planned. Interestingly, the bigger will be your team size, the greater will be the challenges in the field. Your reaction during all these moments will determine the future of your business. In fact, emotional resilience actually differentiates the top network marketers from the rest.

Everyone can shout, clap and give motivational speeches when things are going good and business is growing. The real test of a leader is how he/she behaves when things are not working out, when people are leaving, when business is stagnant or situations are adverse. If you are coming to network marketing looking at the lifestyle and the freedom of your leaders, then please remember they have gone through all the hardships and earned their lifestyle by successfully passing through tough times. They have faced their share of hardships and now is your turn. You will also have to face challenges before you can actually climb to the top and earn love, admiration and financial abundance.

It's very easy to criticize and condemn. You can very easily blame other people, situations, luck etc. and decide not to take any initiatives in the future. But it takes real courage and guts to accept mistakes and recover fast from them. If you want to be a successful network marketer, then you must be able to bounce back better and faster from every setback.

> *Any true champion can bounce back. That's what being a champion is: being able to deal with adversity and being able to bounce back.*
>
> –Floyd Mayweather Jr

Stop complaining and accept total and absolute responsibility of your life. Your attitude should be 'Try Me' instead of 'Why Me'. Everyday there will be situations when your emotional resilience will be put to test. Every single day you will face negativity from people and handle their No. I sometimes tell in my training events that if you really want to build a big network marketing empire, you have to face temporary loss of self-esteem from some stupid people for first 9-12 months.

You will have to face different kind of people and unexpected situations as part of your daily routine. Some people will listen to you and others will rebel. Some will follow the system and some others will try their own ideas. Some will adore you and some others will play games with you. Some will grow faster and some will be stuck in the same situation for years. There will be situations when you will be made accountable for mistakes that you have not committed. But you have to keep your spirit up and keep moving forward. Your emotional resilience will determine if you will allow all of it to stop you or propel you.

Can you quickly change your bad mood to a good mood? Can you maintain peak and resourceful state irrespective of your ongoing situation? How fast you can cheer up your team? You will have to be your own cheerleader and keep moving.

It's simple, if you cannot bounce back fast from crisis, you cannot be a leader in the network marketing business.

> *I don't measure a man's success by how high he climbs but how high he bounces when he hits bottom.*
>
> –George S Patton Jr

> *All legends have one common quality—emotional resilience.*
> I have studied and met some of the founders of legendary network marketing companies and each one of them have gone through some really tough challenges and resistance. In fact the higher is the level of difficulty you surpass the greater will be size of your achievements. Everytime you go through difficulties, crisis and setback, thank God for it because God wants you to go to next level. Some of the men for which I have deep admiration in this industry are Rich DeVos, Jay Van Andel, Rex Maughan, Robert and Jonas Affochnick, Mark R. Hughes, David H McConnell, Mary Kay Ash, Pravin J Chandan, Gautam Bali and T C Chhabra.

SECTION-VI

9 CORE ACTIONS

9 CORE ACTIONS

Lifeline of your Business

A man who works regularly, in a systematic fashion, never feels overworked or tired. It is not hard work that kills a man, but irregularity or lack of a system.

–Mahatma Gandhi

These are the actions that are to be performed on a regular basis by every distributor for speed and stability in the business. These are seemingly insignificant activities, but the key lies in two things—consistency and duplication. Some people work with this myth that if they just stay in the business, it will keep running. That's far from the truth. The plan will work only if you work as per the plan. These are some easily doable activities that can be performed by each and every associate. Consistently taking these 9 actions will ensure massive success in the business. Whatever be your rank and income level, I highly recommend you do these activities regularly.

1. **At least one business opportunity presentation daily:**

   Howsoever busy you may be, share your opportunity with at least one person everyday. Even if you miss some days, make sure that the weekly total adds up to a minimum of seven opportunity presentations. Product presentations should be over and above this number.

2. **Add one name to your list every day:**

   Your list is your biggest resource. Remember, people don't quit this business because others say 'No' to them, but because they have small lists. Bigger the list, the more profitable will your business be. It's mandatory to add seven new names to your list weekly.

3. **100% product/service usage:**

   You should be the #1 brand ambassador of your products/services. You should be the biggest fan of your company. Whatever your company makes, you should be their number one customer. Whatever products your company makes, you should use them.

4. **Attend weekly hall meetings with guests:**

   Weekly events are the lifeline of our business. Every profession, job or business requires daily working hours. In our business, the weekly meetings are our office. Weekly meetings maintain the momentum and consistency in the business. Make it your top priority to attend the weekly meetings with new guests every week. If no guest or associate turns up, then you should go alone.

5. **Attend all programs with teams:**

   People can get into this business by a variety of ways, but they start building the business only through one way—programs. Programs set people up for working in this business the right way. Develop the art of inviting people to programs and make sure your numbers grow from program to program.

6. **Read the recommended books/watch the recommended videos daily for 30 minutes:**

   You need to prepare your mind for massive success. The right books and audio/video programs daily can program your minds for success. It's food for your mind and this investment will yield the highest returns on your investment.

7. **Every week personal sponsoring:**

   Your team will not do what you tell them to do; your team will do what you do. If you want your teammates to do massive personal sponsoring, you should also be doing at least one personal sponsoring every week. Whatever income model your company follows, personal sponsoring will always lead to the highest profits.

8. **Monthly counseling with the upline:**

   You must have a one-to-one counseling meeting with your active upline once every month. You need it when the business is not doing great and you need it even more when the business is doing extremely well. This is an overlooked area, but can give you an edge and can save you a lot of time and money.

9. **Add a minimum of two new customers every month:**

    A good customer base gives stability to your business, and happy customers are more probable to become successful business associates in the future. So, promote your products or services aggressively and make it a practice to personally add a minimum of two new customers every month to your business.

And remember, do these actions with absolute faith and in the best of state.

SECTION-VII

BUSINESS CODE OF CONDUCT

BUSINESS CODE OF CONDUCT

What you do not want done to yourself, do not do to others.
                                                            –Confucius

It really pains me when people build a large business after great efforts but it comes crashing down due to some silly mistakes by some of the associates. I have lost some of my best leaders due to some totally avoidable actions. While I rebuilt my teams, I don't want you to go through the same pain. Hence, here are 11 guidelines that everyone in this business must follow as a strict code of conduct. Adopt these practices and make your entire team strictly follow them for a stable and growing business.

The 11 practices recommended here will serve as a guide for your daily decision-making and for the right conduct required while building this business.

1. **Never mess with people's money:**
   People have given their money to the company and not to you; you are only an intermediary or caretaker. Make sure whatever money you receive on behalf of the company goes to the company's account immediately. Similarly, if you receive money for products or event tickets or for any other work, make sure you deliver the products or tickets in time and the money is rightfully used for the purpose it is intended for.

2. **Never hurt people's ego:**
   When egos are hurt, people make wrong decisions and adamantly stand for those wrong decisions. Discussions turn into arguments when egos are hurt. To prove you are right, don't make others wrong. People are free to choose their opinions and professions. You have no right to judge them. Don't demean their profession or job in order to make your business look better. Think before

you speak. Egos are fragile; never say anything that hurts the ego of the other person.

3. **No accounts between upline and downline:**
   Network marketing is a pay and collect business. Be it products, event tickets or tools, or anything you want to buy from your Upline, please pay and collect it. No accounts are to be maintained between the upline and the downline.

4. **Maintain appropriate conduct while dealing with someone's spouse:**
   Ours is a family business that flourishes at homes. Hence, it is of utmost importance to respect the family values and maintain appropriate conduct while dealing with anyone's spouse. Every culture and place is different; behave appropriately and earn their respect.

5. **Stay away from negative influencers:**
   Since ours is a people's business, it is important to identify the right people and even more important to recognize whom to avoid. Stay away from negative influencers. Don't make it your life's mission to make every person on earth positive about this business, that's not your job. Your job is to find some like-minded people and work with them for mutual benefits with a genuine intention to serve.

6. **Don't criticize and complain:**
   It's a virus. It's an addiction. It will cost you relationships that you've built over years. It's a black spot on your reputation. Never ever talk about someone behind his or her back. Some people have become professional complainers by doing it for years. They complain even without realizing it. If you are one of them, change yourself immediately.

7. **Never talk negative about your upline or company in front of your downline:**
   No company or upline is perfect. At times, there will be things, situations or policies that you may not agree to or understand, but the right place to discuss them is with your upline. Never ever talk negatively about your upline or company in front of your teammates.

Their reaction may not be visible at that moment, but the consequences will be seen over time. It takes just a small hole to sink a giant ship; likewise, small seeds of doubt or mistrust can make people even leave the business. Most of the times, these problems are temporary and corrected later, but if discussed in front of the team, the damage will be permanent.

You should be careful about this not only when you are on stage, but also when you are off it. Be even more careful about this when you are in casual interaction with your teammates.

8. **Avoid unnecessary interactions with your cross-lines:**

   Many good people have made wrong decisions or bad judgments because of their excessive interactions with their cross-lines. Howsoever good the relationship may seem, a cross-line doesn't have any interest in your business growth; rather, most of them are competing with you. So, avoid excessive interactions with cross line distributors. Also avoid discussions with associates in other companies.

9. **Regular communication between upline and downlines:**

   Communication is the thread that keeps Uplines with Downlines together in this business. We don't have official or formal relationships in our business. Regular and healthy communication between the upline and downlines plays a vital role in building a big business. Lack of communication is the beginning of the end. Stay connected.

10. **Never work like a manager or boss:**

    In this business, everyone is a partner or an associate. Managers are not required. We are not paying anyone to be in this business. There is a thin and delicate line between being an upline and a manager, never cross that. Respect is not given to a position here, but to the person. Everyone needs to earn his or her own respect in this business.

11. **Consult your upline before doing anything for the first time:**

    Since most of the people start building this business part time with their job or profession, I highly recommend people to use the experience of their active uplines. It can save you a lot of time and effort. I am not here to kill your creativity, but the idea is to use the experiences of one's uplines and achieve your goals faster. If your upline has made some mistakes, he or she can save you from making the same.

Build a big business on the foundation of this code of conduct and you will happily enjoy the fruits of your hard work for years and decades to come.

SECTION-VIII

TOOLS FOR EXCELLENCE

1
596 System for Massive Success

I always tell people there is no secret to success, but there is a system to success. Given below is a time-tested and doable system for anyone to be wildly successful in the network marketing business and to fulfill his or her dreams in record time. This system will work in any network marketing company in any country with any product or service. I have seen countless people getting success with this system in the past 11 years. This entire system is explained at length in this book and we cover it extensively in our workshop. It's summarized here for you in a simplified format.

596 SYSTEM FOR MASSIVE SUCCESS

5 Steps Success Process
1. List building and selection
2. Approaching your list and securing appointments
3. Sharing the opportunity
4. Follow through and sales closing
5. Right takeoff for the new associate

9 Core Actions - Lifeline of your Business
1. Share at least 1 business opportunity presentation daily.
2. Add one name in your list everyday.
3. 100% product/service usage.
4. Attend weekly hall meeting with guests.
5. Attend all Programs with team.
6. Read recommended books/watch recommended videos daily for 30 min.

7. Atleast 1 new distributor every week.
8. Monthly counseling with upline.
9. Add minimum two new product customers every month.

6 Business Values
1. Never mess with people's money, ego or family.
2. No accounts between upline and downline.
3. Consult your upline before doing anything for the first time.
4. Never talk negative about your upline, company or team in front of your downline.
5. Avoid unnecessary interaction with your cross-lines and other negative influencers.
6. Regular communication between upline and downlines.

2
Universal Framework for Choosing the Best Network Marketing Company

There are four pillars for a network marketing company. If any one of these pillars is weak, either the company will shut down or the distributors will not make big money. For the distributors to earn big money and for the company to run for generations to come, all four of these pillars have to be really strong. Whenever anyone proposes that you start business with a network marketing company, you simply evaluate the company on these four parameters and you must choose a company that is strong on all of them.

Four Pillars of a Network Marketing Company	
1	Credibility and Track Record of the Company
2	Products or Services
3	Income Plan and Reward System
4	Professional Training and Support System

1. **Credibility and Track Record of the company:**
   Check how long the management has been in the business. Check the general goodwill of the company, track record of the directors, other family businesses and history, customer and distributor friendly policies, latest technology, payment history, innovation and adaptability, offices, certifications from the government and other bodies, transparent practices, training and development set up, support to distributors, etc.

2. **Products or Services:**

   The company must have good quality products or services that are marketable even without the business opportunity. The products should be of good quality, ones that can be used regularly, worth recommendation even without the income model, offer good value for money, priced appropriately, having all the necessary certifications and standardizations, manufactured at factories following good standards and giving results.

   Many fraudulent companies who are basically into money circulation, keep dummy products to fulfill the government regulations. Dummy products can easily be identified as they don't give any value for money to their customers and are given just for the sake of it. Stay away from such companies. Such companies will ultimately shut down, spoiling your personal reputation with them.

3. **Income Plan and Rewards:**

   Look for a doable and sustainable income plan with possibilities of big income—a plan that suitably rewards efforts, is not complicated, easy to understand and easier to explain, transparent with no hidden conditions and based on a genuine revenue generation model. There should be genuine sale of products or services out of which the commissions will be paid. Income should be given in the bank accounts after TDS or other applicable taxes. One should be able to earn income purely on product sales without making distributors and on repurchase of products by existing distributors also. It should have a nomination facility. I would consider a plan simple and powerful if it can be explained in 60 seconds to any common person.

   Stay away from plans that look too lucrative. Remember, the income can be given only from the sale of products or services. Use your common sense and intellect. Never be lured into a fraudulent idea of unbelievably good returns without much hard work.

   An excellent reward system is a proven way to encourage high performers. Regular rewards like foreign trips, a car fund, performance-linked bonuses, etc. motivate distributors to achieve big targets and serve as a catalyst for big growth.

Many companies offer plans that look good on the face but are loaded with lots of hidden conditions. Read all the documents or visit the company's website to get complete details of the same.

4. **Professional Training and Support System:**

    Other things being similar, this one factor will give you an edge and will enable you to achieve big success in network marketing. There are institutions to become a doctor, lawyer, chartered accountant, engineer, teacher etc. but for this amazing business, there are no formal schools or colleges. On top of it, most of you will start this business part time along with your other job or profession. Professional training and the support system of your team will be your learning and development institution for this business. Programs organized by your team, business tools and one to one support provided by the seniors are critical for success in this business. So, always join a company or a team with a professional training and support system that has an excellent track record.

3
Write your Million Dollar Story

People love to buy from people they trust.
                                            –Deepak Bajaj

Your story is the place where your prospects start trusting you. They connect with you and relate to some of the things you say through your story. They might have heard about the network marketing business or your company before and may have a variety of opinions about it, but your story is your chance to make a difference. Your story is the most important component of the entire meeting. Remember, people don't join a company or a product; people join people. Learn the art of story telling and win your way to success.

All great network marketers are great storytellers.
                                            –Deepak Bajaj

These are the 7 components that make a good story and in this exact same order:-

1. **What were you doing before starting this business?**

   Your background, education, location and work profile. If you have moved places, changed jobs or had different academic experiences, mention everything briefly here. People look for similarities. Be truthful about everything.

2. **What was your condition? What was good and what was bothering you?**

   Tell the good things but highlight what you were not happy about in your job/profession in simple words. This is the point where people connect with you and will realize the need for this business.

3. **What was your first reaction to this business presentation?**

   Truthfully and briefly tell what was your opinion about the business. You can tell if you had any doubts or concerns. If you had already tried some other network marketing business, tell that here too.

4. **What convinced you to get started and what mind blocks did you remove?**

   State all those things that you found good in this business opportunity and what all solutions you found for your problems/challenges. Highlight one most important thing that made you start this business. Also, talk about some of your wrong beliefs that got changed after meeting some person or after attending some event.

5. **Your achievements and journey so far:**

   Share your income, team size, feelings, recognitions, trips, new friends you got to make and any other good changes you have experienced so far. Be truthful. You may add some significant achievements of your teammate also.

6. **What are your long-term and short-term goals with this business?**

   This is the time to give your listeners a vision. Boldly state your top 2-3 short term and long term goals with full faith and conviction. Don't just say anything to impress others, be truthful. Declarations are powerful.

7. **Your personal commitment to your prospect and your team:**

   Restate your commitment to give the best possible support to your teammates and anyone else who starts with you.

Please remember that all this is to be done in your natural style and in simple words. Be truthful and brutally honest. I am not asking you to cook a story, but learn to present your truth in a way that is effective. You will not get the same amount of time every time for sharing your story. So, it's smart to prepare your story in 3 different time durations and share your story as per the time availability. Make a detailed story taking 5-7 minutes, a shorter one for 2-3 minutes and a quick 60-second one. Make sure to keep the same sequence for all three durations.

Along with the content of the story, what really makes an impact are the non-verbals like your energy, the spark in your eyes, a confident voice, posture, eye contact and your conviction when you are making a declaration or giving assurance to your team and to new prospects.

You can listen to my story for your reference on my website or on my YouTube channel.

4
Top Success Drivers (TSD) Chart

Each one of us has got dreams and we aspire for a lot of things for ourselves and for our families, but a few things are closer to our heart than the others and these are different for different people. For some, it may be cars; for some others, it may be a house; some may find joy in playing with their kids while some others get excited about receiving recognition on stage. These are our Top Success Drivers. Top Success Drivers are the purpose behind our work and we do everything in our capacity to achieve them.

What is the benefit of identifying the TSDs of our prospects? It's simple: All of us love to do things that help us in the achievement of our TSDs. Hence, a business presentation will be effective only if it provides solutions to the prospects for achieving his or her TSDs. If the prospect gets this conviction that doing this business will enable him or her to achieve his or her TSDs faster, your prospect will sign up right away.

We are blessed to be in this business that offers a multitude of benefits. Once you have identified the TSDs of your prospect, every time you wish to highlight the benefits of your business, you can highlight them in terms of the TSDs of your prospects. Talking more about those 3 TSDs at appropriate places during the presentation will help you connect more with the prospect and will multiply their chances of starting business with you. Also remember; never ever assume that the TSDs of your prospects will be the same as yours. Learn to appreciate and respect different perspectives and opinions. Once you have got the TSDs of your prospect, please forget about yours and focus only on their TSDs. It's about them.

Below is a list of 13 main Success Drivers. Please determine what are the 3 TSDs for your prospect using this chart. You will need a print out or image of this card. You can keep it in your mobile or in your laptop or as a printed form in your folder.

Top Success Drivers

1	Extra income/second income source	
2	Financial freedom	
3	Entrepreneurship (Being your own boss)	
4	Being rich and famous (Being a celebrity)	
5	Luxury lifestyle – car, vacations, luxury brands, etc.	
6	Secure future for family/Legacy for kids	
7	Early retirement/More spare time	
8	Your own dream house	
9	Quality time with family	
10	Meeting new people/developing a social circle	
11	Helping others	
12	Contributing towards nation building	
13	Your personal growth and personality development	

My way to identify top 3 TSDs for your prospects:-

1. Start by saying, 'Before we tell you what exactly we do, let me show you why people do this business.'
2. Produce your TSD card and ask the following questions
3. **Ques. 1** Ask them – 'Out of this list, what are your top 3 priorities?'
4. **Ques. 2** Then ask – 'Which one would be the most important of these 3?'
5. **Ques. 3** Wait for the answer and ask – 'Why is it important to you?'
6. **Ques. 4** Wait for the answer and ask – 'What would happen if you don't get this?' It should not be an interview but a genuine desire to know the other person to serve them better. Be compassionate and listen properly.

7. Now, repeat their answers to all the 4 questions and get their Yes/head nod by saying this, 'Okay. Great. So you are working everyday to get these 3 things...'
8. Then say, 'If you seriously look at our presentation for the next 30 minutes, you will find out how we can help you achieve these 3 priorities in a very short time.'

The basic idea behind this is that if you start giving the presentation to people without understanding what they want, it will just be a boring presentation that they will simply wait to end. The objective of our meeting is to be a solution provider and help them see what is good for them. We want them to listen with the right attitude. We want to shift the perspective from 'it's about us' to 'it's about them'. The whole quality of the presentation will magically change if the prospects start looking at it with an intention to get some benefit from it. The key is to know what they are looking for before you start presenting the solutions.

5
5 Lists for Success

Your success in this business depends on your lists. Every serious distributor in this business must have 5 updated lists with him or her at all times. I highly recommend these lists to be updated every week or fortnight.

1. **List of prospects:** This is the list of new people whom you want to approach for business. Add names to this list everyday.
2. **List of pending follow-ups:** These are the people with whom you have already shared the opportunity but they are yet to start the business and you are in the process of following through with them. Update it after every meeting.
3. **List of active distributors:** This list is your real strength and will determine your income in network marketing. The telecom industry works on Metcalfe's law that states that the value of a telecommunications network is proportional to the square of the number of connected users of the system (n^2). Likewise, the income of a network-marketing distributor is directly proportional to the square of the number of active distributors in his or her team.

    Income (I) ≅ Number of active distributors in the team (N^2)

    A detailed guideline on how to identify an active distributor is given in the Tools for Excellence section of this book.
4. **List of customers:** This is the list of people who are active users of your products/services. They use the product and sometimes recommend it to others, but have not yet decided to be a distributor in the business. They give you volume and since they

are satisfied customers, they will become very good partners whenever they choose to be so.

5. **List of all distributors:** This is a comprehensive list of everyone who has started business in your team. Everyone will not start building the business as soon as they start. Many people wait and watch before they actively start building the business. It's always a good idea to be in touch with all of these associates as they may start building the business anytime in the future. Invite them for all the events and keep them updated on the new products, new achievements, etc.

6
Power Connectors

Business is all about relationships and connections. As I have already said at several places in this book, sales is simply the transfer of your conviction to the other person. So many books and trainers will suggest you to make the other person talk more but remember, for the other person to continue talking, he/she has to like you. That will happen only when that person is in a good rapport with you. While dealing with thousands of people and by learning from many of my mentors (Tony Robbins, Antano Solar John, Robert T Kiyosaki, Allan Pease, Richard Bandlar and many more), I have identified and verified several ways to establish a quick rapport and connection with the other person in a meeting. What I have learnt by paying millions of rupees and by investing more than a decade with people, I am giving you here, in the form of my favorite tools to stay connected to your teammates or prospects or anyone else during a meeting. Here are my 9 time-tested power connectors:

Power Connectors

Smile	Magic words	Mirroring
Eye contact	Head nod	Progress makers
Yes stacks	Point out similarities	Genuine listening

1. **Smile:** A smile is the universal symbol of love and appreciation. A smile opens doors that logic and reasoning can never do. In my own team of thousands of people, I have realized that the more you smile, greater are the chances that the other person will like you, trust you and would like to associate with you. A smile is your asset in this business and in life too. Make smiling

your second nature. Smile as often as you can during the entire meeting.

2. **Magic words:** Each one of us has our own vocabulary. We express our basic emotions like happiness, joy, pain etc. by different sets of words. If you ask someone how he/she is doing and the person wants to say—he or she is doing fine, this expression can itself be expressed in countless ways like good, awesome, excellent, fine, great, incredible, etc. Whatever unique words any person is using to express his or her emotions are called Magic words and everyone has got their own unique magic words. There are no right or wrong words; they are just different expressions of the same emotion.

Whenever you are interacting with someone, just observe which words he or she repeatedly using during the conversation. Once you have identified those magic words, just use those words wherever appropriate during the conversation, even when you are giving a complement to the other person. Your connection with that person and the impact of your words will be much better this way.

3. **Mirroring:** When two people are in a good rapport with each other, their bodies start taking similar postures and gestures. This is called mirroring. Mirroring simply means that the mental rapport gets reflected in physical movements. Mirroring need not be developed, we humans are born with the ability to mirror and intuitively copy the person with whom we have a good rapport. To turn this around, if you start mirroring the body posture, seating position, gestures, expressions and voice of the other person, you will quickly get in a good rapport with him or her. When you are in a good rapport, there are more chances of the other person liking and trusting you.

4. **Eye contact:** Maintain eye contact with other people in the meeting. It reflects your honesty and confidence.

5. **Head nod:** A Head nod is a commonly acknowledged gesture for yes or acceptance. If you feel positively about something or if you are in agreement with something/someone, your head will start nodding. Likewise, if you start nodding your head, you will start feeling positive.

Also, a head nod is contagious. If you start nodding your head, the other person will also start doing it. A head nod is a very simple yet powerful tool to stay in rapport and get the desired results. Frequent head nods during the meeting will increase your chances of getting the main head nod when you ask them to start business with you.

6. **Progress makers:** There are certain words or phrases that can keep the flow of conversation going. If you can master the use of these words, you will be able to continue the conversation without talking much. You will give the prospect more opportunity to talk and make them feel good. As per my experience, the meetings where the prospects do more talking than the presenter, the results are excellent. These progress making phrases are: *Tell me more, for example, alright, meaning?, Oh really, and then?, for example, so then, isn't it, that means, and what after that?, therefore, that's right, fair enough, I see, etc.*

7. **Yes stack:** Research shows that once you start saying 'yes' in a meeting, the more likely it is that you will continue to do so. A 'Yes stack' is created by asking several simple questions that can be answered only in a yes. If your prospect has said Yes a few times to a few questions, his or her chances of saying Yes to what you are going to ask them to do next get multiplied.

   A Yes stack is created when a salesperson asks you a couple of simple questions like, 'Is it 29th March today?' or 'It seems to be quite hot today, isn't it?' or any other simple statements that will generally produce a Yes response.

8. **Point out similarities:** Our mind tends to trust those who are like us and with whom we can find some similarities. Try to find some similarities (the more the merrier) and state them. Same school, college, favorite food, movies, companies you've worked with, same style of house, kids, education, holidays, hobbies, etc. the list is endless. Do it in a flow as you move forward in the meeting.

   Some people try to prove themselves better or superior in the meeting, but it doesn't work. What works are the similarities. The best thing to do is to allow the other person to talk more, especially in the first 10-15 minutes and during that conversation, identify the similarities and talk about them. The more the other person talks, the greater are the number of similarities that you may find.

9. **Genuine listening:** Even if you don't use any technique, a genuine desire to listen and understand the other person itself is enough to build a good rapport. Listen not to reply, but listen to listen.

7
Programs Progress Monitor (PPM)

Network marketing runs on programs and program numbers are the pulse of our business. The strength and stability of our business is directly proportional to the number of people from our team in the program. One question that every distributor must ask oneself, 'Am I growing in numbers from program to program?'

The simple format mentioned below can be used to monitor the progress in program numbers from time to time. There are a lot of programs that keep happening all through the year, but I recommend we monitor 4 key programs—2 weekly programs and 2 quarterly programs. We should fill the data in this sheet after every program.

We can take a printout of this sheet and fill it, or we can just draw this table in our diary and fill it. We can make it in Microsoft Excel or Mac Numbers applications in our laptops or in a variety of other mobile apps. The trend of these numbers from program to program will give us a clear idea about which direction our business is heading towards. To have the same numbers or declining numbers in the programs is alarming and we must accelerate and multiply our efforts. We want only one direction for our program numbers to head in, and that is upwards.

PROGRAMS PROGRESS MONITOR (PPM)

WEEKLY PROGRAMS	Week 1	Week 2	Week 3	Week 4
Basic training program				
Hall business opportunity presentation				
QUARTERLY PROGRAMS	Qtr 1	Qtr 2	Qtr 3	Qtr 4
One day advance training program				
Two days residential program				

8
Active Distributor Scorecard (ADS)

There has always been a debate on who should be called an active distributor. Active Distributor Scorecard (ADS) is a proven solution for that. The ADS is a unique comprehensive self-assessment tool that will work in any network marketing organization dealing with any product or service. It lists all the basic qualities required to be an active distributor. Anyone can evaluate himself or herself by just scoring on this sheet, and can see for themselves where he or she stands in terms of the various requirements of this business. You can also use ADS in your training programs for the assessment of your teammates. Self-realization is the best form of realization and ADS can be a turning point for your team by becoming the first step towards self-realization and transformation.

Evaluate yourself at the beginning of every month on this scorecard and identify 1-2 development areas for that month from this list. Improve yourself on all these 15 parameters one after the other. You can inspire each of your teammates to use this tool and work for their improvement. Our aim is to get a score of 15 on 15 and improve the score of our teammates on this scorecard.

ACTIVE DISTRIBUTOR SCORECARD (ADS)

Name of the Distributor:	
Questions	Score
1 Do you give the business opportunity presentation yourself?	
2 Do you wear formal dress in every program?	
3 Do you reach before/on time in every program?	
4 Are you using 100% products/services of your company at your home/office?	
5 Do you talk to min. 1 new person everyday (Prospecting)?	
6 Do you make 2 minute phone calls everyday for setting appointment?	
7 Do you add min. 1 new name to your list everyday?	
8 Do you give at least 1 business presentation everyday?	
9 Do you have appointments for next 1 week in your calendar?	
10 Do you have product display at home?	
11 Do you deliver a good experience sharing in programs?	
12 Do you read recommended books?	
13 Do you conduct at least 1 Home meeting every week?	
14 Do you attend at least 1 Basic Training with team every week?	
15 Do you attend at least 1 Hall Opportunity Presentation every week?	
TOTAL SCORE:	/15
Give yourself a score of 1 for every Yes and 0 for every No.	

9
Getting the Best Results from Programs

Programs are the lifeline of your business. We build our business program to program. But we don't do programs for the sake of doing programs; we do programs to multiply our business. There is absolutely no benefit of a program if our income and volume doesn't increase after the program. Here are the guidelines for getting the best results from every program you organize or participate in:-

Pre-Event
1. Promote the program as if your life depends entirely on this program. Learn the art of program promotion. If you have any tools like videos, brochures, etc. to promote the program, use them. Do whatever it takes to ensure you have maximum people attending the program from your team.
2. Promotion of the event is not complete till the tickets are sold and the payment collected.
3. Program promotion and regular sales should go together. Don't stop the business because you are promoting a program. In fact, you should increase the sales volume during the program promotion period and the week/month before the program should be the highest business week/month.
4. Make sure all your key distributors attend the event. Make lists before the program and ensure that everyone is covered.
5. Programs are good opportunities to activate passive distributors. Send message and meet up with people who have become passive and make them active through the programs.
6. You should also have a list of all the expected guests from your team.

7. Send reminders to everyone before the event.
8. Make the necessary travel arrangements, like booking cabs or buses wherever required.
9. Network Marketing programs are the platforms for the recognition of achievers. Make sure you achieve the best possible rank and go on stage as an achiever. If you have a team, make sure that maximum people become achievers and go on stage.
10. If there are special seats available closed to the stage, even at a higher price, get those tickets. It's worth it.
11. Tell everyone about the duration and conduct of the program. If they need to carry food or water bottles etc., inform them well in advance.

The Event

- Sit in the front rows and keep your mobile phone switched off.
- Be in formals.
- Reach before the scheduled time.
- Make sure everyone in your team reaches on time and attends the whole event.
- You should be the most excited person in the hall. Clap, shout and click pictures, as if this is your first program.
- If something is not right, don't complain in front of your teammates. Rather, handle the situation and make sure no one leaves the program before completion.
- Introduce your teammates to some seniors and click their photos with the seniors.
- If tools are on sale, make sure everyone in your team buys the maximum tools there.

Post Event

For the event organizers, the program is over on the day of the event but for you and your team, the real work has begun now. Now is the time to get results. A program is not an end in itself; a program is only a means to an end.

- Within 24 hours of the program, you should get a list of all those who attended the program.

- ✓ Someone should meet every person who attended, within the next one week of the program and start working with him or her. A program does two things—it motivates people by building their faith in the business, and it creates a mindset to start working seriously on the business. Before this motivation fades, we should start the action.
- ✓ If there were new guests, follow-ups must be completed within the next 2-4 days.
- ✓ For all the distributors who attended, we must do a planning meeting and make an action plan for getting big business in the next few weeks. We must set new goals for everyone and kick start action on the same.

10
Recommended Books

You can read the following books to build the right mindset for growing big in this business. All these books are classics and can be read again and again too.

1. Awaken the Giant Within by Tony Robbins
2. How to Win Friends and Influence People by Dale Carnegie
3. Rich Dad, Poor Dad by Robert T Kiyosaki
4. Secrets of the Millionaire Mind by T Harv Eker
5. Think and Grow Rich by Napoleon Hill
6. The 21 Irrefutable Laws of Leadership by John C Maxwell
7. The Business of the 21st Century by Robert T Kiyosaki
8. The Greatest Salesman in the World by Og Mandino
9. The Greatness Guide by Robin Sharma
10. The Magic of Thinking Big by David Schwartz
11. The Science of Getting Rich by Wallace D Wattles
12. The Seven Habits of Highly Effective People by Dr Stephan R Covey
13. The Success Principles by Jack Canfield

11
Things to Do Immediately After Starting the Business

These are 10 simple actions that need to be done immediately after starting:-

1. Make sure you have got all the products and services for the money that you have paid. Get information on all the products through videos or brochures and quickly start using your products or services.
2. Get all the tools and study them—videos, mobile Apps, brochures, business presentations, etc.
3. Make sure all your registration formalities and documentation is completed and updated in your account.
4. Have a meeting with your upline and understand the products, income plan, rewards, rank system, any running contests or promotions, and most importantly the working system of your team.
5. Get information about all the programs that are happening over the next 3 months and attend them. Buy tickets, if required for any event. Attending programs should be your number one priority.
6. Make a list of prospects, do the selection and set up the first batch of meetings in consultation with your upline.
7. Define your dreams. Write down your short term and long term dreams that you want to accomplish through this business.
8. Set your business goals in consultation with your upline and make an action plan for their accomplishment.

9. Be a student of the business. Be committed to attend all the events and work in close association with your upline.
10. Start reading any one book from the list of recommended books given in this book and on my website.

12
Action Plan for the First 90 Days in the Business?

The first 90 days are critical for the business. Those who successfully survive and thrive in the first 90 days generally continue to build good business. Personally, Whatever heights I have touched in this business, are because of working on a right action plan in first 90 days of my business. In fact I resigned my job and took this business full time on the 93rd day of my business because of right working in those first 90 days. I was in a high profile job and was one of the top performers of my company. I was at the peak of my career and it was not easy to make such a fast shift to this business. But a strategic 90 days plan and its flawless execution with my coach for this business in my first 90 days set up my network marketing career forever and in fact shot me to the league of top performing leaders of the business in the country.

Your action plan entirely depends on your goal from this business because every achievement requires a different level of time and commitment. You need to determine what is your goal and then make an action plan in consultation with your upline.

Fundamentally for everyone, there are three goals in the first 90 days: Education, continuation and achievement.

1. **Education and understanding:**
   Attend all programs and meetings in these 90 days. Make it a top priority and be committed to travel if required.
   Read the recommended books and watch the recommended video and audio programs.

Meet with different leaders and observe what they say and what they do.

The real education comes from implementation. Do maximum presentations. Irrespective of whether the person starts with you or no, every meeting will be a learning experience. In the early stages of the business, you need to talk to everyone possible and show maximum plans because you need practice.

2. **Don't quit:**

   Make a commitment to survive the first 90 days, come what may. Just be a student of the business and keep going strong for the first 90 days. Do a minimum of 30 business opportunity presentations or product presentations in this period. Don't analyze the results till you complete these 30 meetings. Take the help of your upline wherever required. Attend programs, meet uplines regularly, read books and never quit.

3. **Achievement:**

   Initial achievements are critical for the development of a big business. Set your goals in consultation with your upline and work aggressively for their achievement. If any contest is going on, plan to achieve it. Initial achievement will strengthen your confidence to successfully run this business. Also, your teammates will be watching your growth. If your income and other achievements are good, they will also start building the business seriously. Many prospects will make a decision to start business with you looking at your achievements. If you have initial achievement, your sales conversion will be better.

Most of the network marketing income plans and rewards are designed keeping in mind that a majority of people in the business are part timers. So, good achievement is possible with the right planning and disciplined weekly actions. Also, achievement in network marketing is the result of teamwork. If you can have some right people in the right structure in the first few weeks, any achievement is possible.

While education and understanding should be top priority, your can decide your level of achievement in the first 90 days based on your goals. Bigger goals will require a bigger commitment and more working hours.

Be committed, follow the system, give your 100% and never quit.

My mission is to empower all network marketers to get better results and to fulfill all their dreams. In this quest, we keep upgrading our tools and keep creating new tools. You can learn and download them on my website www.deepakbajaj.biz.

Social Media Planning Guide for Big Success in Network Marketing

1. Always remember that the genuine intention to add value is critical to success in social media. Put best quality content that benefits your audience.
2. It takes time. Look at the long term and keep adding useful content everyday.
3. Don't keep checking for likes or comments every half an hour. Keep posting good content and keep doing your regular work.
4. Be consistent. One or two posts everyday is good.
5. Keep at least 2-3 videos out of every 10 posts. Videos are working better these days.
6. Avoid putting posts directly for sale of products or asking people to join you. Focus on building relationship and credibility.
7. Keep it entertaining. Add variety and spice to your posts.
8. Experiment. Try new things and then do more of what works
9. Be yourself. Everyone is unique and that is the beauty. Learn from your ideals and influencers but have your own genuine style. People will connect more with your true self.
10. Keep 4:3:2:1 ratio in your posts as per the guideline below:-

Events of your life/Lifestyle	Value adding content	Business events	Product testimonies/ Business success stories
4	3	2	1

SECTION - IX

FREQUENTLY ASKED QUESTIONS (FAQS) ANSWERED

FREQUENTLY ASKED QUESTIONS (FAQS) ANSWERED

This section aims to answer a few basic questions that keep coming to the minds of many distributors. A very useful and effective guide on handling questions and objections have also been given in the chapter on 'Follow Through and Sales closing' in The Success Process section of this book. This section here covers some specific questions that are simple and natural, but not getting the right answers to them, make people quit the business or they do the business half-heartedly, producing not so encouraging results. These answers are purely based on my beliefs and my many years of experience in this business. You can give your own answers that you find suitable for that person.

Question: How to make my teammates positive and active for this business?

Programs are the only way to make and keep people positive and active in the business. Starting this business is very easy; deciding to build this business is tough. It needs faith and people need to understand what this business can do in their lives. This realization can come only in the programs. The best of the leaders also need a program to really deliver their best. If your people are continuously attending programs, they will stay in the business and gradually start performing in the business. Remember the power of five—it generally takes five programs for people to trust this business and start working on it. So make sure all your people are attending programs repeatedly.

Question: What to do when the business goes really slow?

Show more and more business presentations. Increase the level of activity in your personal work as well as in your team's. Motion propels emotion and emotion brings the momentum. Lead from the front by showing maximum business presentations and by creating maximum new achievers personally. Within a few weeks, the team will pick it up and the business will start growing again. Increased activity is a one-stop solution for all your business problems.

Question: How to balance between customers and distributors?

While both are important for the business and we should have both distributors and customers in our team, I would recommend investing 70-80% of your time in adding distributors and 20-30% of the time in adding new customers. Customers need a lot of time in providing them the service and there is no business multiplication on the spot, but distributors can multiply really fast and bring in big volume. We can achieve a big rank and income with a big distributor base. A customer base gives stability and the customers keep converting into good distributors gradually. So, always keep an eye for good distributors while maintaining good volume through the customers.

Question: When should one come a full-timer in the business?

Since you have realized that this business is a better way to live life and fulfill your dreams, you should plan to do this business full-time as early as possible. In fact, the lifestyle and the quality of life this business can give you in 3-6 years is very difficult to get even after 30 years of working in a typical job or profession. But more than full time or part time, the key is to do this business properly. I know several people who earn more income part time than many so-called full timers.

The key is to follow the system 100%. I have repeatedly seen that if someone cannot do this business properly as a part timer, he or she can never do this business well as a full timer either. Build a good business while keeping your job/profession and once you start making good income and have the right structure, decide to be a full timer after consultation with your upline. Also, if you love what you are doing, then keep doing that along with successfully building this business.

Attend all events and trainings and master the business basics. While building this business part-time, do business opportunity presentations every day and build a strong team of active and committed leaders in the right structure. Make sure you have a supporting upline, a team with a proven training and development system, and you have chosen the right company as per the four parameters we had discussed in the Tools section. Now, if you are committed to work 100% as per the system and have 12-24 months of your household and other expenses in your bank today, you can decide to do this business full time immediately.

Question: What is the right structure for the business?

Every company has a different income model and our objective is to maximize our income and rewards today and for the future. So, the right structure is one that gives you the maximum income as per the income plan of your company. So, understand your company's income model and then create the required structure.

Fundamentally, there are two principal components of the structure that you need to manage – depth and width. While depth gives you stability and volume, width generally gives you more profit and security. Both are critical for the development of the business. Invariably in every company, rewards are higher as you develop the width.

So, maintain your depth with the depth building principles given in the section, Principle to give a solid foundation to your business. Keep supporting the depth of your existing teams through programs and by occasionally putting personal sales to keep the group momentum.

Gradually, keep expanding your width with regular personal sponsoring. Done consistently and properly, this combination will empower you to build a strong, stable and highly profitable business.

Question: How to make my family positive for this business?

Firstly, you should stop this quest of making them feel positive by telling them to be positive or by worrying about their lack of positivity. There are only two ways to make anyone feel positive about this business or for any business: Understanding and achievement. Understanding can happen only in the programs. Programs develop faith and when anyone has faith, he or she will definitely be positive about this business.

Secondly, instead of focusing on their lack of positivity, focus on your achievement. Work hard to earn a good income and achieve a good rank. When money comes in the house and the family gets recognition on a big stage, positivity will automatically come. Positivity is the effect; a lack of understanding and achievement from the business is the root cause. You work on the cause, the effect will automatically be fine.

Question: I can't do this business because I think it is very tough to build this business.

Nothing is easy or tough. Whatever you are committed to do and willing to learn is easy for you. It's not that this business is tough; it's just the lack of willingness to learn how to do it. Whatever we find easy today and can easily do without even thinking about it, seemed tough at one point of time. Riding a bicycle or car was something we found terribly difficult when we started, but with our resolve to learn it somehow, anyhow, we became a master at it. If there is a problem in my phone, I take it to a customer care center where someone fixes it in minutes. Now, fixing the phone is tough for me but easy for the phone expert. I can happily and easily talk to a 100 more people for my business, but I dread fixing problems in my kitchen/AC/car or many such things. Everyone who is successfully doing anything is able to do it well only because he or she learnt it. So, if you are willing to put in the time and commitment to learn this business, you will be a master within a few days or weeks for sure.

Question: Such businesses don't last. How do I trust this company?

Go to the chapter on 'How to choose the best network marketing company' in the Tools for Excellence section of this book. Also, I highly recommend that you attend some events. Events will build your trust in the business.

Question: There is no respect in this profession.

You show me any profession where respect is guaranteed. Please remember, a profession never guarantees you respect and income, it's how you do that profession that determine your income and respect in that profession. There are good doctors and then there are bad doctors too who indulge in wrong practices, good teachers and bad teachers, good accountants and bad accountants, good insurance sales agents and bad insurance sales agents, etc. In every profession, there are people who become role models due to their personal values and conduct; while in the same profession, there are many others who bring a bad name to themselves and the profession due to their bad practices.

Respect will come only when you do the profession with the right values, integrity, honest practices and business/professional ethics. If you are ready to follow this, you will see for yourself that the respect that anyone can get in this business is the best possible on earth. In fact, you have to be a network marketer to really understand what genuine respect and love means in a profession.

Question: What to answer when people say, 'I don't have the time or money'?

I know that, that's why I have come to you with this business proposal. I was also facing the same problem and was desperately looking for a solution so that I could have an abundance of time and money at my disposal. This business is clearly a time-tested and doable solution for people like you and me to have more money and more time to do things that we have always wanted to do.

Don't make a lack of time or money your excuse for not starting this business. Rather, make it your reason to do it.

Question: How to answer when people say, 'I don't know if I will be able to this business successfully. I have never done anything like this before'?

I totally understand what you are feeling. I also felt the same when this business came to me. I was a lawyer/teacher/doctor or (your profession) and I had never done any selling or ever built a team. But during one of the discussions like the one we are having now, my Upline helped me realize that I became a successful lawyer because of two things – my in depth education in the subject of law for many years, and then my law practice for many years. Why did I study and practice law for several years is because I thought that being a lawyer, I would have a secure career, make good money, fulfill my dreams, get the job satisfaction, etc. Now, if the same things are possible here in this business, why shouldn't I devote some time into learning and practicing this? The best part is, I need to devote only a few hours every week initially, and that too along with my current profession. I need not leave my current work to do this.

Whatever we all are doing today, we were new to it at some point of time. We decided to learn it and got better at it with regular practice. It was not easy in the beginning, but we gradually mastered it as we started doing it.

It is the same for this business. When it appears to be a better way to achieve…(use the TSDs of your prospect here)…, let's try it together. If so many people can achieve such great success here, why not you and me. Let's learn it and do it. Anyway we will be doing our regular work as we have been doing.

Question: I feel like quitting at times. I feel too frustrated and that I will not be successful in this business. What to do in such situations?

There are broadly two situations in such cases. Many a times people quit without even trying. They sometimes do 1-3 meetings or phone calls, that too half-heartedly without learning exactly how to do it. Looking at the first reaction of people, they just feel frustrated and feel like quitting. To all those people I can say that *you can come into this business by chance, but you cannot be successful by chance*. You have to understand, this is a business and success takes time and effort. You need to learn the basics and work as per the system for a few months to taste the success. If you are serious about fulfilling your dreams from this business, go to the programs and get to the field doing the work. If you want success without paying the price, you better quit right now.

A few other people feel like quitting when they do not get encouraging results despite doing everything. I understand their situation, I also felt like quitting many a times, but each time I thought of quitting, I asked myself, 'If not this, then what else? Quitting this business is very easy. It takes a second to quit, but what else will I do to fulfill my dreams then?' Also, I used to remind myself of why I started this business in the first place. Sometimes, you need to just pull yourself up and drag yourself. Remember, prosperity is simply one distributor away. One new person can change your business situation altogether. Attend programs and do counseling with your active uplines. You can consult some senior uplines also. Increase the level of activity, show more plans, pull your people along and soon you will be doing better than ever before.

Never stop attending the programs. Even if there is nobody with you, go to the programs alone. Always be in touch with your upline and meet them often. If you do these things, you will never quit and if you don't quit in this business, you will be successful for sure.

Conclusion

These are some of the questions that I have heard repeatedly. You may have to answer many different questions when you conduct your presentations. As a thumb rule, never get upset when people raise objections. Acknowledge the question with a smile and answer it gracefully in a pleasant tone. We don't want to argue or put someone down. The other person might have tried something and got a bad experience or have heard about someone's bad experience. Questions and objections are the beginning of a relationship. It's like you hold a Rs 2000 currency note in one hand and a chocolate in the other hand, and you ask a baby to pick one. The baby will immediately pick the chocolate. It's not because the chocolate is better, but because of the ignorance of the baby about how many chocolates he or she can buy with Rs 2000. The prospect is not choosing your business opportunity even though it is better, simply because of ignorance. The moment people understand the power of this business and what this business can do in their lives, they will come looking for you to start the business. Remember, our job is educating them and starting a relationship.

THE NEXT STEPS

Congratulations. You have just completed a full course on network marketing by reading this book. You proved that you have dreams and you are committed to do everything it takes to be a top income earner.

Now is the time to take action. Be compulsive and obsessive to implement everything you have learnt and surprise yourself with your performance. Unleash your hidden potential and rise for the skies. Now you are a genius and you know everything it takes to be at the top.

But remember network marketing business runs on a simple principle that your income is directly proportional to the number of active distributors in your team. The biggest task of every network marketer is to create an army of active distributors. This book can be your greatest help in creating a powerful team that will continue to give you big volume week after week. Just make sure that everyone in your team reads and implements this book.

As every reader of this book felt, this book gives you several benefits:

- It reduces your training workload. This book teaches the right system to your team.
- It helps you to train people even without meeting them. They can read the book and you can discuss the points on phone or video calling.
- This book can train your people in new locations where there is no training program.
- With this book, your teammates will get training even after the training program is over. Spreading this book in your team will work as if you have opened a training center in 1000s of homes in your team.
- This book can be your key to getting big passive income. A well-trained team will produce sales even without your

active involvement and that is the biggest reward of network marketing.

All these benefits are yours at less than the price of one pizza or a movie ticket.

To get these benefits you need to ensure that all your teammates are using the principles and techniques given in this book. Here are some ideas from successful leaders who have multiplied their incomes by spreading this book in their teams:

- Use this book like a workbook and teach your teammates to refer to this book for every field issue.
- Prime minister of India once said that we should give a book in place of a bouquet. Life of a flower bouquet is 2-3 days but a book lives forever. You can make it a practice in your team to give this book to chief guests or achievers in place of bouquets.
- This book can become part of your welcome kit that is given to all new distributors when they start the business.
- This book can be given as an award in small contests. It's the best gift you can get in this price.
- You should give this book to all the participants of a residential training program or a leadership training program.
- It's a great gifting idea. You can gift this book to your prospects or teammates on their birthdays, new achievements, special moments, festivals, etc. with your best wishes written on it.
- New distributors can be awarded with this book when they achieve first level or some simple targets.

You can buy this book for your whole team at special bulk quantity discounted prices. Please speak to our representatives on the contact numbers given on our website www.deepakbajaj.biz.

Use this book like a dictionary or encyclopedia of network marketing. Read it fully once and come back to it every time you need a solution for anything. Everyone must always have one book at home. Any product, any company, any income plan, anywhere in the world, this book will work like magic.

I also invite you to attend my live event – **Network Marketing Millionaires Academy**. This program will make you achieve in 2-3 years what many people struggle to achieve in 8-10 years. Everything

I have learnt by paying millions of rupees to world's best trainers and everything I learnt by working with lacs of people for more than a decade, I will pass it on to you to set you up for a life of your dreams. It's the best program available to actually make you and your teammates network-marketing millionaires. The details of this program are given on next few pages and on our website.

For high dreamers who want to achieve big success in a record time, I have very exclusive **High Performance Coaching** sessions. These are one to one sessions where we will make customized action plan for you and empower you for successful execution of those strategies. You will come out to be a different human being after these sessions. More details are available on our website.

In addition to the above, we have lot of live events happening throughout the year like, Launch your Dream Life, Live your Best Life, etc. Our participants have experienced total life transformation in these lives events. Health, happiness, career, relationship, money or success, whatever you are looking for, these live events will help you achieve your dreams faster. Please speak to our staff or book online at www.deepakbajaj.biz.

Your feedback is important to us. Please take time to give all your feedbacks at our website. If you are looking for some solutions that are not available in this book now, please give your suggestions at www.deepakbajaj.biz.

Stay in touch for latest tools and techniques to improve your life and to multiply your businesson my website www.deepakbajaj.biz and on various social media channels like YouTube, Facebook, Instagram, LinkedIn, etc.

Work like a committed businessperson and follow the system 100%. Stay focused and keep improving yourself. Legendary success takes time. I want to see you at the top. Your happiness and success is my greatest reward. Be a multi-millionaire and create millionaires in your team. Don't forget to write me your success story. Wish you super success.

Your partner in success.

Deepak Bajaj

DEEPAK BAJAJ'S
NETWORK MARKETING MILLIONAIRES ACADEMY

10x your Income. Create a Millionaire Mindset. Scale up your Skills & Strategies.

Network Marketing Millionaires Academy is a must attend event for every network marketer. Achieve total mastery of network marketing/direct selling business and achieve top rank of your company at a record speed. In this life-changing, deeply immersive and high-energy event, Deepak will work with you and your team to make you a millionaire in network marketing. This live event is full of life changing knowledge, tools, exercises, worksheets and activities to really empower you and your teammates to fulfill all your dreams.

Everything Deepak has learnt by paying millions of rupees to world's best trainers and everything he has learnt by working with lacs of people for more than a decade, he will pass it on to you to set you up for a life of your dreams. The principles, tools and techniques covered in this event will give amazing results in all different companies with different products and income plans.

Objective of the event:
To multiply your income by creating the right mindset and belief system, by developing your leadership and by enhancing your skills and strategies.

Key Benefits:
✓ Learn what the top earners actually do to multiply income and team size in record time

- ✓ Build the right foundation to earn ongoing passive income
- ✓ Develop the right mindset and belief system to be a top achiever in your company
- ✓ Master the hidden psychology of customers
- ✓ Master the right duplication system for building a big and growing team
- ✓ Make your team a leaders creation factory
- ✓ Build your personal brand to attract best people to you
- ✓ 90 Days game plan to turn around your business
- ✓ Social media strategy for big success
- ✓ New age time management system to get best results
- ✓ Learn the tracking system to monitor and multiply your business
- ✓ Create never ending list of prospects
- ✓ Secret techniques to convert every meeting to sales
- ✓ How to promote programs and get maximum results from programs

All this LIVE with Deepak Bajaj

Deepak Bajaj is the best man to set you up for success in network marketing. As on the writing of this book in 2019, Deepak has already trained and empowered more 7 lac people in last 16 years. His book has is followed as the textbook or guidebook of network marketing industry and has been on the bestsellers list for months in a row. Deepak is an International NLP master practitioner and has got trainings from the world's best trainers and coaches in USA, Portugal, Singapore, Bangkok and India. His videos get more than 3 million views every month and people across the globe are following them.

Network Marketing Millionaire Academy is conducted in an absolutely safe environment without mentioning any company or product's name. So you can attend it with your team without any worries. We have zero tolerance policy and anyone found giving plans or recruiting other attendances is immediately expelled from the event.

Our goal is simply to uplift the profession of network marketing and genuinely empower the network marketers around the globe. We want to positively impact the world by producing better leaders. Join us in this mission with your team and we will create a better world together. The world needs your brilliance.

Reserve your Seat at www.deepakbajaj.biz.

DEEPAK BAJAJ'S
HIGH PERFORMANCE COACHING
Customized action plans. Flawless execution. Time linked Results

There are a small percentage of people who not only have big dreams, but also they are committed to achieve their dreams in a short time. For all those people, who value their time and who believe they deserve nothing but the best, there is Deepak Bajaj's High Performance Coaching.

Deepak is a high performance coach to individuals and organizations in the area of business growth, life and stress management, network marketing, career development, holistic living, etc. His coaching empowers people and organizations to be happier, healthier, profitable and more successful.

At these sessions, Deepak himself evaluates your goals and current situation and makes a customized time bound action plan for you. He empowers you to execute the plan and monitors the progress. Since life and businesses are dynamic in nature and situations keep changing really fast, he makes necessary modifications at every stage and keeps you on track. Whatever gets monitored gets improved. Deepak and his team, work like your accountability partners who monitor your progress periodically through a proven system.

Since coaching needs Deepak's personal time and commitment, only limited slots are available on first come first served basis. You will become a totally different human being after these High performance coaching sessions. It will be a journey worth going on together. You can check the availability and book your sessions at www.deepakbajaj.biz.

ACKNOWLEDGEMENT

This book is indeed the result of massive teamwork of thousands of people who have influenced my life in different ways. A million thanks to all my live event participants, teammates, readers, social media followers, channel subscribers and everyone of you who have given your love, support and prayers. I can't mention everyone individually, but there are some significant few who have played a vital role in the creation of this masterpiece book.

My family is at the core of all my accomplishments. I believe I am the chosen one because God has given me the vision, the capability to make this vision a reality and a family to give me all the support. It all started with the invisible blessings from my father Late Mr Basant Kumar Bajaj and my maternal grandmother, Late Mrs PushpaWanti, two most amazing human beings who are taking of me from the heaven. I have always got immense strength from Ma and Babu, Late Dr S K Banerjee and Late Mrs Anjali Banerjee.

My mother, Mrs Raj Rani Bajaj, is the only God I know. She is my source of inspiration and strength. All my success is just the manifestation of her prayers and blessings. My beloved wife, Dr Tanima, has been my partner and pillar of strength throughout my transformation journey. I can never thank my brother Gaurav enough for everything he is to me. He is my friend, advisor, partner, my strongest support system and my lifeline. He is the best network marketer on earth and this book would not have been possible without his unconditional support and inputs. My little sister, Divya, who always brings so much joy to our family. Being a joint family, we have the privilege of living with five angels, our children—Saksham, Nirbhay, Prashansa, Cheeraayu and Devanshi. My kids are my cheerleaders. They always inspire me and are always waiting for me to bring home more trophies and bigger achievements. They are my power bank and they make me feel like a king.

I would also like to thank some other God sent angels who have done more for me than I could ever say thanks for – Dr K L Khurana, Late Mrs Susheel Khurana, Mr Dayal Dass Arora, Mrs Seema Vij, Mr Deepak Satija, Mrs ReenaSatija, Mrs Anita Manchanda, Mr Gulshan Bajaj, Mrs Poonam Bajaj, Mrs Naresh Dhir, Dr Vishesh Dhir, Mr Subhash Srivastava, Mrs Chandrima Banerjee, Mr Basudev Nandi and divine blessings of Late Dr D P Dhir.

Thanks to my friends and pillars of strength—Gaurav Mehra, Vikas Garg and Sanjay Jindal. I am alwaysgratefultomy Uplines.I am blessed to have the best team on earth. I would like to extend my heartfelt gratitude to each and everyone in my team who have given me unconditional support, unparalleled love, affection, prayers and rich experiences all through my career. Blessed to have you all in my life.

A million gratitude to a man who stood with mel ike a Banyan tree and who is my inspiration—Mr Pravin J Chandan. My 24x7 support system, great men who always support me like elder brothers and never say no to anything I ask for—Mr Kailash Bhattad, Mr Salil Mathew, Mr Alok Pandey, Mr Sunil Singh and Mr K K Rajesh.

My sincere gratitude to my publisher, Manjul Publishing House and especially to Mr Vikas Rakheja. Thanks to my first publisher, Invincible Publishers.

A million thanks to my countless fans and supporters whose love, affection and support is my strength as well as my inspiration. I love you all.

My sincere gratitude to the network marketing industry, which has made me the person I am today. My salute to every network marketer who is moving forward everyday towards his/her dreams overcoming every obstacle. I am one among you and I know what you are going through every single day. This book is my token of appreciation for all the love you have given me. You are my inspiration to keep going and I will do everything possible to make you a winner.

My life has only one mission—to empower each and every one of you to fulfill your dreams faster. Keep rising.

Deepak Bajaj

ABOUT DEEPAK BAJAJ

Bestselling author, motivational speaker, breakthrough trainer and high performance coach

Having trained more than 7 lac people in past 16 years, Deepak is passionately pursuing his life mission everyday to inspire and empower people in fulfilling their dreams. Deepak is an International NLP master practitioner and has got trainings from the world's best trainers and coaches in USA, Portugal, Singapore, Bangkok and India. His MBA from a top Management Institute, 4 years of record breaking corporate experience and 12 years of super successful entrepreneurship makes him the best trainer, speaker and coach.

Deepak's training programs are designed and delivered to bring desired results at jet speed. Deepak is famous for his life changing training events that are always jam-packed. He also conducts customized corporate training programs for sales multiplication, leadership, high performance teams, creating an empowering organizational culture, organizational productivity and profitability, fast growth and setting up of startups, etc.

Deepak is a high performance coach to individuals and organizations in the area of business growth, life and stress management, network marketing, career development, holistic living, etc. His coaching empowers people and organizations to be happier, healthier, profitable and more successful.

He is a powerful speaker who brings amazing transformation and lasting impact in every speech he delivers. His unique 6-component formula of content, delivery, state and engagement has been inspiring, entertaining and bringing desired results from every speech since more than 16 years. He is regularly invitedas keynote speaker at various events at corporates, government bodies, dealer conventions, sales meets, colleges, universities and various entrepreneurship promotion forums

Deepak is a leading social media influencer and his videos get more than 3 million views every month. Deepak is a bestselling author in two languages and work has already started for translation of his books in several languages this year. He also received the Best Debut Author 2018 award. Recently he was on the cover of a leading magazine and his articles are regularly published in leading magazines.

Deepak is an avid reader, runs marathons and is an adventure sports freak. He loves travelling and has already travelled to 25 countries with his family. He lives in Gurgaon (Delhi NCR), India with his wife, Dr Tanima and 3 kids.

www.deepakbajaj.biz

www.ingramcontent.com/pod-product-compliance
Lightning Source LLC
Chambersburg PA
CBHW031608210526
45464CB00004B/1481